Express Publisher

Version 2.0

Power Up Software Corporation
2929 Campus Drive
San Mateo, California 94403

Table of Contents

Chapter 3 *Fundamentals*   **55**

Introduction

Welcome to Express Publisher Express Publisher is a page-design program that lets you easily combine graphics and text to create professional-looking documents. Use Express Publisher to create great-looking newsletters, reports, flyers, announcements, invitations, or presentation materials. You can import pictures and text from your favorite graphics and word processing programs; or use Express Publisher's powerful drawing and text-handling features to create documents from scratch. If you want complete artistic control, you can create your own page layouts; or use one of the provided templates to get professional results fast. Either way, you won't have any trouble creating impressive work with Express Publisher.

Layout Page layout in Express Publisher is as simple to understand as using scissors and tape, but much less aggravating. Once you learn the simple automatic layout functions, you'll be able to create great-looking pages in a fraction of the time you might spend using a word processor. While you work, Express Publisher displays your document on the screen as it will appear on the printed page. Feel free to experiment and make mistakes. You can move and change every element in a document. Don't worry about your drawing ability: you can draw perfect boxes, lines, and circles without any special skills using the drawing tools.

Graphics Unlike other entry level publishing programs, Express Publisher can import several types of high resolution graphics. These include scanner-generated TIFF, the most popular standard for professional clip art; CGM, a popular standard for presentation graphics; EPS, the highest quality graphics standard; and PCX, created by best sellers PC Paintbrush® and Publisher's Paintbrush®. Express Publisher can also load MacPaint®, PrintShop®, and First Publisher® pictures. To help you get started, we've included a large collection of high quality TIFF pictures in both 150 and 300 dpi. Once pictures are imported, they can be cropped, flipped, inverted, or scaled to fit in with the rest of your work.

Text Express Publisher includes all the text-handling abilities you need to create professional documents: several justification options, search and replace, automatic hyphenation, cut and paste, leading, and kerning are just a few of the options. You can choose between your printer's native fonts and the typeset quality AGFA Compugraphic® fonts, CG Triumvirate™, CG Times™, and Univers™. If you want more fonts to work with, you can purchase additional Express Fonts™ font portfolios. Express Publisher also supports softfonts (see Appendix I for more information). For super-fast formatting, Express Publisher's style sheets can apply several formatting commands at once. Express Publisher can keep track of several stories at once in a single document, flowing text from column to column, and even skipping over other stories and pages. Create all the text you need for your work inside of Express Publisher, or import files directly from several of the more popular word processors. Microsoft Works®, Microsoft Word®, WordPerfect®, and WordStar® files can all be imported directly.

TextEffects This tool lets you create eye-catching headlines or logos with advanced typesetting effects. You can have text fill a polygon, bend along a curve, or increase in size along a distortion field.

Room to grow Unlike some entry-level products, Express Publisher offers powerful features that will keep you satisfied as you become more advanced. Some entry-level programs are easy to use because they can't do very much. Express Publisher is easy to use because of its strengths, not its limitations.

System requirements

Express Publisher requires the following software and hardware:

- An IBM PC®, XT®, AT®, PS/1®, PS/2®; Tandy 1000, 1200, 3000; or 100% compatible computer
- 640K of RAM
- A VGA, MCGA, EGA, CGA, Hercules or compatible graphics adapter
- A Microsoft, Logitech, IBM, or Mouse Systems mouse, (or 100% compatible)
- A hard disk with at least 3 MB of available disk space
- Version 3.0 or later of DOS

Express Publisher automatically takes advantage of the following types of extra memory:

- Extended memory on IBM AT, PS/2, or 386 compatible computers
- Expanded memory that adheres to the Lotus-Intel-Microsoft standard version 4.0 or later (LIM EMS)

Supported Mouse Drivers

The following mouse drivers are supported by this version of Express Publisher:

- LOGITECH 3.2, 3.42, and 4.0
- Dexxa 3.43
- Microsoft 6.14 and 7.04
- Tandy (with Microsoft driver version 6.36)
- Mouse Systems 5.50
- Kensington Expert Mouse 1.0

If you have an earlier version, call your mouse vendor's Technical Support department to get upgrade information for your version of the mouse and driver.

Upgrading from version 1.1

Before you install your new copy of Express Publisher version 2.0, we recommend that you delete the Express Publisher version 1.1 program files from your \EXPRESS directory. If you placed any files you want to keep — such as document or template files (files ending in .EPD or .EPT) — in this directory, move them to another directory before continuing. To make sure you delete only the correct files, check the list of files in Appendix C.

Important

Delete these files only if you are installing an upgrade of Express Publisher.

These installation instructions assume that you used the default directories for your original installation.

1. Make sure you are in the EXPRESS directory to prevent deleting any necessary files. To make sure, type cd \express and press ENTER. You should see the prompt C:\EXPRESS>.

2. If, and only if, you see the C:\EXPRESS> prompt, type erase ep*.* and press ENTER.

3. Type erase *.prd and press ENTER.

You are now ready to install Express Publisher version 2.0.

The setup program

Before you begin using Express Publisher, you need to set it up for your hardware. You also need to make sure that your mouse and mouse driver software are correctly installed according to the manufacturer's instructions.

The setup program copies Express Publisher on to your hard disk, and configures the program for your hardware. Express Publisher will not work if you to try to run it from the master disks. The only time you should use the master disks is to run the setup program or to make backup copies.

Note   Make sure that you have 3 MB of disk space available on your hard disk before using the setup program to install Express Publisher. If you plan to install a lot of clip art, you may need considerably more space. You will need an additional 2 MB to install all of the clip art.

1. Start your computer.

2. Put the disk labeled "Disk 1" in drive A.

3. Make sure that the A> prompt appears on the screen. If it doesn't, type A : and press ENTER.

4. Type SETUPEP and press ENTER.

5. Follow the directions on the screen.

Appendix C, "Trouble shooting," contains information on possible problems with the setup program and a list of the directories the setup program creates. It also explains options for optimizing memory.

Note   If they are not already present, add the lines FILES = 20 and BUFFERS = 20 to your CONFIG.SYS file. See the DOS appendix and consult your DOS manual if you don't know how to do this. You will need to reboot after making this change.

Setting up directories

Express Publisher stores your data in one of three user-selectable subdirectories in your EXPRESS directory. The default direc-tories (those that are automatically set when you run SETUPEP the first time) are as follows:

- C:\EXPRESS\DOCS holds all documents and templates
- C:\EXPRESS\ART holds all clip art
- C:\EXPRESS\TEXT holds word processing and ASCII text files for importing

"Changing the default directories" in Chapter 3 explains these directories in more detail.

To change one of the default directories, run SETUPEP and choose "Set up file locations" on the main setup screen. The following section explains how to run SETUPEP.

Modifying an existing setup

The setup program copies itself onto your hard disk so that you can use it later to modify your configuration after installation.

- To run setup from your hard disk, change to the \EXPRESS directory and type SETUPEP. Follow the instructions on the screen to perform the various setup functions.

Windows compatibility

Express Publisher is not a Windows program, but it can function in the Windows environment. To make Express Publisher work in the Windows environment, you must install the Express Publisher EP.PIF file and add the Program group and the Program Item to the Windows Program Manager. Follow these steps:

1. Copy EP.PIF to your Windows directory by typing copy c:\express\ep.pif c:\windows and pressing ENTER. If you have Express Publisher or Windows in directories other than those mentioned, substitute the appropriate pathnames.

2. Open the Windows Program Manager and choose File. If you are not sure how to get to the Program Manager, press CTRL-ESC to bring up the Task List. Select Program Manager and press ENTER.

3. New should be highlighted. Click New to select it or press ENTER.

   The New Program Object dialog box appears. Use the arrow keys or the mouse to select Program Group. Click OK or press ENTER.

4. The Program Group Properties dialog box appears. Type Express Publisher in the Description field. Click OK or press ENTER.

5. Choose File from the Windows program Manager.

6. New should be highlighted. Click New to select it or press ENTER.

   The New Program Object dialog box appears. Select Program Item. Click OK or press ENTER.

7. The Program Item Properties dialog box appears. Type Express Publisher in the Description field. Type EP.PIF in the Command Line field. Click OK or press ENTER.

8. Express Publisher is now set up to start from Windows. To do so, double click the DOS-Express Publisher icon or select it and press ENTER.

Note If Express Publisher is not located in C:\EXPRESS you will need to use the Windows PIF editor to change the path in EP.PIF. See your Windows manual for more information.

What's new in Version 2.0

- Express Publisher 2.0 allows you to create special typesetting effects with TextEffects. You can make text bend in a curve, run along an angled line, increase or decrease in size from one character to the next, and fill with any available pattern. You can save the special text images created with TextEffects for use in a number of documents.
- A new Text Frame tool is included that allows you to draw a text frame and immediately enter text.
- With the Zoom In and Zoom Out commands you can change the view of your document without losing any of the editing features of Express Publisher. Zoom In doubles the size of your document so you can work on small type or make minute adjustments. Zoom Out shrinks your document in half so you can move large objects around.
- Express Publisher 2.0 can create and print documents in landscape perspective. All available paper sizes in the Create a New Document dialog box can be inverted from portrait to landscape orientation.
- You can now select more than one object to move, cut, copy, or paste at any time.
- Version 2.0 can duplicate a text frame and its text.
- The Headers and Footers command creates headers and footers on every page of your document. Page numbers are intelligently updated when you add or remove pages.
- You can crop TIF images with the Crop Image command.
- The toolbox in version 2.0 has changed slightly. The Magnify tool has been removed and replaced with the Edit Bit Image command on the Objects menu. The Crop tool has been removed and replaced with the Crop Image command. The Send to Front and Send to Back tools have also been removed and replaced with menu commands.
- The CGM utility allows you to use CGM graphics files with Express Publisher.

Where to go from here

Be sure to fill out and send in the postage-paid registration card. This helps establish your warranty commencement date and lets us keep you informed of program upgrades and enhancements.

Guided tour   Express Publisher version 2.0 includes a self-paced, interactive overview of Express Publisher's features. To use the guided tour, click the File menu and choose Open. From the list of files that appears, double-click LEARN_EP.EPT and follow the instructions.

Using the manual   If you have used another desktop publishing program, you probably won't have any trouble learning Express Publisher. Express Publisher follows many conventions established by other programs. If you are new to desktop publishing, you should read the whole manual from start to finish. If you're more advanced, read through the descriptions of the chapters below and decide what you need to read.

The Express Publisher manual contains eight chapters. The information is presented in order from the most basic to the more specialized. There is a narrative from start to finish, but each chapter can also be read on its own if you feel you already understand what came before it.

Chapter 1, Beginning, explains everything you see on the screen—including how to use commands, dialog boxes, and tools—and introduces you to the concept of stories and text frames.

Chapter 2, Tutorial, contains four lessons that convey a general sense of how Express Publisher works. The first two lessons provide a free-form introduction to working in Express Publisher. Lessons three and four lead you through the construction of a simple two-column newsletter using the program's main features, and points out a few tricks and techniques along the way.

Chapter 3, Fundamentals, explains how to create and save documents, and how to resume work on existing documents. It also documents optional performance features.

Chapter 4, Objects, details every function related to working with objects in Express Publisher: creating them, selecting them, and changing them.

Chapter 5, Text, explains all of Express Publisher's text-related functions: importing text, typing text, editing, linking text frames, style sheets, and other text-related special features.

Chapter 6, TextEffects™, explains this type styling feature and how to use its functions. It discusses using TextEffects to create special typesetting effects and provides some design-related tips.

Chapter 7, Printing, discusses all of Express Publisher's printing options and offers a few printer-specific recommendations.

Chapter 8, Layout, offers general advice on page layout. It includes examples of how best to use Express Publisher to create a menu and a newsletter.

The first appendix offers a review of basic DOS concepts. The next three appendices suggest ways you can use the templates, resolve problems, and specify printers. The other appendices display clipart, fonts, and alternate characters you can use with the Express Publisher package.

Typographical conventions

This manual displays keys that you press in small caps, such as ENTER, F1, TAB, and ESC. UP is the up-arrow key. DOWN, RIGHT, and LEFT are the down-arrow, right-arrow, and left arrow keys. PGUP and PGDN are the page-up and page-down keys, respectively.

Anything that you type is shown in Courier typeface, for example, `Write project proposal`.

Italics are used to introduce new terms.

▨ is our end of chapter symbol.

Product support

Be sure to read Appendix C, "Trouble shooting," for help with specific problems.

If you have a question about using the program that is not addressed in this manual, our product support staff will be glad to help you. To help answer your questions quickly and accurately, please have the following information ready before you call:

- Your name and address
- The version number of the program (the version number appears on the screen briefly when you start the program.)
- Version number of DOS you are using (see Appendix A)
- Computer make and model
- Amount of RAM installed and type of extra memory
- Type and capacity of hard disk
- Graphics adapter and monitor type
- Printer make and model
- List of any special peripherals installed
- Contents of your CONFIG.SYS and AUTOEXEC.BAT files (see Appendix A)
- A concise and clear description of the problem, including all error messages

The product support phone number is (415) 345-0551. Call between 8 AM and 5 PM Pacific Standard Time, Monday through Friday. In the United Kingdom, call 0252-376000. We find that telephone calls are more productive, but you may write to this address:

Power Up Product Support
Express Publisher
PO Box 7600
San Mateo, CA 94403

▨

Beginning

This first chapter introduces you to the basics of working with Express Publisher. It explains how to start Express Publisher, what the words and pictures shown on the screen mean, how to choose commands, how to use the mouse, and how to move around in the file. It also explains how Express Publisher flows your text through the document so that when you edit portions of the text, the page layout you created is not disturbed. We highly recommend that you at least skim through this chapter to see if there is anything new to you.

With Express Publisher, you can create unique, flexible, and dynamic page layouts for newsletters, brochures, presentation graphics, and the like. Import text and graphics prepared in other programs, or use Express Publisher's text and graphic tools to enter text and create simple graphics and page designs. Once the information is in the file, you can resize the graphics, format and reformat the text, and direct the flow of text through your document as you desire.

This chapter assumes that you have already installed Express Publisher using the setup program. If you have not, follow the instructions for the setup program found in the introduction.

Here is a list of the sections in this chapter:

- Starting Express Publisher
- Understanding the Express Publisher screen
- Using the mouse
- Moving in the document window
- Using commands
- Using dialog boxes
- Using the toolbox
- Introducing stories and text frames
- Help

Starting Express Publisher

Follow these steps to start Express Publisher:

1. Turn on your computer.

2. When the DOS prompt appears, type `cd\express` to change to the EXPRESS directory and press ENTER.

3. Type `EP` and press ENTER.

After loading, the Express Publisher screen appears.

Note   If you see the message, `Unable to create working copy`, it means there is not enough free space on your hard disk to run Express Publisher. The program needs at least 135K of free hard disk space to make temporary working copies of your document while you are creating it (300K is reccomended). See "Problems starting Express Publisher" in Appendix C for more information.

Understanding the Express Publisher screen

You won't have to decipher several screens full of information to learn your way around Express Publisher. Most of Express Publisher's features are available directly from the screen you see when you first start the program.

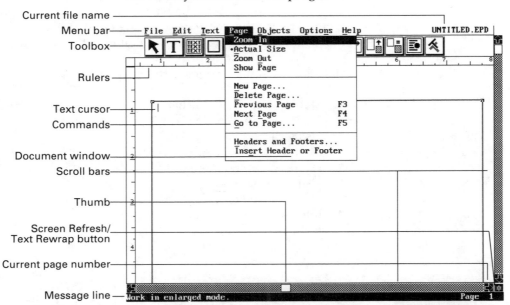

Note Express Publisher looks different on different types of monitors. The pictures in this manual were created using one type of monitor. See Appendix C for more information on graphics adaptors.

Express Publisher may look familiar to you even if you haven't read this part of the manual before. It uses pull-down menus and tools to execute commands. The system that a program uses to communicate with users is called a *human interface.* Many software developers have come to realize that a human (or user) interface combining icons, pull-down menus, and dialog boxes is one of the easiest ways for human beings and software to exchange information. If you have used another program with a similar human interface you may only have to skim this chapter.

- **Menu bar:** The menu bar lists the menu names. Each of these menus contains a list of commands that relate to a single topic, such as text. To find out how to use the menu bar to select a command, see "Using commands" later in this chapter.
- **Commands:** Each of the commands on the various menus tells Express Publisher to do a different task, such as saving a file, or creating a new page.
- **Toolbox:** The toolbox contains a row of pictures, or *tools,* that represent various commands. Moving the pointer onto a tool and pressing the mouse button activates that tool. Many of Express Publisher's most basic functions can be executed by tools in the toolbox. For a complete list of the tools and what they do, see "Using the toolbox" later in this chapter.
- **Rulers:** The vertical and horizontal rulers help you measure objects in your document. The units of measure can be either in inches, centimeters, or picas. For more information about rulers, see "Setting Options" in Chapter 3.
- **Current file name:** The file name of the document you are currently working on appears in this area. All new files are opened as UNTITLED.
- **Document window:** The document you are currently working on appears in the document window. Whenever you start Express Publisher, the program automatically creates a one-column, one-page document. The lines you see within the document window in the picture above show the edges of the text column. To learn how to create a new document, work through the lessons in Chapter 2, "Tutorial."
- **Message line:** The message line offers extra information you may need to make a decision while using Express Publisher. It describes the function of each command and sometimes prompts you to take an action.

- **Pointer:** The pointer moves as you move the mouse; it allows you to point to tools, menus, or to the place on the current page where you want to work next. The shape of the pointer changes depending on the tool you are using.
- **Scroll bars:** Use the Scroll bars to move up and down, or side to side in the document window.
- **Thumb:** The position of the thumb in the scroll bar indicates what part of the current page is visible in the document window.
- **Current page number:** The number of the page you are currently viewing is always displayed in the lower right corner of the document window.
- **ScreenRefresh/Text Rewrap button:** Click this button (marked with an asterisk) in the lower right corner of the screen to tell Express Publisher to redraw the screen or rewrap text around pictures.

Using the mouse

You only need to learn a few basic procedures to use the mouse with Express Publisher. Moving the mouse moves the pointer on the screen. The shape of the pointer often changes to reflect the kind of work you are doing. The most common pointer shape is the arrow.

- **Pointing:** Pointing to an object is usually only the first step in performing one of the mouse routines described below. You point to an object by moving the pointer on top of it. If you are trying to indicate a very precise location, make sure that the pointer's *hot spot* is exactly where you want it to be. The hot spot is the precise point on the screen indicated by the active part of the pointer. With the arrow pointer, for example, the hot spot is always under the very tip of the arrow. Different pointers have different hot spots; you will become familiar with them as you work with Express Publisher.

- **Clicking:** Clicking means to press the mouse button and release it immediately while pointing to a specific location on the screen. Clicking initiates an action, such as selecting part of your document, or starting a command or displaying a different part of the screen. For example, to move the document window down you place the tip of the arrow pointer in the vertical scroll bar and click.

- **Double-clicking:** Double-clicking is pressing the mouse button twice in rapid succession. Beginners often don't click fast enough. Press the mouse button twice in about the time it takes to say "express." Double-clicking is usually used as a shortcut. For example, to open a file you can double-click it instead of selecting it and then clicking Open.

- **Dragging:** Dragging means to press the mouse button and hold it down while moving the mouse. Drag the mouse to define an area or move an object.

Pointer shapes

As you use different tools, the shape of the pointer changes to help you remember what you are doing. Here are the different pointer shapes.

The arrow pointer

The most common pointer shape is the arrow. It allows you to select objects for layout. The pointer always changes to the arrow whenever you move the pointer off the document window to scroll, select a tool, or pull down a menu.

The I-beam pointer

The pointer looks like an I-beam when you are working with text.

Four-headed arrow pointer

While moving objects the pointer changes to a four-headed arrow.

The watch pointer

The watch pointer informs you that you must wait while Express Publisher carries out your last request. You cannot do anything with the watch pointer other than move it around.

There are other pointer shapes associated with more specific functions. They are explained later along with the function.

Moving in the document window

When you create a document with Express Publisher, you are working on pages that correspond to the pages that you print. However, most computer screens can only show one part of the page at a time. *Scrolling* and *paging* allow you to see different parts of the page.

Scroll bars

The scroll bars at the right side and bottom of the document window allow you to see different parts of the current page. Use the vertical scroll bar to move the document window up and down on the current page and the horizontal one to move from side to side.

Each scroll bar has an arrow at each end and contains a small square box called a *thumb*. The position of the thumb in the scroll bar represents your location in the document.

- Click the mouse on the gray (or cross hatched) area of the scroll bar to move your view of the document in the chosen direction by one full screen.

- To move in smaller steps, click the arrow that points in the direction you wish to go.

- Drag the thumb to move to a certain location more quickly, such as the top or bottom of the page.

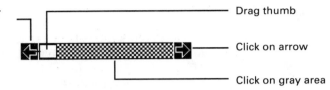

A scroll bar — Drag thumb

Click on arrow

Click on gray area

Page up/down   Use PAGE UP and PAGE DOWN to move the document window up or down the page by one full screen.

Using commands

All Express Publisher commands are available directly from the main screen on pull-down menus. The row of words across the top of the screen is called the *menu bar*. Each of the words represents a pull-down menu. These pull down menus are similar to the pull-down maps and diagrams used in classrooms. They stay out of the work area while you're not using them.

You can pull down menus and select commands using either the mouse or the keyboard. Function keys also activate many of the most commonly used commands.

With the mouse   These steps tell you how to select a command using a mouse:

1. Point to one of the words on the menu bar and click the mouse button.

   The menu drops down from the menu bar. The menu stays open until you pull down another menu, or click somewhere in the document window.

2. Click the command you want to use.

The command is activated.

With the keyboard   The following method activates any command in three keystrokes. For example, to use the Cut command on the Edit menu, you need only press ALT-E, and then C. Follow these steps to select a command using the keyboard:

1. Press ALT to activate the menu bar while you are working in the document window.

   One letter in each of the menu names that appear on the menu bar is underlined, usually the first letter. The underlined letter is that menu's *hot key*. Each of the commands on all of the menus has an underlined hot key.

2. Press RIGHT and LEFT until the menu name you want is high-lighted (displayed in reverse video). Once the menu you want is highlighted, press ENTER or press the hot key for the menu.

   The menu drops down from the menu bar.

3. Use UP and DOWN to select one of the commands on the menu, and press ENTER. Or, press the underlined hot key for the command you want to use.

   Pressing either LEFT or RIGHT closes the current menu and pulls down the next menu to the left or right.

Closing a menu   To close a pull-down menu, move the pointer into the document window and click the mouse button, or press ESCAPE.

Function keys   Some of the commands on the menus have function keys listed next to them. You can press these function keys to activate the commands instead of pulling down the menu. (The function key method will not work if the menu on which it appears is pulled down.)

F1	Help
F3	Previous Page
F4	Next Page
F5	Go to Page
F9	Scale Object
F10	Save

The following function keys also activate commands, but they do not appear on the menus because of space limitations. To activate a command with a SHIFT function key, hold down SHIFT as you press the function key.

F2	Zoom Out (zooms out one level)
F6	Next story frame
F7	Search again
F8	Begin text selection
SHIFT-F2	Zoom In (zooms in one level)

SHIFT-F3	Import Text
SHIFT-F4	Import Picture
SHIFT-F5	Print
SHIFT-F6	Previous story frame
SHIFT-F7	enables Snap to Grid
SHIFT-F8	Choose Font
SHIFT-F9	Choose Style
SHIFT-F10	Insert alternate character

Screen refresh   Occasionally, you may want Express Publisher to redraw or refresh the screen, or rewrap text around a graphic. Click the screen refresh button or press CTRL-F1.

Using dialog boxes

When Express Publisher needs more information to carry out a certain command, it presents a dialog box. All commands that invoke a dialog box are followed by an *ellipsis* (...) on the menu. The dialog box usually displays the name of the command that invoked it and lists the options available for that command.

The basic method for using a dialog box is always the same.

1. Use a command that invokes a dialog box.

2. Follow one of the methods outlined below to set the options according to your needs.

Note   The options in many dialog boxes are preset to their *default* setting, that is, the one most commonly used. If an option is already set the way you want it, you don't have to change it.

3. Click the button that executes the command (usually labeled OK).

You can always click Cancel or press ESCAPE to cancel a command from a dialog box.

There are several ways to select options from dialog boxes.

Check boxes: Check boxes let you turn off or on one or more options that modify the command you are using. An X in the box indicates that the option is on; an empty box means that the option is off. Click a check box to toggle between on and off. You can also use the arrow keys to toggle between on and off: UP and LEFT turn the option on; DOWN and RIGHT turn the option off.

Option boxes: Option boxes present a series of options that are mutually exclusive. Option boxes are similar to the row of buttons on car radios that only allow one button to be pressed at a time. An option is on when a dot appears in the parentheses next to it. Clicking one of the options in an option box turns on that option and turns off any other that was selected earlier.

Dialog boxes

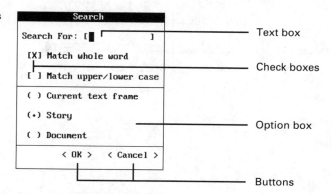

Text boxes: Text boxes are areas where you can enter information to tell Express Publisher what you want it to work on. This could be the name of a new file you are saving, a range of pages to be printed, or a measurement.

A text box will often appear with default information already in it. To accept the information, click OK. To change it, click the text box, delete the information in it, and type in your own. (Usually all the default text is highlighted so that you may delete it by pressing DELETE.) The following keystrokes are helpful:

- BACKSPACE deletes the character to the left of the cursor.
- DELETE deletes the character at the cursor.
- LEFT and RIGHT arrows move the cursor.
- END moves the cursor to the end of the text in the box.
- HOME moves the cursor to the beginning of the text in the box.
- INSERT switches between (toggles) insert and overstrike modes. In insert mode, typing new characters pushes existing characters to the right. In overstrike mode, you type new characters over existing characters.
- TAB moves the cursor to the next Text box.

List boxes: List boxes list options by name, such as files or type fonts. Since many lists do not fit entirely within the list box, there is a scroll bar that lets you scroll through the list. Click an item in a list box to select it. In many cases, double-clicking the item will carry out the command you are using.

<u>Icons:</u> Icons appear when visual information is helpful in making a choice between options. Each icon is a picture that represents an option relating to the command you are using. Clicking one of the icons selects the option. Frequently, double-clicking an icon carries out the command.

Pressing a letter on the keyboard while in a list box immediately selects the first item on the list beginning with that letter.

Dialog boxes

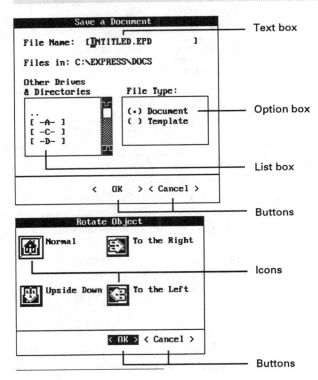

Text box

Option box

List box

Buttons

Icons

Buttons

Dialog box control keys

In addition to all the mouse functions mentioned above, most dialog boxes can be controlled from the keyboard without using the mouse.

In dialog boxes that have more than one active list box, such as Choose Printer and Choose Font, you need to select one of the list boxes with the tab key or the mouse before you can use PGUP and PGDN to move the cursor up or down the length of the list box.

- TAB moves the cursor between list boxes and from option to option. SHIFT-TAB moves the cursor in the opposite direction.
- LEFT and RIGHT arrows change the options in an option box, or change the selected icon.
- PAGE UP and PAGE DOWN move the cursor up or down the length of a list box.
- ENTER is the equivalent of pressing a button that is highlighted. If no button is highlighted, ENTER is the equivalent of clicking OK.
- ESCAPE cancels the command and closes the dialog box without making any changes.

File utility dialog boxes

This type of dialog box appears when you open or save files. A text box is provided for entering a file name or wild card search characters. An alphabetical list of the files in the current directory is displayed in a Files list box that you can scroll through. Another list box, labeled Other Drives and Directories, usually displays all of the currently available drives and directories. When you double-click a new drive or directory, the list of files in the other list box changes. Clicking the two dots, "..", at the top of the Other Drives and Directories list box tells Express Publisher to change to the parent directory. For example, if you are in \EXPRESS\ART and you double click the "..", the program changes to \EXPRESS. Look up directory structure in Appendix A or your DOS manual if you don't understand this.

You shouldn't have to change drives or directories very often while using the program. Express Publisher automatically changes to the \EXPRESS\DOCS directory every time you save or open a document; it changes to the \EXPRESS\ART directory when you import a picture.

The Import Text dialog box

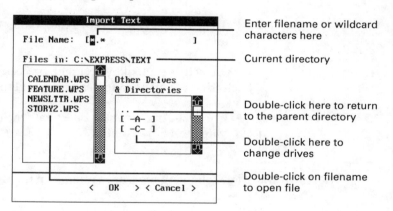

Enter filename or wildcard characters here

Current directory

Double-click here to return to the parent directory

Double-click here to change drives

Double-click on filename to open file

Wild card characters

You can enter wild card search characters in the File Name text box to change the list of files shown in the File list box. Express Publisher recognizes the same wild card characters as DOS, so check your DOS manual if you're not sure how to use them. If you don't understand wild card characters at all, don't worry about them. They can help out in some cases but they are not required to use any Express Publisher functions.

These are the wild card characters recognized by Express Publisher:

? Stands for any single character in the exact same position.

* Stands for any number of characters in that position.

The name *.* stands for any file name regardless of file name or extension. In computer jargon *.* is called *star dot star*.

Using the toolbox

The Express Publisher toolbox appears directly beneath the menu bar. It contains tools that help you perform the most common desktop publishing tasks. This section identifies all the tools in the toolbox and tells you how to activate a tool. Each of the tools is fully explained later, in the section covering the tasks that it performs.

- To activate any tool, move the pointer onto the desired tool and click the mouse.

If you activate a tool by accident, or decide not to use it after selecting it, you need to deactivate it before doing anything else.

The Arrow tool

- Click the Arrow tool to deactivate the current tool and activate the arrow pointer.

The toolbox   The following tools are available in the toolbox:

Arrow	Text	Text Frame
Box	Rounded Box	Ellipse
Line	Set Line	Set Fill

Link Unlink Align

Equate Text Wrap TextEffects

- **Arrow** activates the arrow pointer described in "Using the mouse" in this chapter.

- **Text** allows you to start typing text in a text frame.

- **Text Frame** allows you to draw a box and immediately start typing text in it.

- **Box** allows you to draw a rectangular object.

- **Rounded Box** allows you to draw a rectangular object with rounded corners.

- **Ellipse** allows you to draw ellipses and circular objects.

- **Line** allows you to draw vertical, horizontal, and diagonal lines.

- **Set Line** allows you to set the line type and width for lines and rectangular objects.

- **Set Fill** allows you to fill an object you have drawn with a shade or pattern.

- **Link** connects, or links, stories on different parts of a page or on different pages so that text can flow between them.

- **Unlink** disconnects, or unlinks, frames so that text no longer flows between them.

- **Align** allows you to line up two objects.

- **Equate** allows you to make two objects the same size.

- **Text Wrap** wraps text around one side of a picture.

- **TextEffects** opens TextEffects so you can create special typesetting effects.

Introducing stories and text frames

Express Publisher groups and stores text in a way that allows it to flow smoothly through your file. The formatting levels are

- Document
- Story
- Text frame

These levels work together to produce the final page. Although this concept is described in more detail throughout the manual, the following description provides an overview.

When you type or import text into Express Publisher, all of the text you enter is one *story*. You can have up to 64 separate stories in one Express Publisher *document*. Whether you type text directly into Express Publisher or import it from a word processor, Express Publisher enters the text in *frames*. A text frame is simply a window through which you can view your text. A *document* consists of all the frames and stories in your file.

See "About stories and text frames" in Chapter 5 for additional information, including how to apply commands to the various formatting levels.

Help

Almost all of the crucial information in this manual is available in the on-line Help Index. This help is organized by topic.

1. Pull down the Help menu and choose Help Index, or press F1.

   The Help Index dialog box appears. Use the scroll bar to get to the desired topic, or press the first letter of the topic that you want and that item is selected.

2. Double-click the topic on which you want help in the list box.

3. Click Cancel when you're done.

For more information on using Help, pull down the Help menu and select Getting Started.

Tutorial

This chapter leads you through a few simple lessons that illustrate most of Express Publisher's important features. You should make sure that you understand what was covered in Chapter 1, "Beginning," before you try to follow the tutorial.

The tutorial contains four lessons. You can do them all at once or one at a time. The first two lessons offer a free-form introduction to the program. They provide examples of the major concepts that you need to understand in order to work with Express Publisher. The third and fourth lessons guide you through the construction of a simple document.

The lessons in this tutorial are as follows:

- Getting started
- Lesson 1: understanding objects
- Lesson 2: entering text
- Lesson 3: creating a newsletter
- Lesson 4: advanced layout functions, including TextEffects

Getting started

1. Start your computer as you usually do.

2. Change to the EXPRESS directory on your hard disk by typing CD \EXPRESS and pressing RETURN.

3. Type EP and press RETURN.

When you first start Express Publisher, you see the menu bar and toolbox across the top of the screen. Since you did not specify a document to be opened when you started the program, Express Publisher creates a one-page, one-column document. Notice that the file name UNTITLED.EPD appears at the right side of the menu bar.

Creating a new document To learn about Express Publisher from the ground up, it's best to start with a completely empty document. To get started, put away the one-column document and use the New command to create a blank, one-page document.

1. Click the File menu, and then click the New command.

   The Create a New Document dialog box appears.

The Create a New Document dialog box

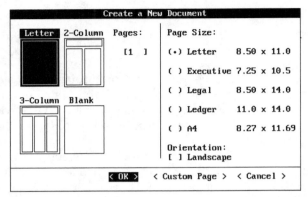

2. Click the Blank icon (it looks like an empty page).

3. Click OK.

Express Publisher creates a blank, one-page document.

Lesson 1: Understanding objects

In Express Publisher, an object is any shape that you can place on a page and then change with a command or move with the arrow tool. Objects may be boxes, ovals, lines, boxes with text in them, or pictures. In this lesson you will learn how to create, import, and handle objects. Later, you will learn how to use them as elements in constructing a document.

Creating objects   The simplest way to create objects is to draw them with the drawing tools. In the first exercise, you'll use the Box tool to draw a box.

The Box tool   1. Click the Box tool.

   The shape of the pointer changes to a pencil. This is to remind you that you are drawing. While you are using the Box tool, or any of the drawing tools, tick marks appear on the rulers to show you the exact position of the pointer.

2. Move the pointer somewhere inside the document window.

3. Press and hold down the mouse button.

   This marks the box's anchor point.

Drawing an object   Anchor Point

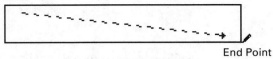

End Point

4. Without letting go of the mouse button, move the mouse down and to the right as shown above.

5. When the box is the right size and shape, release the mouse button. This position is called the *end point*.

All the drawing tools work the same way. After you click a drawing tool, the position where you click the mouse marks the object's anchor point. You then drag the mouse and release it to mark the end point. Express Publisher draws the object between the two points that you defined. Little black squares appear around an object right after you draw it; they will be explained shortly.

The drawing tools

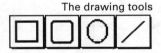

To get a better understanding of how the drawing tools work, try drawing an object using each of the drawing tools. Don't worry about making a mess, this is a learning experience.

Objects

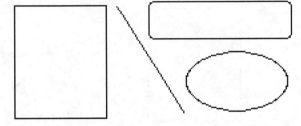

Selecting and deselecting objects

So far you have only created objects. If you could only create objects and not change them afterwards, your work would be very difficult. Express Publisher lets you move and change objects in many different ways.

In order to do anything to an object you have to *select* it. Selecting an object tells Express Publisher that you want to change it with your next action.

When an object is selected, little squares called *handles* appear around it, and the lines around it become heavier. You may have noticed this with the practice objects you have just drawn, because right after you draw an object, it is selected for you automatically. The squares are called handles because they are used to manipulate the object.

Deselecting is almost as important as selecting. If you inadvertently leave an object selected, your next action may affect the selected object instead of doing what you actually want.

Follow these steps to learn how to select and deselect objects:

1. Move the pointer over one of the objects that you drew earlier and click the mouse button.

A selected object

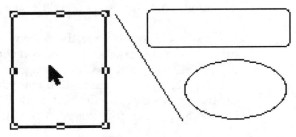

Handles appear around the object that you selected, and the lines around it get thicker. Now try to select another object.

2. Move the pointer over another object and click the mouse button.

Another selected object

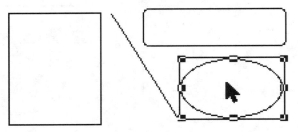

Notice that the handles around the object you selected earlier disappear, and new handles appear around the object that you just selected. When you select an object, any object that was previously selected is deselected.

3. Move the pointer so that it is not over any object and click the mouse button.

This deselects any selected object without selecting a new one. You can tell that no objects are selected because none of them have handles around them.

Changing objects
You should understand how to create and select objects by now. Once you understand these concepts you shouldn't have any trouble moving objects or changing their appearance. Express Publisher can change objects in many ways, but these functions are the most basic: moving, grouping, resizing, reshaping, filling, and deleting.

Moving an object

All Express Publisher objects can be moved around the document, either with the mouse or with a command. Start by using the mouse to move one of the objects you've been working with.

1. Move the pointer over the center of one of the objects that you drew earlier.

2. Press and hold down the mouse button.

Moving a box

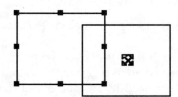

The pointer should change to a four-headed arrow as soon as you move the mouse. If it doesn't, make sure that you are holding down the mouse button and that the pointer is over the object. Also, be sure to place the pointer in the center of the object and not over one of the handles when you press the mouse button.

3. Without releasing the mouse button, move the mouse in any direction.

   This is called *dragging*. The object's outline moves with you as you move the mouse.

4. When the object is where you want it, release the mouse button.

Express Publisher redraws the object in its new location. Try moving several objects around to get a feel for how this works. Notice that while you are moving an object, tick marks on the ruler show you the position of the object's edges. This is very useful for placing an object in a precise location.

Moving lines

Moving lines is slightly different than moving other objects. To move a line you have to drag the center handle, as shown in the picture below.

Moving a line

Cutting and pasting objects

Another way to move an object is to use the Cut and Paste commands.

1. Select one of the objects on the screen.

2. Pull down the Edit menu and choose Cut.

   The object disappears.

3. Scroll to another part of the page.

4. Pull down the Edit menu and choose Paste.

   The object is pasted in the center of the document window.

Grouping objects

When you need to move several objects, you may find it convenient to select them as a group. You can use the Cut, Copy, and Paste commands with grouped objects just as with individual objects. As long as they are selected, Express Publisher treats them as one object.

1. Move the pointer over the first object and click the mouse button to select it.

2. Hold down the SHIFT key and select the second object.

3. While still pressing SHIFT, select a third object.

4. While still pressing SHIFT, click one of the selected objects and drag the group of objects to a new location.

5. Release the SHIFT key; the objects remain selected. If you want to move the group of objects again, press the SHIFT and drag them to a new location. If you want to move only one of the objects, drag it as you normally would; the other objects do not remain selected.

Sizing and shaping objects

Not only can you move an object to a new location, you can change its size and shape.

1. Select an object.

2. Move the pointer so that the very tip of the arrow is on the lower right handle.

3. Hold down the mouse button and drag the handle up and to the right as shown below.

Stretching a box

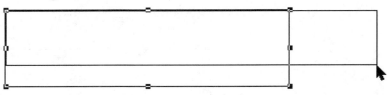

The outline of the object should move to indicate its changing size and shape. If the pointer changes to a four-headed arrow and the whole box moves without changing size, then you did not have the tip of the arrow exactly over the handle when you pressed the mouse button. Let go of the mouse button and try again.

4. When the object is the right size and shape, let go of the mouse button.

Express Publisher redraws the object in the new dimensions. Try dragging different handles to change the size and shape of various objects in different ways. The handles in the middle of an object's sides let you change only one dimension at a time. The corner handles let you change both dimensions at once.

Using fills

You can fill an object with shading or patterns. When an object is filled, it becomes opaque. This means that you can't see the parts of your document that are covered by filled objects.

Try changing one of the objects you created earlier so that it is filled.

1. Select an object that you created earlier.

The Set Fill tool

2. Click the Set Fill tool.

The Set Fill Pattern dialog box appears.

The Set Fill Pattern dialog box

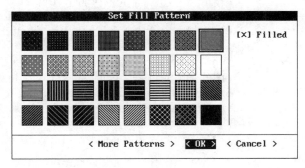

3. Double-click one of the fill types.

The dialog box disappears and the object displays the fill type you just chose. (If you chose white, you may not notice the change unless the object was covering some other objects.)

A filled box

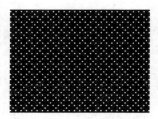

If you want to remove the fill pattern, click the Set Fill tool again, click once in the Filled check box to remove the check mark and click OK. The fill setting changes back to unfilled, and the object becomes clear again.

Deleting objects

After experimenting with what you've learned so far, you may find that your document is becoming cluttered with objects. You may want to delete some objects to clear up some space.

1. Select an object.

2. Press the DELETE key on your keyboard.

   If a portion of the deleted object remains on the screen, click the Refresh button in the lower right corner of the screen, or press CTRL-F1

Bring to Front/ Send to Back

Express Publisher stacks all objects in the order in which they are created. The first object you draw is at the bottom of the stack, and the last is on the top. Moving an object has no effect on its position in the stack. The last object you draw stays in the front until you draw a new object. If you draw an object and then move another object to the same location, the older object will be placed behind the object that you just drew.

While creating documents, you may need to change the stacking order of objects. This is especially true if you use background images. The Bring to Front and Send to Back commands allow you to change the stacking order.

1. Draw a box and choose a fill pattern.

2. Draw another box overlapping the first box and fill it with another pattern, as shown in the following picture.

Overlapping objects

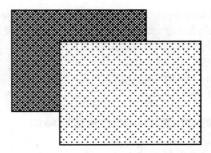

The second box covers the first box because it was drawn later.

3. Draw a larger box that completely covers the others and select a different fill pattern.

   The box you drew last is at the top of the stack, so it covers the earlier objects. Now use the Send to Back command to send the last box to bottom of the stack.

4. Select the larger box, pull down the Objects menu and choose Send to Back (or press CTRL-E).

   The larger box is sent to the bottom of the stack and the other two objects now cover it.

Overlapping objects

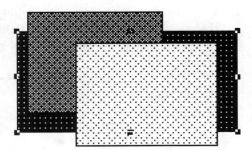

5. With the larger box still selected, pull down the Objects menu and select Bring to Front (or press CTRL-F).

   The larger box is returned to the front of the stack.

Importing pictures   Express Publisher can import pictures from several graphics programs. Once a picture has been imported, Express Publisher treats it as an ordinary object. You can select, move, and size pictures in the same way as other objects. When you change a picture with Express Publisher, it does not change the original picture on disk. Express Publisher only changes the picture within the document you are working on.

1. Pull down the File menu and select Import Picture.

The Import A Picture dialog box appears. It displays an alphabetical list of all of the files in the \EXPRESS\ART directory. The ART directory contains all of the clip art that you chose to install with the setup program. The files that show up on your screen may not match those shown in the picture below.

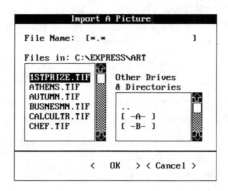

```
            Import A Picture

 File Name:  [*.*                  ]

 Files in: C:\EXPRESS\ART

 1STPRIZE.TIF       Other Drives
 ATHENS.TIF         & Directories
 AUTUMN.TIF
 BUSNESMN.TIF        ..
 CALCULTR.TIF       [ -A- ]
 CHEF.TIF           [ -B- ]


        <   OK   > < Cancel >
```

2. If you don't see the file FLAPPER.TIF in the Files list box, click the arrow at the bottom of the scroll bar to scroll through the list (see the picture above).

3. Double-click the file FLAPPER.TIF.

While Express Publisher is importing the picture, it displays the watch pointer. The hands on the watch go around as long as the program is working. When it is finished importing the picture, Express Publisher displays it in the middle of the document window. Handles appear around the picture to indicate that it is selected.

FLAPPER.TIF

Moving a picture

You can move a picture in the same way as any other object.

1. Move the pointer over the picture.

2. Press and hold down the mouse button.

3. Without releasing the mouse button, move the pointer.

   The picture's outline moves as you move the mouse.

4. When the picture is in the desired location, release the mouse button.

Scaling a picture

You can size a picture by dragging its handles, just like you did with other objects, but you will find that pictures become distorted unless you scale them proportionately. The Scale Object command preserves the original proportions of an object while reducing or enlarging it. You can use the Scale Object command to scale any object, but it is most useful for imported pictures.

1. Select the picture that you imported earlier.

2. Click the Objects menu to pull it down and click the Scale Object command.

   The Scale Object dialog box appears.

The Scale Object dialog box

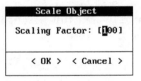

3. Type 50 and press DELETE to get rid of the extra zero.

4. Click OK.

Express Publisher reduces the picture to 50% of its original size, maintaining its original proportions.

Summary of Lesson 1

You have already learned some of the basic concepts in Express Publisher.

- An object is a shape that you can move or change. Documents are made up of objects.
- To change an object you must first select it by clicking on it with the mouse. By holding down the SHIFT key, you can select objects as a group.

- Once you have selected one or more objects, you can move them, delete them, or cut and paste them.
- You can change an object's size and shape, and specify a new fill type.
- All objects are stacked in the order in which they were created. You can change the stacking order with the Bring to Front (CTRL-F) and Send to Back (CTRL-E) tools.
- Express Publisher can import pictures from other graphics programs. You can select, move, and size pictures in the same way as other objects. The Scale Object command sizes pictures proportionally.

How to continue
You have now completed lesson 1. You may now leave Express Publisher or clear the screen and go directly on to lesson 2.

Exiting

1. Click the File menu.

2. Click Exit.

3. You don't need to save this practice document, so when the warning prompt appears, click No. You return to the DOS prompt.

Continuing

1. Click the File menu.

2. Click Close.

3. You don't need to save this practice document, so when the warning prompt appears, click No.

Express Publisher removes your practice document and provides you with a new, empty document for lesson 2.

Lesson 2: Entering text

This lesson focuses on entering and editing text in an Express Publisher document. You can type text directly in the document or import text created by most of the popular word processors.

Feel free to experiment with entering text. If you know another desktop publishing program, or how to operate a word processor, you may find that Express Publisher works in many of the same ways.

Text frames

To enter text in Express Publisher, you must first use the Text Frame tool to create a box that you can type or import text into. The box with text in it becomes a special kind of object called a *text frame*. You can apply most of the commands you learned in Lesson 1 to the text frame; you can also use the Text tool to edit the text itself.

This exercise shows you how to create a text frame.

1. Draw a box at least 2" by 2" using the Text Frame tool.

The Text Frame tool

The shape of the pointer changes to an I-beam and a blinking line appears in the upper left corner of the box. This line is called a te*xt insertion point* or simply a *cursor*. The cursor marks the position where text will go when you start typing.

2. Type Had I known who awaited me I never would have answered the door on that April morning.

Text frame

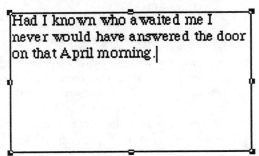

When you reach the end of the line in the text frame, keep on typing; Express Publisher automatically starts a new line. This *word wrap* feature, common to many word processors, means that you don't have to press ENTER at the end of every line. You should press ENTER only at the end of paragraphs.

Note

The I-beam pointer allows you to type and select text. You cannot select or move objects with the I-beam, and you cannot select text with the arrow pointer. If you are working with text and click the mouse while the I-beam is outside of a box, the arrow pointer reappears. If this occurs, click the Text tool, move the I-beam pointer inside the box, and click the mouse button. This procedure can be used to change any box into a text frame.

Moving the cursor

As you enter text, the cursor moves to the right of each new character. You can move the cursor using either the arrow keys or the mouse. You cannot move the cursor outside of a text frame or beyond the end of existing text.

Moving the cursor with the arrow keys

Pressing an arrow key on the keyboard moves the cursor in the direction of the arrow. If you hold down an arrow key, the cursor moves continuously in that direction.

Try adding a new word to the sentence that you just typed.

1. Use the arrow keys to move the cursor between the words "April" and "morning."

2. Erase the word "April" by pressing BACKSPACE.

   The BACKSPACE key deletes the character to the left of the cursor. Notice that the other characters to the right are pulled back as you delete characters.

3. Now type `December` to replace April.

   As you type the new characters, the existing characters move to the right.

Moving the cursor with the mouse

For moving longer distances, it is much faster to use the mouse to move the cursor. Just move the I-beam pointer to where you want to place the cursor, and click the mouse button. The cursor then moves to the place where you clicked. You can only place the cursor within the text that is already in the frame. You can't place the cursor in an area that does not already contain text.

1. Move the mouse so that the I-beam pointer is between the words "who" and "awaited" and click the mouse.

2. Backspace over the word "who" and type `what`.

Quick keys

Here are a few keystroke shortcuts for moving the cursor:

- The HOME and END keys move the cursor to the beginning or end of the current line, respectively.
- The key combinations CTRL plus PGUP or CTRL plus PGDN moves the cursor to the beginning or end of the text in the current frame, respectively.

Selecting text and changing fonts

Just as when you are working with objects, you must select text in order to change it. Once you have selected some text, you can move it, delete it, change its font, or change its style. In this exercise you will select all of the text that you've entered so far and then change the font.

Selecting text involves the same technique that you use when drawing objects: you establish an anchor point and an end point.

1. Use the mouse to move the I-beam pointer just to the left of the first character in the sentence.

2. Press the mouse button, and without releasing it, move the mouse down and to the right.

   As you move the mouse, the selected text is highlighted. If the first few characters are not highlighted, release the mouse button and try again, moving the mouse more slowly.

3. When all the text is highlighted, release the mouse button.

Selected text   Anchor point —

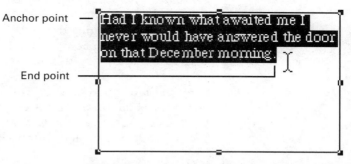

End point ————

Any change you make at this point affects all of the selected text.

4. Pull down the Text menu and select the Choose Font command.

   The Choose Font dialog box appears, listing all of the available fonts. (The fonts available on your system may not match those shown in the picture below.)

The Choose Font dialog box

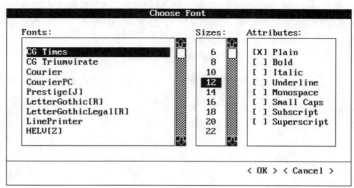

5. Click CG Triumvirate in the Fonts list box, select 12 in the Sizes list box, and click OK.

All of the selected text changes to the CG Triumvirate font.

Deselecting text

To deselect text, move the mouse to another part of the document window and click. If you move the pointer over some other text, the cursor moves to where you clicked the mouse.

Now that you know how to select and deselect text, try selecting different parts of the text you've entered so far. Notice that you can drag the mouse in any direction to select text. As you drag the pointer, all of the text between the anchor point and the current location of the pointer is highlighted. As this lesson continues, you'll learn some other ways to select text.

Changing font attributes In addition to changing the font, you can make text italic, bold, underlined, monospaced, small caps, subscript, and superscript. These are called font attributes.

Note Some of the attributes do not work with fonts that are specific to certain printers. All of the attributes work with CG Triumvirate, CG Times, Univers, and the other CG fonts sold in the Express Fonts Classic, Stylist, and Flair packages.

To apply a font attribute, you need only select the text that you want to change, and choose an attribute. Start by practicing a shortcut for selecting whole words.

1. Move the I-beam pointer so that it is over the word "never."

2. Double-click the mouse button.

   This should select the whole word. If it didn't, you may not have clicked fast enough. Press the mouse twice in the time it takes to say "express." Also make sure that you don't move the mouse as you double-click.

3. Select the Choose Font command from the Text menu.

   The Choose Font dialog box appears.

4. Click the Italic check box on the right side of the dialog box, and then click OK.

   The word "never" is italicized and the rest of the text is unchanged. When changing selected text, the change you make affects all of the selected text, and only the selected text.

Cutting and pasting text The Cut and Paste commands are very useful for moving text around. The Cut command removes the selected text from your document and places it in a temporary storage area called the clipboard. The Paste command places a copy of the text on the clipboard back in the document at the cursor position.

1. Select the text "Had I known what awaited me."

2. Pull down the Edit menu and choose Cut.

   Express Publisher removes the selected text from the text frame and puts it on the clipboard. If you want to make sure that it is on the clipboard, pull down the Edit menu again and choose Show Clipboard. Click OK when you are done looking at the clipboard.

   Now paste the text in a different location.

3. Using either the mouse or the arrow keys, move the cursor to the very end of the existing sentence, between the word "morning" and the period.

4. Pull down the Edit menu and choose Paste.

   The text that you cut earlier is inserted at the cursor position. You will have to adjust the spacing and capitalization to make the sentence correct. You should end up with, "I never would have answered the door that December morning had I known what awaited me."

Putting away the text tool

While you are using the Text tool to work with text you can't move or select objects with the pointer; you can only work with text.

- Click the Arrow tool to put away the Text tool, or move the I-beam pointer outside of any box and click the mouse.

The Arrow tool

This changes the pointer back to the black arrow, so you may again select and move objects. Anytime you have selected a tool and you want to change the pointer back to the arrow, click the Arrow tool.

Changing a text frame

Once you are working with the arrow pointer, you may select, move, and resize a text frame as if it were an ordinary object.

1. If the text frame you've been working with is not already selected, move the arrow pointer inside the text frame and click the mouse button.

2. Move the pointer inside the box, press and hold down the mouse button as you drag it any direction, and then release the mouse button.

   The text frame's outline moves as you move the mouse. When you release the mouse button, Express Publisher redraws the text frame in its new location.

3. Drag one of the text frame's corner handles to change the size and shape of the box.

Resizing a text frame

Express Publisher reformats the text to fit in the resized box.

Resized text frame

4. Resize the text frame so that it is too small to hold all of the text you entered.

The More Text marker

Although some text disappears from the document, it has not been permanently lost. Express Publisher puts the More Text marker (shown at left) in the lower right corner of the text frame to tell you that there is more text than will fit in the text frame. If you stretch the box back to its original size, the text reappears.

Summary of lesson 2   Lesson 2 covered the most basic elements of text entry.

- Express Publisher handles all text within boxes called text frames, which you create with the Text Frame tool.

- You can also create a text frame by drawing a box, clicking on the Text tool, and then clicking inside the box with the I-beam pointer.
- Use either the mouse, the arrow keys, or one of the keyboard shortcuts such as HOME or END to move the cursor within a text frame.
- While you are working with text, the pointer is shaped like an I-beam. You cannot select or move objects while working with text. If you click the Arrow tool, the pointer changes back to the arrow and you may again select and move objects.
- To change text after it has been entered, you must select it with the I-beam pointer. Selecting text involves using the same technique of dragging the pointer from an anchor point to an end point that you use when drawing objects.
- Once you have selected text, you can cut it to the clipboard, change its font, or change its style. Any change you make affects all the selected text, and only the selected text.
- You can select, move, and resize text frames just like ordinary boxes. If you change the size or shape of a box, Express Publisher reformats the text to fill it.

How to continue   You have now completed lesson 2. You may now leave Express Publisher or go directly on to lesson 3.

Exiting

1. Click the File menu.

2. Click Exit.

3. You don't need to save this practice document, so when the warning prompt appears, click No. You return to the DOS prompt.

Continuing

Go on to Lesson 3.

Lesson 3: Creating a newsletter

You now know enough about Express Publisher's basic features to create a simple document. This lesson leads you through the creation of a simple newsletter called "Club Talk." Along the way it tells you how to display an entire page of your newsletter on screen, import text from a word processor, apply a preset style, zoom out to make layout change, add a text frame, align objects to each other, import a new story, add a second page to your newsletter, and link text frames.

Completed newsletter

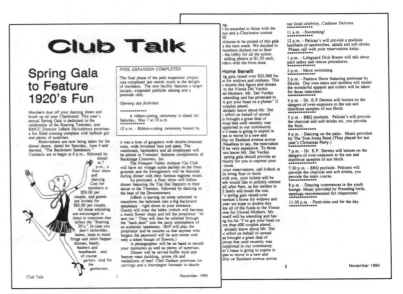

Note — Express Publisher looks different when run on different types of graphics display adapters. Don't be concerned if your document doesn't look exactly like the screen shots in the next two lessons.

Creating a new document

The New command lets you define the number of columns, the number of pages, and the page size for a new Express Publisher document.

1. Pull down the File menu and select New.

   The Create a New Document dialog box appears.

The Create a New Document dialog box

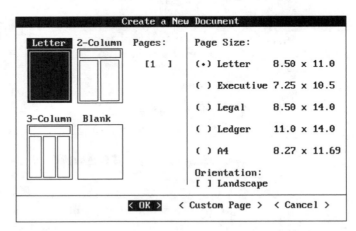

2. Click the 2-column icon, enter 1 in the Pages text field, and make sure Letter (8.5" by 11") is selected as the page size. Click OK when all the options have been set.

   Express Publisher creates a blank page according to your specifications. The frames on the page match the number of columns that you specified. A picture appears in the middle of the document window to show how text will flow through the new document; press any key to remove it.

Importing a story

Until now, you have only entered text yourself. It is much faster to use an external word processor to write a long story, and then import it into Express Publisher using the Import Text command. The text for your newsletter is in a file called NEWSLTTR.WPS. This file was created by one of the word processors that Express Publisher supports.

1. The column on the lower left side of the document window should be selected.

   Make sure that the column is selected before going on to the next step; otherwise the text you import won't be put in the right place. The selected frame should have heavy lines and handles around it as shown in the following picture.

Selected text frame

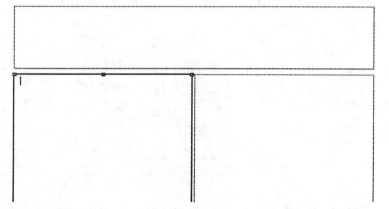

2. Pull down the File menu and choose Import Text.

   The Import Text dialog box appears.

The Import Text dialog box

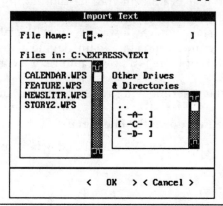

3. The file you want to import is in the \EXPRESS\TEXT directory. If the name on the Files In line is not C:\EXPRESS\TEXT, use this method to change it. If it is, go on to the next step.

   Double-click ". ." in the Other Drives and Directories list box until you are in C:\EXPRESS. Then scroll down the list until the directory name TEXT appears. Double-click TEXT to display a list of the files in it. The file name box should list the same files shown in the picture above.

   If you get lost while changing directories, re-read "Using dialog boxes" in Chapter 1, "Beginning."

4. Double-click the file NEWSLTTR.WPS in the Files list box.

   Express Publisher imports the text into your document. Notice that the text flows automatically from the left to the right text frames.

Imported text

Spring Gala to Feature 1920's Fun

Members dust off your dancing shoes and brush up on your Charleston! This year's annual Spring Gala is dedicated to the celebration of the Roaring Twenties, and RMCC Director JoBeth McAndrews promises a fun filled evening complete with bathtub gin and plenty of surprises.
     Reservations are now being taken for the dinner dance, slated for Saturday, June 4 and themed, "The Backroom Speakeasy." Cocktails are to begin at 6 p.m., followed by dinner at 7 p.m., a floor show and dancing. Cost for members is $50.00 per couple, and

Dinner will be served buffet style and feature roast duckling, prime rib and medallions of beef. Chef Dodson promises ice carvings and a champagne fountain to dazzle all those attending.
     Prizes will be awarded to those with the best 20's costumes and a Charleston contest will begin at 9:30.
     Look for pictures to be posted of this gala event as early as the next week. We decided to display all our members decked out in their finest. So check the lobby for all the action. We will also be selling photos at $1.50 each, so leave your orders with the front desk.
     Last year's spring gala raised over

Saving your work   You should save your work every time you make a significant change to the document. Saving means that you tell Express Publisher to make a copy of the document on the screen and store it as a file on your hard or floppy disk. Saving frequently allows you experiment with confidence; if you make a big mistake you can always re-open the latest saved version of the document and start again. Saving also protects you from losing work if there is a power failure or a computer problem.

The first time you save a document you need to enter a name.

1. Pull down the File menu and choose Save.

   The Save a Document dialog box appears.

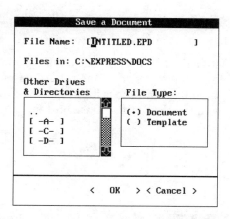

2. Type CLUBTALK in the File Name text field, and click OK.

Express Publisher saves your work. Notice that the file name displayed in the upper right corner of the screen now reads "CLUBTALK.EPD." The document has been stored in the \EXPRESS\DOCS directory.

Press F10 to activate the Save command.

Now that you have saved the document once, every time you use the Save command, Express Publisher saves the document, using the same name and directory.

Creating a story headline

Your document is starting to look like a newsletter, but you need to make the story headline stand out more clearly. To do this, you are going to apply a preset style to the headline.

Using a style

You already know how to change fonts and character sizes, but Express Publisher allows you to make several formatting changes at once with the Choose Style command.

A *style* is a group of formatting characteristics that are identified by a single name. When you select a paragraph of text and apply a style, all of the formatting characteristics within the style are applied to the selected text. This means that with a single command you can change the type face, character size, character attributes, justification, spacing, margins and indents.

Express Publisher comes with a number of preset styles that offer paragraph and character formats suited for particular purposes. For example, the Headline style instantly changes the text in the current paragraph to a larger bold font with extra space below the line. Try using the Headline style on the text that you just imported.

1. Make sure you are using the I-beam text cursor. Use the mouse to move it to the top of the left text frame.

2. Move the I-beam pointer just left of the word "Spring," hold down the mouse button and drag down and to the right. When the headline is highlighted as shown in the following picture, release the mouse button.

Selecting the headline

Spring Gala to Feature 1920's Fun

Members dust off your dancing shoes and brush up on your Charleston! This year's annual Spring Gala is dedicated to the celebration of the Roaring Twenties, and RMCC Director JoBeth McAndrews promises a fun filled evening complete with bathtub gin and plenty of surprises.

Reservations are now being taken for the dinner dance, slated for Saturday, June 4 and themed, "The Backroom Speakeasy." Cocktails are to begin at 6 p.m., followed by dinner at 7 p.m., a floor show and dancing. Cost for members is $50.00 per couple, and

Dinner will be served buffet style and feature roast duckling, prime rib and medallions of beef. Chef Dodson promises ice carvings and a champagne fountain to dazzle all those attending.

Prizes will be awarded to those with the best 20's costumes and a Charleston contest will begin at 9:30.

Look for pictures to be posted of this gala event as early as the next week. We decided to display all our members decked out in their finest. So check the lobby for all the action. We will also be selling photos at $1.50 each, so leave your orders with the front desk.

Last year's spring gala raised over

3. Select Choose Style from the Text menu.

The Choose Style dialog box appears.

The Choose Style dialog box

Choose Style

< No Style >
Banner
Bulleted 1
Bulleted 2
Bulleted 3
Caption
Headline
Mouse Type

< OK >   < Cancel >

4. Double click Headline in the list box.

Express Publisher increases the type size and changes the headline font to CG Triumvirate bold.

Adding a subhead   Subheads make it easier for a reader to find specific information in a story, and they also make the page look a little livelier. Let's add a subhead to this story.

1. Move the mouse so the I-beam is at the beginning of the sentence "Last year's spring gala" in the second column and click once.

You may have to scroll down the document to find the sentence. To do so, press PGDN.

2. Press RETURN twice to create two blank lines and press UP once.

3. Type Del Vechio Home Benefit.

Now change the font of the subhead so that it's different from the story. Use the mouse and the I-beam pointer to select the line you just typed in the same way that you selected the headline earlier.

Selecting the subhead

Spring Gala to Feature 1920's Fun

Members dust off your dancing shoes and brush up on your Charleston! This year's annual Spring Gala is dedicated to the celebration of the Roaring Twenties, and RMCC Director JoBeth McAndrews promises a fun filled evening complete with bathtub gin and plenty of surprises.

Reservations are now being taken for the dinner dance, slated for Saturday, June 4 and themed, "The Backroom Speakeasy." Cocktails are to begin at 6 p.m., followed by dinner at 7 p.m., a floor show and dancing. Cost for members is $50.00 per couple, and guests are invited for $65.00 per couple.

All those attending are encouraged to dress in costumes that reflect the "Roaring 20's." In case you don't remember, ladies, keep in mind fringe and short flapper dresses,

sent me." They will then be ushered through the "back door" into the jazzy atmosphere of an authentic speakeasy. (Biff will play the proprietor and he assures us that anyone who forgets the password will be sent home with only a token bouqet of flowers.)

A photographer will be on hand to record your memories as well as plenty of surprises.

Dinner will be served buffet style and feature roast duckling, prime rib and medallions of beef. Chef Dodson promises ice carvings and a champagne fountain to dazzle all those attending.

Prizes will be awarded to those with the best 20's costumes and a Charleston contest will begin at 9:30.

Look for pictures to be posted of this gala event as early as the next week. We decided to display all our members decked out in their finest. So check the lobby for all the action. We will also be selling photos at $1.50 each, so leave your orders with the front desk.

Del Vechio Home Benefit

Last year's spring gala raised over $20,000 for Emerson's home for widows and orphans. This year we hope to double this figure and donate all of the funds to the Vinnie Del Vechio Home

4. Select Choose Font from the Text menu.

The Choose Font dialog box appears.

5. Click CG Triumvirate in the Font list box, select 14 points as the size, and click bold.

6. Click OK.

The text you selected changes to the new font and size.

7. Click the Arrow tool to put away the Text tool.

Adding a second story

To make room for a second story, you need to clear some space on the first page of the newsletter. It's easier to do this when you can see the entire page on the screen.

1. Pull down the Page menu and select Zoom Out.

The page shrinks so almost the entire page shows on the screen. Now you can shorten the second text column and add a frame for more text.

2. Select the text frame on the right side of the page.

3. Move the pointer over the center handle at the top of the frame.

   You may have to scroll up the document window: drag the thumb in the vertical scroll bar to the top of the screen.

4. Drag the handle down so that the top of the frame ends up 5″ from the top of the page. Use the tick marks on the vertical ruler to measure the distance as you drag.

Spring Gala to Feature 1920's Fun

Members dust off your dancing shoes and brush up on your Charleston! This year's annual Spring Gala is dedicated to the celebration of the Roaring Twenties, and RMCC Director JoBeth McAndrews promises a fun filled evening complete with bathtub gin and plenty of surprises.

Reservations are now being taken for the dinner dance, slated for Saturday, June 4 and themed, "The Backroom Speakeasy." Cocktails are to begin at 6 p.m., followed by dinner at 7 p.m., a floor show and dancing. Cost for members is $50.00 per couple, and guests are invited for $65.00 per couple.

All those attending are encouraged to dress in costumes that reflect the "Roaring 20's."

"back door" into the jazzy atmosphere of an authentic speakeasy. (Biff will play the proprietor and he assures us that anyone who forgets the password will be sent home with only a token bouqet of flowers.)

A photographer will be on hand to record your memories as well as plenty of surprises.

Dinner will be served buffet style and feature roast duckling, prime rib and medallions of beef. Chef Dodson promises ice carvings and a champagne fountain to dazzle all those attending.

Prizes will be awarded to those with the best 20's costumes and a Charleston contest will begin at 9:30.

Look for pictures to be posted of this gala "back door" into the jazzy atmosphere of an authentic speakeasy. (Biff will play the proprietor and he assures us that anyone who forgets the password will be sent home with only a token bouqet of flowers.)

A photographer will be on hand to record your memories as well as plenty of surprises.

Dinner will be served buffet style and feature roast duckling, prime rib and medallions of beef. Chef Dodson promises ice carvings and

The text at the top of the second frame moves down, and some of the text disappears at the bottom. The text isn't lost; Express Publisher stores the rest of the story that no longer fits in the frame. When you make more room, the text reappears. A small crooked arrow, called the More Text marker, in the bottom right corner of the text frame indicates that there is more text than will fit in the text frame.

Now that you have a blank space at the top of the second column, create a new text frame for the second story.

5. Use the Text Frame tool to draw a text frame that fills the space that you cleared. Make sure that the top of the text frame is even with the top of the text column on the left (use the tick mark on the vertical ruler to line it up). Try to make the new text frame the same width as the other text frames (see the figure below).

Creating a new text frame

Spring Gala to Feature 1920's Fun

Members dust off your dancing shoes and brush up on your Charleston! This year's annual Spring Gala is dedicated to the celebration of the Roaring Twenties, and RMCC Director JoBeth McAndrews promises a fun filled evening complete with bathtub gin and plenty of surprises.

Reservations are now being taken for the dinner dance, slated for Saturday, June 4 and themed, "The Backroom Speakeasy." Cocktails are to begin at 6 p.m., followed by dinner at 7 p.m., a floor show and dancing. Cost for members is $50.00 per couple, and guests are invited for $65.00 per couple.

All those attending are encouraged to dress in costumes that reflect the "Roaring 20's."

"back door" into the jazzy atmosphere of an authentic speakeasy. (Biff will play the proprietor and he assures us that anyone who forgets the password will be sent home with only a token bouqet of flowers.)

A photographer will be on hand to record your memories as well as plenty of surprises.

Dinner will be served buffet style and feature roast duckling, prime rib and medallions of beef. Chef Dodson promises ice carvings and

6. Pull down the Page menu and click Actual Size to return to the normal view of the document.

Aligning objects

To look like a professional newsletter, the text frame you just created should line up on the left with the text frame beneath it. Since this is difficult to do by hand, try using the Align tool.

The Align tool

1. Click the Align tool.

The pointer changes to the alignment pointer.

2. Click the text frame at the bottom right of the document window, the same one you resized earlier.

This identifies the text frame as the object to which you want to align another object. The second object that you click is the one that will be moved.

3. Click the text frame that you just drew.

The Align Two Objects dialog box appears. It displays all the different options for alignment. The dotted lines show which edges of the two objects will be aligned. For this example, align the left sides of the two objects.

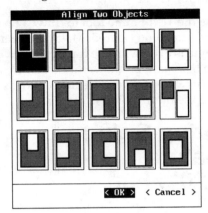

4. Double-click the second icon from the left in the top row.

The left side of the text frame you drew is aligned to the left side of the older text frame.

Now that the new text frame is in the right place, you can fill it with a second story.

1. Click the text frame that you just aligned.

2. Pull down the File menu and select Import Text.

3. Double-click the file STORY2.WPS

Express Publisher imports the file. Notice that the headline at the beginning of the story is italicized. Express Publisher recognized the font attribute that was applied in the word processor. Again, the More Text marker means that there is more text than will fit in the frame. In Lesson 4 you will learn how to make space for the remainder of the story.

Spring Gala to Feature 1920's Fun

Members dust off your dancing shoes and brush up on your Charleston! This year's annual Spring Gala is dedicated to the celebration of the Roaring Twenties, and RMCC Director JoBeth McAndrews promises a fun filled evening complete with bathtub gin and plenty of surprises.

Reservations are now being taken for the dinner dance, slated for Saturday, June 4 and themed, "The Backroom Speakeasy." Cocktails are to begin at 6 p.m., followed by dinner at 7 p.m., a floor show and dancing. Cost for members is $50.00 per couple, and guests are invited for $65.00 per couple.

All those attending are encouraged to

POOL EXPANSION COMPLETED

The final phase of the pool expansion project was completed last month much to the delight of members. The new facility features a larger jacuzzi, expanded poolside seating and a poolside cafe.

Opening day festivities

****
A ribbon-cutting ceremony is slated for Saturday, May 7 at 10 a.m.
****

10 a.m. - Ribbon-cutting ceremony hosted by

sent me." They will then be ushered through the "back door" into the jazzy atmosphere of an authentic speakeasy. (Biff will play the proprietor and he assures us that anyone who forgets the password will be sent home with only a token bouquet of flowers.)

A photographer will be on hand to record your memories as well as plenty of surprises.

Changing the line type

Express Publisher draws text frames with the Text Frame tool with non-printing lines. Non-printing lines appear as dotted or shaded lines on the screen, but they do not show up when you print the document. The text frame you just drew has non-printing lines, as do the other three text frames in your document. In most cases you don't want boxes to appear around all the text in the printed document, but you can use boxes to distinguish one story from another: for example, to set the second story you just imported off from the first story. The Set Line tool allows you to change the line type.

1. Select the text frame into which you imported the second story.

The Set Line tool

2. Click the Set Line tool.

   The Set Line Type dialog box appears.

The Set Line Type dialog box

Set Line Type	
Thickness	**Ink**
▬▬▬	(•) Black
────	( ) White
───	( ) Non-Printing
────	

‹ OK › ‹Cancel›

3. Click the Black option box, and click OK.

Express Publisher changes the lines around the text frame to black lines.

Summary of lesson 3   In lesson 3 you learned some of the first steps you might take in creating a simple newsletter.

- The New command lets you specify the number of columns, number of pages, and page size for a new document.
- It is very important to save your work frequently.
- You can change the font, attribute and type size of any paragraph in a text frame. You may have different fonts and sizes within a text frame.
- Styles can apply a number of text formatting parameters.
- You can import text from other programs, or enter it directly into a text frame.
- Text frames created by the New command are linked together so that text flows from frame to frame automatically.
- Text frames can be resized just like any other object.
- You can use Zoom Out to get a view of the whole document.
- Align any two objects to each other using the Align tool.
- The Set Line tool changes the line type of text frames.

How to continue   You have now completed lesson 3. You may now leave Express Publisher or clear the screen and go directly on to lesson 4.

Exiting

1. Press F10 to save the work you have done in this lesson.

2. Pull down the File menu and click Exit. You return to the DOS prompt.

Continuing

Press F10 to save the work you did in lesson 3 and go on to Lesson 4.

Lesson 4: More advanced functions

Now you're ready to try some more advanced techniques to complete your newsletter: flow stories from one page to another, add a title with TextEffects, wrap text around a picture, and add a page number.

Opening a document   If you closed your newsletter document in Lesson 3, you will have to retrieve it in order to do Lesson 4: Pull down the File menu and choose Open, then double-click CLUBTALK.EPD.

Adding a new page   In Lesson 3 you imported two stories to create the first page of your newsletter. Now you need to add a page to hold the text that wouldn't fit on page one.

1. Pull down the Page menu and choose New Page.

   The Add a New Page dialog box appears. It looks very much like the Create a New Document dialog box.

The Add a New Page dialog
box

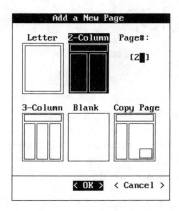

2. Click the 2-column icon and click OK.

   Express Publisher adds a new two column page to your document and displays it in the document window.

Linking text frames   When you imported the first story on page one, the text flowed from the left to the right frame because they were *linked* together. Now you will learn to use the Link tool to make the second story continue on page two of your newsletter. The Link tool can link together text frames on a single page, or across different pages.

The Link tool   1. Press F3 to go to the previous page.

2. Click the Link tool.

   The shape of the pointer changes to remind you that you are linking.

3. Click the text frame containing the second story.

   While you are using the Link tool you can change from page to page to find the frames you want to link. The Next Page and Previous Page commands let you move between pages. F4 activates the Next Page command, and F3 activates the Previous Page command. The number of the current page appears at the lower right corner of the screen.

3. Select Next Page from the Page menu, or press F4.

---

4. Click the text frame on the right side of the page.

Express Publisher fills the text frame with the remaining story text. Now use the same method to link the text frame on the lower right side of page one, to the text frame on the left side of page two.

5. Press F3 to move to the first page.

The Link tool 6. Click the Link tool.

7. Click the text frame on the lower right side of the page.

8. Press F4 to move to the next page.

9. Click the text frame on the left side of the page.

Note   If you get confused while using the Link tool, click the Arrow tool to deactivate the Link tool.

Add a title   Your newsletter still lacks a title. Express Publisher's TextEffects allows you to manipulate type to create very distinctive titles for publications, announcements and advertisements.

1. Move back to page one by selecting the Previous Page command on the Page menu, or pressing F3.

2. Select the empty frame above the two text frames at the top of the page.

Frame selected

Spring Gala to Feature 1920's Fun

Members dust off your dancing shoes and brush up on your Charleston! This year's annual Spring Gala is dedicated to the celebration of the Roaring Twenties, and RMCC Director JoBeth McAndrews promises

POOL EXPANSION COMPLETED

The final phase of the pool expansion project was completed last month much to the delight of members. The new facility features a larger jacuzzi, expanded poolside seating and a poolside cafe.

Opening day festivities

****
A ribbon-cutting ceremony is slated for Saturday, May 7 at 10 a.m.
****
10 a.m. - Ribbon-cutting ceremony hosted by

TextEffects Icon

3. Using the arrow tool, click the TextEffects icon at the far right side of the toolbox.

TextEffects opens and its screen appears. You'll notice it bears a strong resemblance to the Express Publisher screen. A menu bar listing TextEffects's pull-down menus appears at the top of the screen. Below the menu bar are TextEffects's tools. While most of the tools allow you to perform different functions than the

Express Publisher tools, they work similarly. The text frame you selected appears in the document window still selected, but the rest of your document is not there. Don't worry, it hasn't been lost. If you were to exit TextEffects now, your document would reappear along with the Express Publisher screen.

A headline may be made up of several TextEffects objects.

Entering text

While TextEffects looks and functions similarly to Express Publisher, a few of its features are significantly different. The greatest difference between the two is how you enter text. In Express Publisher, the text you type appears on the screen as it will when it prints. In TextEffects, you have to enter text into a dialog box before it appears on the screen. This dialog box, the Text Input dialog box, also lets you to create typesetting effects.

The Text tool

1. With the text frame selected, click the Text tool.

   The Text Input dialog box appears.

The Text Input dialog box

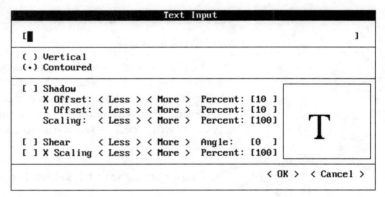

2. Enter the newsletter headline in the Text Input text box by typing Club Talk.

   Now you'll use the special typesetting commands available in the Text Input dialog box to give the headline a shadow and widen the headline's letters.

3. Click the Shadow check box.

   The X and Y Offsets control the placement of the shadow in relation to the headline. The X Offset is the amount of horizontal distance between the shadow and the headline; Y Offset is the amount of vertical distance. Both the X and Y Offsets default settings are 10 percent. The Scaling option controls the size of the shadow in relation to the headline. Its default makes the shadow the same size as the headline. For now, leave the default settings.

4. Click the X Scaling check box.

   The X Scaling option allows you to distort the headline's width in relation to its height. An X Scaling factor of 100 percent retains the font's natural width to height relationship. A factor larger than 100 widens characters while retaining their original height, a factor smaller than 100 thins characters.

5. Make the X Scaling factor 200 percent by clicking the arrow pointer in the X Scaling text box and typing 200.

6. Click More to preview the font. The T is updated to display the font and text effect.

7. Click OK.

   TextEffects places the headline according to the selections you made in the selected box.

Club Talk headline

Saving the headline

The headlines you create in TextEffects can be saved like documents in Express Publisher. Whenever you make significant changes to your work in TextEffects, make sure to use the Save command. This way you can experiment freely without losing previous work, or lose work due to computer malfunction or a power outage.

The first time you save a headline file you need to give it a name.

1. Pull down the file menu and select Save.

   The Save TextEffects Image dialog box appears.

The Save TextEffects Image dialog box

Save TextEffects Image

File Name: [UNTITLED.EPI   ]

Files in: C:\EXPRESS\ART

Other Drives
& Directories

..
[-A-]
[-B-]

< OK > < Cancel >

2. Type CLUBTALK in the File Name text field, and click OK.

TextEffects saves your headline. Don't worry about naming your headline file the same as your newsletter because the images you create with TextEffects are saved with the file name extension .EPI. The file name CLUBTALK.EPI now appears in the right corner of the screen. Your headline has been saved in the \EXPRESS\ART directory.

Now that you have saved your headline once, every time you use the Save command, TextEffects saves your headline using the same name and location.

Formatting the headline

Now that you have your headline text on the screen, you can manipulate it. The first action you'll take is to reduce the amount of space between the characters, then enlarge their size. Making characters fit closer together is a common technique when using large type sizes.

Before you can format the headline, you have to select it. But rather than select text with the I-beam pointer, in TextEffects all you have to do is select the object the text is in. In this case, it means selecting the box.

1. Select the box your headline is in.

2. Pull down the Text menu and select Character Spacing.

The Character Spacing dialog box appears.

The Character Spacing dialog box

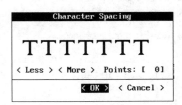

3. Click Less until the Points text box is at -4 and click OK.

Now you need to make the font size larger.

4. With the box still selected, pull down the Text menu and select Choose Font.

The Choose Font dialog box appears. It is identical to the Choose Font dialog box in Express Publisher.

5. Change the font to 60 point CG Triumvirate, and click OK.

TextEffects changes the headline according to your selections. It should look like the following picture.

Club Talk

Changing the line type

The final step to complete your headline is to change the line type of the box to non-printing lines.

1. Select the box.

2. Click the Set Line tool.

   The Set Line Type dialog box appears.

3. Click the Non-Printing option box, and click OK.

   When TextEffects changes the box's lines to non-printing, they appear as shaded or dotted lines.

Exit TextEffects

Now that your headline is complete, you can exit TextEffects.

1. Pull down the File menu and choose Exit.

   If you haven't saved your headline recently, TextEffects asks if you want to save the changes. Click Yes.

2. TextEffects closes and the Express Publisher screen appears. Your newsletter appears on the screen. Express Publisher automatically imports your headline into your newsletter and places it in the middle of the screen.

Move the headline into place

For more ideas on using TextEffects, see Chapter 6, "TextEffects," and Chapter 8, "Layout."

To quickly move a headline into place, line it up with the empty frame at the top of the page by following these steps:

1. Click the Align tool.

2. Select the empty box and then the "Club Talk" headline.

3. When the Align option box appears, click the Center option in the lower right-hand corner and click OK.

The headline is centered over the empty frame.

Importing a picture

So far, your newsletter contains only text; it needs a picture to liven it up. This exercise shows you how to use the Text Wrap tool to wrap text around irregular pictures or any object.

Start by importing a picture and placing it at the bottom left column of page one.

1. If necessary, use the Previous Page command to change to page one.

2. Press PGDN until you are at the bottom of the document.

3. Use the horizontal scroll bar to move to the very left side of the document.

4. Pull down the File menu and select Import Picture.

   The Import A Picture dialog box appears.

The Import A Picture dialog box

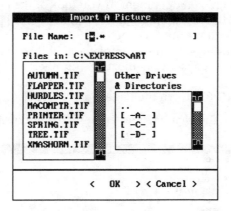

```
┌──────────────── Import A Picture ────────────────┐
│                                                  │
│   File Name: [█.*                    ]           │
│                                                  │
│   Files in: C:\EXPRESS\ART                       │
│                                                  │
│   AUTUMN.TIF          Other Drives               │
│   FLAPPER.TIF         & Directories              │
│   HURDLES.TIF                                    │
│   MACOMPTR.TIF        ..                          │
│   PRINTER.TIF         [ -A- ]                     │
│   SPRING.TIF          [ -C- ]                     │
│   TREE.TIF            [ -D- ]                     │
│   XMASHORN.TIF                                   │
│                                                  │
│                                                  │
│         < OK  > < Cancel >                        │
└──────────────────────────────────────────────────┘
```

5. Double-click the file FLAPPER.TIF.

   Express Publisher imports the picture and places it in the middle of the document window.

6. Move the picture into the following position.

FLAPPER.TIF in the correct position

dress in costumes that reflect our "Roaring 20's." In case you don't remember, ladies, keep in mind fringe and short flapper dresses, beads, feathers and headbands - and, of course, garters. And for the gentlemen, it was a time of gangsters with double-breasted suits, wide-brimmed hats and spats. The waitresses bartenders and all employees will be attired in Twenties' fashions complements of Backstage Costumes, Inc.

The Freeport Antique Car Club will have six vintage autos parked on the front grounds and Swingtimers will be featured during with their famous ragtime music.

A professional show will follow dinner featuring the Hat Dancers in their salute to the Twenties, followed by dancing to the beat of the Downtowners. JoBeth is leaving no stone unturned to transform the ballroom into a big backroom speakeasy - right down to your entrance. Guests will enter the lobby (which will become a mock flower shop) and tell the proprietor "Al sent me." They will then be ushered through the "back

who forgets the password will be sent home with only a token bouqet of flowers.)

A photographer will be on hand to record your memories as well as plenty of surprises.

Dinner will be served buffet style and feature roast duckling, prime rib and medallions of beef. Chef Dodson promises ice carvings and a champagne fountain to dazzle all those attending.

Prizes will be awarded to those with the best 20's costumes and a Charleston contest will begin at 9:30.

Look for pictures to be posted of this gala event as early as the next week. We decided to display all our members decked out in their finest. So check the lobby for all the action. We will also be selling photos at $1.50 each, so leave your orders with the front desk.

Last year's spring gala raised over $20,000 for Emerson's home for widows and orphans. This year we hope to double this figure and donate all of the funds to the Vinnie Del Vechio Home for Unwed Mothers. Mr. Del Vechio himself will be

7. Click the Text Wrap tool.

8. Click the text frame, beyond the edges of the picture, but not outside of the frame.

If you click the picture by mistake, a dialog box appears telling you that you must select a text frame first.

9. Click the picture.

The text wraps around the picture.

Adding a footer

The last step in finishing your newsletter is to add a footer. Footers are single lines of text that appear at the bottom of every page of a document. If you look at the bottom of this page, you will see a footer. Footers can be used to provide essential information, such as page numbers, publication names, chapter titles, or dates. In this example, you will create a footer that contains the newsletter name, page number, and publication date.

1. Pull down the Page menu and select Headers and Footers.

The Headers and Footers dialog box appears.

The Headers and Footers dialog box

```
                        Headers and Footers
 Header:
   Left Text    [                                      ]
   Center Text  [                                      ]
   Right Text   [                                      ]

 Footer:
   Left Text    [Club Talk                             ]
   Center Text  [#                                     ]
   Right Text   [November 1990█                        ]

 Use the # symbol to place a page number in text.

 Page Number Style:  (•) 1, 2, 3    ( ) I, II, III
                     ( ) A, B, C    ( ) i, ii, iii
                     ( ) a, b, c    ( ) one, two, three
 Starting Page: [  1]

                               < OK >  < Cancel >
```

2. Type Club Talk in the Footer Left Text box.

This aligns Club Talk to the left margin of the document.

3. Type the pound symbol (#) in the Footer Center Text box.

Express Publisher will place a page number at the bottom center of every page in the newsletter. If you enter a number in the text box, that same number will repeat on every page. Express Publisher adjusts the page numbering as you add or delete pages.

4. Type November 1990 in the Footer Right Text box.

This aligns November 1990 to the right margin of the document.

5. Click OK.

Inserting a footer   To place the footer in your document,

1. Pull down the page menu and select Insert Header or Footer. The Insert Headers and Footers dialog box appears.

2. The option boxes, Insert Header and Insert Footer, are already checked. You are placing a footer, so click in the Insert Header check box to turn that option off, and click OK.

Show Page   Your newsletter is ready for printing, but before you print you might want to see both pages of your newsletter at once on the screen. The Show Page command allows you to display single or double pages (but you won't see the footers on screen).

1. Select the Show Page command on the Page menu.

   Express Publisher reduces the view of the document.

2. Click the Two Pages button at the bottom of the screen.

   Express Publisher reduces the view of the document so that both pages are visible in document window.

Note   Although you can read the type on the pages, you can't make any changes to the document in this view. If you want to see an entire page while you edit, use the Zoom Out command explained in Lesson 3.

3. Click OK when you are done viewing the page.

   If you want, make adjustments based on what you saw.

Printing   Now that the newsletter is complete, you're probably eager to see what it looks like on a printed page.

1. Pull down the File menu and choose Print.

   There are a number of printing options available on the Print dialog box, but the default options are suitable for your current needs. All of these options are explained in Chapter 7, "Printing."

2. Click OK.

   The Printing Progress dialog box appears. It indicates the current page number and the number of objects still to be printed on the page.

```
Processing page #1

  5 of  11 objects have been printed.


Press ESCAPE to stop printing
```

If you've never printed from a desktop publishing program before, it may seem as though Express Publisher takes a long time to print. Express Publisher needs to send about a thousand times more information to your printer than an ordinary word processor. If you're printing on a laser printer it may seem like nothing is happening. As long as the hands on the watch pointer are going around, you know that information is still being sent to the printer.

Summary of lesson 4

In lesson 4 you began to learn about some of Express Publisher's more advanced features.

- You can add a new page to a document at any time.
- Text frames can be linked so that text flows from frame to frame. Text frames can be linked across pages.
- TextEffects lets you create special effects with type.
- Express Publisher can wrap text around a picture.
- You can add page numbers with the Headers and Footers commands.
- The Show Page command displays a reduced view of an entire page in the document window.

How to continue

You are now ready to start using Express Publisher to create your own documents. If questions arise as you work, look up the subject in the index and read the section of the manual that discusses it.

Exiting

You may want to save this document to refer to as you practice some of the skills you have just learned. When you feel comfortable with your new ability, you can delete it.

1. Press F10 to save the work you have done in this lesson.

2. Click the File menu.

3. Click Exit.

   You return to the DOS prompt.

Fundamentals

This chapter covers many of the basic functions you need to understand before beginning work on your own documents. Most of these features relate to creating and saving documents. The chapter also explains how to move around in a document, and how Express Publisher's optional display settings work.

- Creating a new document
- Saving your work
- Resuming work on an existing document
- Using templates
- Document viewing options
- Moving between pages
- Adding and removing pages
- Undoing
- Rewrapping text around a graphic
- Setting options
- Closing and quitting

Creating a new document

The New command allows you to create new documents. When using the New command, you can choose between preset column layouts and page sizes or the Custom Page option to create your own columnar format and page size. In all documents created by the New command, text flows automatically from column to column and from page to page. If you are learning Express Publisher, you probably should start with the preset options.

Note You don't have to use the New command to start working. If you start Express Publisher without specifying a file to work with, it creates a one page, one column document.

Using Presets Using the preset options you can create professional-looking documents quickly without having to do a lot of calculations or designing. The presets allow you to choose between blank, one, two, and three column layouts. Text flows automatically from column to column in documents created by the one, two, and three column presets. The two and three column formats include space at the top of the page for a headline. The Blank option creates a document with no preset columns or first page header. Each of these column layouts can be placed on any of the five page size options. These include Letter (8.5" x 11"), Executive (7.25" x 10.5"), Legal (8.5" x 14"), Ledger (11" x 14"), and A4 (the European standard, approximately 8.27" x 11.69"). The Landscape option inverts the page dimensions so the width is larger than the length. Any page size can be created in Landscape orientation. You can create a document of up to 32 pages.

Follow these instructions to create a new document:

1. Pull down the File menu and select New.

    The Create a New Document dialog box appears. It contains four icons representing each of the column layout options, a text field for entering the desired number of pages, an option box for choosing the page size, and a check box for selecting Landscape orientation.

The Create a New
Document dialog box

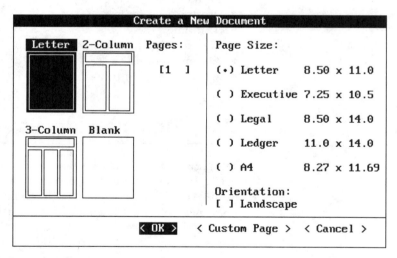

2. Click the icon representing the number of columns you want. If you don't want any predefined columns, click Blank.

3. Type the number of pages you want in the Pages text field, or leave the default setting.

4. Choose one of the preset page size options, or leave it set to 8.5" x 11". Click the Landscape check box if you to create your document in Landscape orientation. Then click OK.

Express Publisher creates the new document according to the options you selected. If you selected the two or three column presets, a picture appears in the document window showing you how the text flows through the document. You can press any key to delete the picture.

Note If you want to get rid of the pictures that appear when you use the two or three column presets, delete the files EP.CL2 and EP.CL3. They are in the \EXPRESS directory.

Custom Page If none of the presets meets your needs, or if you simply want to specify your own page size and column layout, the Custom Page option lets you specify all of the new document's settings. Choose the document's margins, create up to eight columns, and specify the amount of space between each column (the *gutter width*). You can decide whether you want a header on the first page and specify the header height. You can also include crop marks, a title, and copyright statement on each page.

Crop marks, titles, and copyright statements are used on professional printing galleys to identify every page of your document. Crop marks are corner markers that define the actual page size when the page is smaller than the paper the document is printed on. The title and copyright statements appear at the top and bottom of every galley, beyond the edge of the real page. For crop marks, title, or copyright statements to work, the document must be smaller than the paper: for example, a 7" x 9" document on 8.5" x 11" paper. The picture below shows you where the title and copyright will be placed, and what parameters the other Custom Page options control.

Custom Page parameters

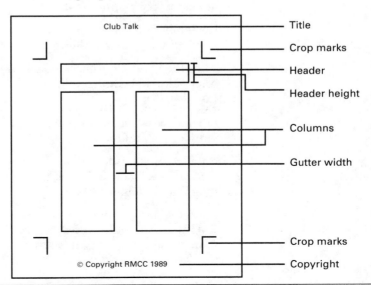

Club Talk ———— Title

Crop marks

Header

Header height

Columns

Gutter width

Crop marks

© Copyright RMCC 1989 ———— Copyright

1. Pull down the File Menu and select New.

   The Create a New Document dialog box appears. None of the options in this dialog box affect the Custom Page parameters.

2. Click the Custom Page button at the bottom of the dialog box.

   The Custom Page dialog box appears.

```
┌──────────────────────────────────────────────────────────────────┐
│                            Custom Page                             │
├──────────────────────────────────────────────────────────────────┤
│   # of Pages: [1 ]                        [ ] Crop Marks           │
│   Page Width: [8.500] (inches)                                     │
│  Page Length: [11.00]                     [ ] Landscape            │
├──────────────────────────────────────────────────────────────────┤
│ # of Columns: [4 ]                                                 │
│ Gutter Width: [0.062]                                              │
│ Header Height: [1.250]                    [X] First Page Header    │
│                                                                    │
│ Margins - Top: [0.750]   Bottom:[0.750]                            │
│          Left: [0.750]   Right: [0.750]                            │
├──────────────────────────────────────────────────────────────────┤
│       Title: [                                                  ]  │
│   Copyright: [                                                  ]  │
├──────────────────────────────────────────────────────────────────┤
│                                     < OK >   < Cancel >            │
└──────────────────────────────────────────────────────────────────┘
```

3. Enter the number of pages you want in the Pages text box.

4. Leave the default width and length settings, or type a new page width and length in the Page Width and Page Length fields.

Note The largest page you can create with the Custom Page command is 8.5" by 11". The largest page for Landscape orientation is 11" by 8.5".

5. Click in the Crop Marks check box if you want crop marks to appear in your print-outs.

   Remember that crop marks do not actually appear unless your document is smaller than your printer's paper.

6. Click the Landscape check box if you want your document's orientation to be horizontal.

   When you change the orientation to Landscape, the page dimensions do not change automatically. You must reset the width to 11" and the height to 8.5".

7. If you want a header on the first page, click the First Page Header check box and enter the appropriate measurement in the Header Height text box.

8. Enter the number of columns you want in the Number of Columns text field. Type the desired space between each column in the Gutter Width text field.

9. If you want to change any of the document's margins, change the appropriate numbers in the Top, Bottom, Left, or Right margin text box.

10. If you need a title or copyright statement, enter them in the fields provided. (Crop Marks must be checked.)

11. Click OK.

Express Publisher creates the document according to your specifications.

Saving your work

You should save your document every time you make significant changes to it. If you save frequently, you can always revert to the previously saved version if you are not happy with a change. Do not wait until you have completed the entire document before saving. Anyone who has lost several hours of work after a black-out or machine failure can attest to the importance of this habit.

The Save command   The Save command saves your document to disk. If you are saving a document for the first time, you have to tell Express Publisher what to name the document. After you have saved a document once, the Save command always saves the document using the same name and location you specified earlier.

These steps tell you how to save a document that you haven't saved before:

1. Choose Save from the File menu, or press F10.

The Save a Document dialog box appears. The current file name is displayed in the File Name text box. Below the File Name text box appears the drive and directory the document will be saved to. The default directory for documents is \EXPRESS\DOCS. You'll find it less confusing to store all your documents in the DOCS directory. If you want to save a document in a different location, you can change drives or directories by double-clicking a new drive or directory in the Other Drives and Directories list box. You can also use an option box to specify whether your document should be saved as a normal document or as a template (templates are explained later under the heading "Using templates").

The Save a Document
dialog box

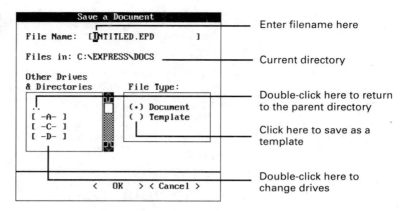

Enter filename here

Current directory

Double-click here to return to the parent directory

Click here to save as a template

Double-click here to change drives

2. Type a name for the document in the text box.

3. If you want to save the document to a different drive or directory, choose the desired drive in the Other Drives and Directories list box. Change directories by double-clicking on a directory name.

4. If you want to save your work as a template, click Template; otherwise leave it set to Document.

   The Template option is fully described in the section titled "Using templates."

5. When all the options have been set, click OK. If a document or template with the same name exists, you are asked if you want to cancel or to overwrite the existing file.

You may now continue working on your document, close your document, or quit Express Publisher. If you changed the name of your document, the new name is displayed at the far right of the menu bar.

The Save As command

The Save As command allows you to change all the Save options of an existing document. There are two main reasons why you might want to change some of the Save options:

- To create a new copy of a document with a different name, leaving the old copy unchanged.

- To save a document to a new location.

The Save As command activates the Save a Document dialog box. This is the same dialog box that appears when you save a document for the first time.

1. Select the Save As command from the File menu.

2. Follow the instructions for the Save command found above.

Naming files

You can name your files using any system that is meaningful to you. There are, however some strict limitations imposed by DOS. A file name can only have eight characters. Express Publisher automatically adds the .EPD extension to every file you save. In the file name DOCUMENT.EPD, DOCUMENT is the file name and .EPD is the extension.

For example, if you type MYFILE in the File Name text box, Express Publisher saves the file under the name MYFILE.EPD.

File names cannot contain spaces. They also cannot contain any of the following characters: * ? / . , ; [ ] + = \ : < >.

Changing the default directory

When you installed Express Publisher on your computer, the setup program, SETUPEP, created default directories to store your documents, word processing files, and clip art. If you didn't reset those directories during setup they are as follows: documents are stored in the \EXPRESS\DOCS directory, word processing files in the \EXPRESS\TEXT directory, and clip art in the \EXPRESS\ART directory. The first time you use a command that opens a file dialog box, Express Publisher looks in the default directory for the corresponding file type you want. For example, the first time you use the Import Text command, Express Publisher lists all the word processing files in the \EXPRESS\TEXT directory in the Files list box. As long as you import a word processing file from that directory, the Import Text command looks to that directory first. But, if you import a word processing file from the \EXPRESS directory, the next time you use the Import Text command it looks to the \EXPRESS directory first.

These are the commands that use a file dialog box and the directories they can change:

Command	Default Directory
Import Text	TEXT
Import Picture	ART
Save As Picture	ART
Open/Save As	DOCS
Open Template	DOCS

Be careful, when using these commands, that you do not inadvertently save data to a directory you don't mean to, making it difficult to locate next time.

For more information about what the default directories are and how to change them, see the instructions in "Setting up directories" and "Modifying an existing setup" in the Introduction. For more information on the DOS directory structure, see Appendix A, "Basic DOS."

Resuming work on an existing document

There are two ways to resume work on an existing document. You can type the name of the file you want to work on when you start the program, or you can use the Open command once you are inside the program.

Using the Open command

These steps tell you how to open an existing document from within Express Publisher:

1. Pull down the File menu and select Open.

   A dialog box appears listing all of the documents in the \EXPRESS\DOCS directory.

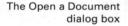
The Open a Document dialog box

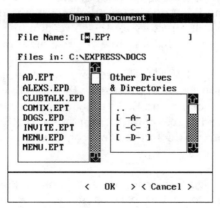

2. If necessary, change the current drive or directory by double-clicking an option in the Other Drives and Directories list box.

   The files displayed in the File list box change when you switch drives or directories.

3. Scroll through the listing of files in the File list box. Select the document you want by clicking on it and then clicking the OK button, or simply by double-clicking on the file you want to open. Express Publisher opens the document to the last page you worked on (not the last page of the document).

Using wild card characters

When opening document files, or importing text or picture files, you can use wild card characters to make your search for the file easier. If you can't remember exactly which file you are looking for, or if you want to look at a certain group of files, use wild card characters to view all the file names that have certain characters in common.

For example, all Microsoft Works word processing files have an extension of .WPS. If you want to view only Works files in a directory that contains several types of files, you could type *.WPS in the File Name text field of the Open a Document dialog box. When you press ENTER the listing in the File list box changes to include only files that end in .WPS.

Specifying a name upon start-up

You can tell Express Publisher what document you want it to load directly from the DOS command line. To do this you must first use the DOS PATH command to set a path to the \EXPRESS directory. If you're not familiar with the PATH command, look it up in your DOS manual or check Appendix A.

- To open a document at start up, type EP FILENAME from the DOS command line, where "FILENAME" is the name of the document you want to work with.

For example, if you wanted to resume work on a document named NEWSLTTR, you would type EP NEWSLTTR. This only opens documents you have saved in the \EXPRESS\DOCS directory.

If you want to open a document at start-up from a directory other than \EXPRESS\DOCS, you must type EP and the complete pathname for the file. Consult your DOS manual if you are unsure of how to specify the complete pathname of a file.

Using templates

A template is a document that contains most of the basic page elements needed to suit a particular purpose. For instance, a template for a weekly newsletter might already have the title in place and all the columns and picture locations defined. To complete the newsletter each week you would only have to import a couple of stories and type a headline or two.

Opening a template is very much like opening an ordinary Express Publisher document, except that all templates are opened without a file name. The file name UNTITLED.EPD appears at the right side of the menu bar until you save the document with a new name. This ensures that you do not accidently overwrite the template.

Included templates

Express Publisher includes several templates, shown in Appendix B, that you may find useful. The setup program installed them in the \EXPRESS\DOCS directory. Most of the templates included with Express Publisher contain brief instructions or advice on how they should be used. You can delete the instructions as soon as you start to work on the document. Templates are stored on disk as separate files. The only way to identify them within Express Publisher is by their file names. Templates have an extension of .EPT.

Creating templates

Any document can be saved as a template and used as a starting point for other documents. If you need to create similar documents every week, such as a schedule or a status report, you should save a template that contains the basic elements of the document.

Saving a document as a new template saves every object in the document, so you should consider carefully whether everything in the document is really necessary. In particular, pictures take up a lot of space on disk and should not normally be saved as part of a template. (TIF, GIF, and EPS picture files are not stored in document or template files. This is discussed in Chapter 4, "Objects.") You can keep working on a document after you have saved it as a template. You can even save it as an ordinary document file.

Follow these steps to create a template:

1. Create a document that includes all the elements that you want in the template.

2. Select Save As from the File menu.

3. Type a name for the template.

4. Click Template in the File Type option box.

5. Click OK.

   Express Publisher saves your work as a template.

Revising templates

To make changes to an existing template, follow these steps:

1. Select Open from the File menu.

   The Open a Document dialog appears listing all the files in the \EXPRESS\DOCS directory.

2. If necessary, change drives or directories by double-clicking options in the Other Drives and Directories list box.

3. Double-click the template you want to open in the File list box.

   Express Publisher opens the template as a document. The name of the template with the extension .EPT appears on the right side of the menu bar.

4. Make changes as necessary.

5. Select save from the file menu, or press F10.

Note   To open a template at start up, add the extension .EPT to the FILENAME. This is equivalent to using the Open command. Otherwise, the file will be opened as UNTITLED.EPD. See the section above, "Specifying a file name upon start-up," for more information.

The Open Template command

Use the Open Template command to create a new document using an existing template. All template names end with the .EPT extension.

1. Pull down the File menu and choose Open Template.

   The Open a Template dialog box appears. It is identical to the Open Document dialog box. It displays all of the templates in the \EXPRESS\DOCS directory.

The Open a Template
dialog box

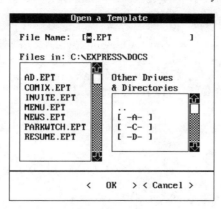

```
┌──────────────────────────────────────────────┐
│              Open a Template                   │
│                                                │
│  File Name:  [█.EPT                    ]        │
│                                                │
│  Files in: C:\EXPRESS\DOCS                     │
│                                                │
│   ┌──────────────┐▲   ┌──────────────────┐     │
│   │ AD.EPT       ││   Other Drives             │
│   │ COMIX.EPT    ││   & Directories            │
│   │ INVITE.EPT   ││   ┌──────────────┐▲        │
│   │ MENU.EPT     ││   │              ││        │
│   │ NEWS.EPT     ││   │ ..           ││        │
│   │ PARKWTCH.EPT ││   │ [ -A- ]      ││        │
│   │ RESUME.EPT   ││   │ [ -C- ]      ││        │
│   │              │▼   │ [ -D- ]      │▼        │
│   └──────────────┘    └──────────────┘         │
│                                                │
│          <   OK   > < Cancel >                 │
└──────────────────────────────────────────────┘
```

2. If necessary, change drives or directories by double-clicking options in the Other Drives and Directories list box.

3. Double-click the template you want to open in the File list box.

Express Publisher opens the template. UNTITLED.EPD appears at the right side of the menu bar. You may start your work as if it were an ordinary untitled document.

Document viewing options

Zoom In and Zoom Out   The Zoom In and Zoom Out commands allow you to change the view of your document while still retaining editing capabilities. Zoom In doubles the page size so you can edit small type and make layout adjustments that are hard to see in the regular view, and Zoom Out reduces the page so most of an 8.5" by 11" page fits on the screen. When you Zoom Out you can still manipulate objects and edit text in your document, but smaller type is more difficult to see.

To use the Zoom In and Zoom Out commands, follow these steps:

1. Pull down the Page menu and select Zoom In to increase the page size or Zoom Out to shrink the page.

   Your view of the document is changed so that either a small part of the page is visible, noticeably larger, or the page is reduced to be almost entirely visible within the screen.

2. All of Express Publisher's commands are functional so you can make the necessary edits.

3. To return to the normal view, pull down the Page menu and select Actual Size.

Note   Press F2 to Zoom Out one level: from reduced mode to Actual Size, or from Actual Size to enlarged mode. Press SHIFT-F2 to Zoom In one level: from enlarged mode to Actual Size, or from Actual Size to reduced mode.

A Zoomed In screen

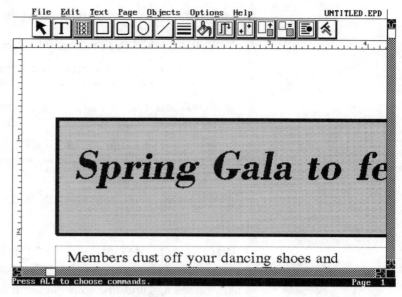

A Zoomed Out screen

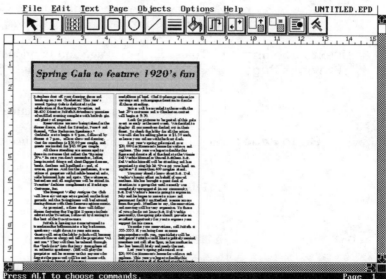

Changing your view of the document

In most cases only a small portion of your document is visible in the document window. You can change your view so that the entire page is shown in the window by using the Show Page command. This allows you to see how all the page elements look in relation to each other. When you are viewing a page using Show Page, you cannot modify the document in any way, you can only look at it. Non-printing objects are not displayed, except for non-printing text frames, which appear as dotted lines.

To use the Show Page command, follow these steps:

1. Pull down the Page menu and select Show Page.

   Your view of the document is changed so that the entire page is visible in a reduced state.

2. While using Show Page you may change from page to page by clicking on the Next Page and Previous Page buttons.

3. If you are working on a document with two pages or more, you can use the Two Pages button to display two pages side-by-side.

4. Click OK to return to normal view.

Moving between pages

The Next Page and Previous Page commands move you from page to page in your document. The Go to Page command lets you jump to any page.

Next Page and Previous Page
- To use the Next Page and Previous Page commands, select either of them from the Page menu; or press F4 for Next Page and F3 for Previous Page.

Express Publisher immediately changes the current page.

Go to Page
The Go to Page command is very useful for moving around in longer documents.

1. Pull down the Page menu and select Go to Page, or press F5.

   The Go to Page dialog box appears.

The Go to Page dialog box

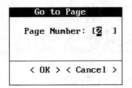

2. Type the page number that you want to move to in the Page Number field and click OK.

   Express Publisher moves to the page you selected.

Adding and removing pages

You can add new pages to your document whenever you like. When you create a new page you have the same options you did when you first created the document. However, new text frames are not linked to any other text frames on other pages and you cannot specify a new page size or orientation. You can also choose to copy the current page. You can insert a new page anywhere in a document.

New Page

Follow these instructions to add new pages to your document:

1. Pull down the Page menu and select New Page.

   The Add a New Page dialog box appears. You have the choice of selecting all the same preset options you did in the Create a New Document dialog box: blank, letter, two, or three column. You can also choose to copy the current page with the Copy Page option.

2. Click the icon representing the style of page you want.

3. Type the page number of the page you want to insert and click OK.

The new page is inserted. If you inserted a new page two, the old page two is now page three. None of the text frames in the new page are linked to any other frames on the other pages; you must do that yourself.

The Add a New Page dialog box

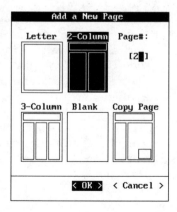

Copy page

The Copy Page option in the Add a New Page dialog copies every object on the current page to a new page. It is useful for duplicating irregular page layouts. If you create an uneven layout on page one of a document, use Copy Page to add identical pages as the document grows.

1. If necessary, change pages so that the page you want to duplicate is displayed in the document window.

2. Select New Page from the Page menu.

3. Enter the page number of the new page in the Page# field, or leave the existing number.

4. Double click Copy Page.

Express Publisher copies every object on the current page to the new page.

Delete page The Delete Page command removes an entire page from your document, deleting every object that was on the page. It deletes all text on the page from the file. It should be used with extreme caution, it is not Undo-able.

1. Pull down the Page menu and choose Delete Page.

2. Enter the number of the page you want to delete. (The current page is the default.)

3. Click OK, or cancel the operation.

Undoing

Being able to change your mind and correct mistakes easily is one of the major advantages of doing almost any type of work on a computer. You can undo many of the operations in Express Publisher by using an opposing command to reverse the operation. For example, when you use the Bring to Front command, in most cases you can use the Send to Back command to undo the change. Or, after you paste an object, you can cut it while it is still selected. Certain operations can be undone with the Undo Move command.

Undo Move The Undo Move command allows you to undo the following actions: moving an object, drawing an object, resizing an object, CTRL-clicking an object (in most cases), and deleting an object (except for a text frame).

• To use the Undo Move command, pull down the Edit menu and select Undo Move.

Your last action is undone, or a dialog box appears informing you that your last action cannot be undone.

Rewrapping text around a graphic

Express Publisher allows you rewrap text around a graphic by clicking the Rewrap Text button in the lower corner of the screen, or pressing CTRL-F1. The Rewrap Text button is that black box abutting both scroll bars. When you force a text rewrap, Express Publisher clears the screen and redraws your document. This can be helpful for two main reasons.

- If you have text wrapped around an object, and the text unwraps because you move the object or text frame, you can force the text to rewrap around the picture.
- If you are moving a number of objects around in your document, some objects are temporarily left behind. When Express Publisher redraws the screen, these phantom objects are cleared away.

Setting options

The Options menu lets you control some of Express Publisher's optional display elements.

Putting away the rulers and the toolbox

If you want to look at your document with no distractions, you can put away the rulers or the toolbox.

- To put away either the rulers or the toolbox, pull down the Options menu and select either Rulers or Toolbox.

Each of these commands works like a toggle switch. If the toolbox is displayed, the Toolbox command puts it away. If it was already hidden, the command makes it reappear. A dot appears next to the command when the option is on.

Units of measure

The Units command changes the units of measure shown on the rulers. This setting determines the units for all the measurements in the program, (except for text character measurements, which are always in points). You can choose between inches, centimeters, and picas (a pica is 12 points, a point is approximately 1/72").

Note

Depending on the type of monitor you are using, the rulers may not be accurate on the screen. However, they correctly reflect the printed document. See Appendix C for more information.

Follow these instructions to set the units of measure:

1. Pull down the Options menu and choose Units.

The Set Units dialog box

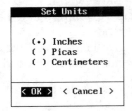

2. Choose either inches, centimeters, or picas from the dialog box.

3. Click OK.

Display settings

The Display Settings command controls six optional operation features. Collectively, they control the degree to which the document you see on the screen looks like the final print out. They are somewhat technical in nature and you may not be interested in them until you become more advanced in using the program.

If you are working on a slower system or a computer with only 640K, you may want to turn off some of the options that use a lot of memory or slow down the program. Each of the Display Settings options is documented below. If you don't understand one of the options, leave it on.

Display actual fonts: With this option on, Express Publisher correctly displays the fonts in your document on the screen. Express Publisher uses a lot of time and memory computing how each character should look and where it should be placed. With the Display Actual Fonts option off, Express Publisher uses your computer's system font to display all text. This speeds up text handling and uses less memory, but makes it hard to see how text will appear in the final print-out. Express Publisher places the system font characters so that they take up the same amount of space as the selected font. The correct fonts appear when you print the document.

Display bitmap Images: Displaying large bit-mapped pictures on the screen takes up large amounts of memory in your computer and slows down the screen display. With this option on, Express Publisher displays all bit-mapped pictures the way they will print out. If you are running low on memory, turn this option off to clear up some space; Express Publisher shows only a gray rectangle to mark the location of the bit-map. The pictures appear when you print the document.

Retain scaled bitmaps: Ordinarily, when you change the size of a picture, Express Publisher stores the resized picture in memory along with the picture in its original size. With the scaled picture stored in memory, Express Publisher doesn't have to resize it every time it draws the screen. This speeds up the program, but it also uses a lot of memory. If you turn this option off, Express Publisher can use the extra memory for other functions, but it must scale resized pictures from scratch every time it draws the screen. This slows down the program considerably, but if you are running low on available memory it is worthwhile.

High definition bitmap display: This option is usually left off. When the option is on, Express Publisher uses a more sophisticated system to display pictures on the screen. This system uses a lot more memory and computing time than the normal system, but it improves the appearance of pictures on the screen. This option has no effect on how pictures are printed.

Display hidden objects: This option makes objects visible, even those that were hidden with the Object Specs command. If you have lost track of a hidden object, turn this option on to find it. Read about the Object Specs command in "Object specifications" in Chapter 4, "Objects."

Make all objects selectable: This option makes all objects selectable, even those that were made non-selectable with the Object Specs command. Read about the Object Specs com-mand in "Object specifications" in Chapter 4, "Objects."

To change the settings:

1. Pull down the Options menu and choose Display Settings.

2. Turn the various options in the dialog box off or on.

3. Click on OK.

Colors The Colors command controls the color options available to users of EGA and VGA systems. All Express Publisher documents are in black and white, but you can set the color of the scrollbar, ruler, menu bar, dialog boxes, and menus. In some cases, choosing a color display will slow down the program considerably.

1. Pull down the Options menu and choose Colors.

2. Set the color for the menu bar, scroll bar, and rulers by clicking a color.

3. Click OK.

Closing and quitting

Closing a document

To close a document is to put the document away without quitting Express Publisher. Close a document at anytime by choosing the Close command from the File menu. Express Publisher closes the document and clears the screen.

If you made any changes to a document without saving, Express Publisher asks you if you want to save these changes.

- If you choose Yes, the document is saved with the current name and location. If the document is untitled, the Save a Document dialog box appears.

- If you choose No, the document is closed and the changes are abandoned.

Quitting Express Publisher

Quitting Express Publisher closes your document, ends your session, and returns you to DOS. If you have made changes without saving, you are asked if you want to save the changes.

This is not a recommended way of saving changes. We prefer that you save your document and then quit. You may lose work if you accidentally choose the wrong option while quitting.

1. Choose Exit from the File menu.

   If you haven't made any changes to a document, or if no document is open, Express Publisher returns you to DOS.

2. If Express Publisher asks you if you want to save any changes, select an option.

If you choose to save changes, Express Publisher saves the document with the current name. If the document is untitled the Save a Document dialog box appears.

If you choose not to save changes, the changes are lost and Express Publisher returns you to DOS.

4

Objects

Creating a document with Express Publisher is similar to creating a collage. Express Publisher handles a page as a collection of many page elements called *objects*. You can move and change every object without affecting surrounding objects. This chapter explains all of the different ways you can create and change objects. Since imported pictures are treated as ordinary objects, this chapter also covers all the issues related to importing and modifying pictures. The basic methods of working with objects in Express Publisher are the same no matter what type of objects you are working with.

This chapter addresses all of the following object-related subjects:

- What is an object?
- Drawing objects
- Selecting objects
- Changing lines and fill patterns
- Moving objects
- Aligning objects
- Changing the size of objects
- Using the grid
- Object specifications
- Cut, Copy, Paste, and the clipboard
- Flipping and rotating objects
- Control-clicking objects
- Duplicating objects
- Importing pictures
- Changing pictures

What is an object?

Objects are the elements in a document that you can change individually. Every image that you create with one of the drawing tools is a separate object; so are, imported pictures, TextEffect headlines, and text frames.

In the picture below, there are three objects: the box containing text, the TextEffects headline, and the picture.

Three objects

This box containing text is an object.

Drawing objects

Every image that you create with one of the drawing tools is an object. The Express Publisher drawing tools are similar to drawing tools in other programs. All of the images, except for lines, are based on *bounding rectangles*. When you draw an object, you are actually drawing a box around what will be its final image. While you are using one of the drawing tools, the pointer shape changes to a pencil.

The drawing tools

This example shows you how to draw a box, but every drawn image can be made in the same way.

The Box tool

1.   Click the Box tool.

The pointer shape changes to a pencil.

2. Move the pointer to where you want to place the upper left corner of your box and hold down the mouse button.

This marks the *anchor point* for the box you are drawing.

3. Drag the pointer down and to the right.

Drawing a box

Anchor Point

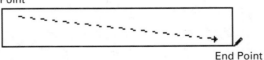

End Point

Notice that tick marks appear on the ruler as you move the mouse. They show the position of the edges of the object that you are creating. These tick marks are useful for measuring objects as you create them.

4. When the box is the desired size, release the mouse button.

The pointer changes back to an arrow. The point at which you released the mouse button marks the box's *end point*.

Every drawn image is created in the same way. After you select the particular drawing tool, the point at which you press the mouse button marks the image's anchor point. You then drag the pointer to define the image. When you release the mouse button you are marking the image's end point. Express Publisher then draws the image within the rectangle you defined. Lines are the only drawn images not based on rectangles. Lines are drawn between the anchor point and the end point.

Note   If you need to draw an object larger than the document window, drag the pointer off the edge of the document window and Express Publisher scrolls the window for you.

Shortcut   If you hold down the SHIFT key as you draw a new object, the current drawing tool remains active. This allows you to draw several objects without having to click a drawing tool between each one.

1. Click one of the drawing tools.

2. Hold down the SHIFT key and do not release it.

3. Draw an object without releasing the SHIFT key. Continue to hold down the SHIFT key when you have finished drawing the object.

   Notice that the pointer does not change back to an arrow after drawing the object. It remains in the pencil shape.

4. Still holding down the SHIFT key, draw another object.

   You can continue using the same drawing tool to draw objects until you release the SHIFT key.

Using the grid   Express Publisher can automatically align objects to grid markers. This is helpful for drawing objects in a certain location or exact size; it's also useful for drawing straight lines. The grid is explained in this chapter under the heading, "Using the grid."

Selecting objects

To select an object is to choose the object that will be affected by your next action. Understanding how to select the object you wish to modify is an important step in mastering Express Publisher.

The Arrow tool

The pointer reminds you of the tool you are working with at that moment. When selecting objects the pointer should be the arrow. If it is not, clicking the Arrow tool restores the arrow pointer.

Selecting an object

- To select an object, move the arrow pointer onto the object then press and release the mouse button.

You can tell that the object is selected when little black squares called *handles* appear around the object.

A selected object

Once you have selected an object, use any of Express Publisher's functions to manipulate the object.

Grouping objects

- To select more than one object at a time as a group, hold down the SHIFT key as you select the first object. Continue holding down the SHIFT key as you select all the other objects you want to group together. As long as you hold down the SHIFT key, Express Publisher treats all the objects as one. You can only move, cut, copy, or paste grouped objects. Moving and cutting, copying, and pasting objects is detailed in the corresponding sections later in this chapter.

Deselecting an object

- To deselect an object, move the pointer anywhere in the document window outside of the selected object and click the mouse button, or select another object.

The object is deselected and the handles disappear.

An Express Publisher page consists of several layers of objects. Think of a page as a stack of transparencies. The stack is in chronological order. The first object you place on the page is at the bottom of the stack, and the last is on the top.

Selecting overlapping objects

Ordinarily, you select an object by moving the pointer to some area within the object that is not covered by another object and clicking the mouse button. It can not be immediately obvious that an object is covering another if there are several objects overlapping. You can always tell which object is selected because handles appear around its borders. It is not possible to select an object that is entirely covered by another object. In some cases, you can have to change the stacking order to be able to select a certain object.

Overlapping objects

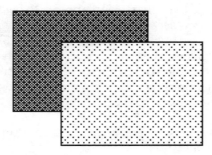

Changing the stacking order

The order in which objects are placed on top of each other can have a big effect on the final appearance of your document. For example, you can want a shaded box to be placed behind a picture. If you place the picture first, when you draw the shaded box it will cover the picture. In this case you would use the Send to Back tool to move the box behind the picture.

Use CTRL-F for Bring to Front and CTRL-E for Send to Back

The Bring to Front, Send to Back, Shuffle Up, and Shuffle Down commands on the Objects menu help you to rearrange the stacking order of objects in your document.

- CTRL-F (Bring to Front) brings any selected object all the way to the top of the stack.

- CTRL-E (Send to Back) sends a selected object all the way to the bottom of the stack.

- Shuffle Up moves a selected object a layer up in the stack.

- Shuffle Down moves a selected object a layer down in the stack.

Bring to Front/Send to Back

To bring an object to the front of the object stack, or send it to the back, follow these steps:

1. Select the object you want to bring to the front or send to the back.

2. Press CTRL-F (Bring to Front) or CTRL-E (Send to Back).

Shuffle Up/Shuffle Down

These two commands are very useful for working on documents that have background images. You might decide that you want one of your foreground images behind another, but not behind the background image. In this situation the Shuffle Down command lets you move an object behind one of the foreground images, but not behind the background. Remember that objects are stacked in chronological order in your document. The first object you create is at the bottom of the stack, and the last is at the top. Even if an object appears to be directly underneath another object, there can be several other objects placed chronologically between the two objects. The Shuffle Up and Shuffle Down commands move selected objects only one layer up or down in the stack, so in some cases you can have to repeat the command several times to move the object to the right position in the stack.

These steps tell you how to use the Shuffle Up or Shuffle Down commands:

1. Select the object you want to change.

2. Pull down the Objects menu and select either Shuffle Up or Shuffle Down.

3. Repeat step 2 until the object is in the desired position.

If you can't select an object

In some cases it can seem as though it is impossible to select an object. There are two situations that could cause this.

Covered objects

The most common problem in selecting objects is that an object is completely covering the object you are trying to select. Remember, many objects are transparent. If you drew an unfilled box or other shape around an object, you won't be able to select the object inside until you send the covering object to the back. The example below illustrates this point.

1. Draw a small unfilled box.

2. Draw a larger unfilled box that completely encloses the smaller box.

   Now try to select the smaller box. You are not able to, you can only select the larger box. Use the Send to Back command to remedy this situation.

3. With the larger box selected, press CTRL-E.

You are now able to select the smaller box. Since the smaller box doesn't completely cover the larger box, you can still select the larger box. You can do the same thing with the Shuffle Down command.

Note   If you draw a box around a large area that contains many objects, make sure that you send it to the back or you won't be able to select any of the enclosed objects.

Non-selectable objects

It is possible to make any object non-selectable with the Object Specs command. This is explained later in "Object specifications."

Changing lines and fill patterns

You can change the line and fill type of existing objects, or reset the default options. When you change the default line or fill type, the new option is used each time an applicable object is created.

Fills   All shapes can be either filled or unfilled. Filled shapes are opaque, they obscure anything that they cover. Unfilled shapes are transparent. The Set Fill tool allows you to specify whether a shape is filled or unfilled. It also lets you choose between the available fill patterns and change the pattern palette itself.

Changing existing objects

The Set Fill tool can change the fill pattern of a selected box, rounded box, ellipse, and certain TextEffects shapes.

1. Select a shape.

The Set Fill tool   2. Click the Set Fill tool.

The Set Fill Pattern Pattern dialog box appears.

The Set Fill Pattern
dialog box

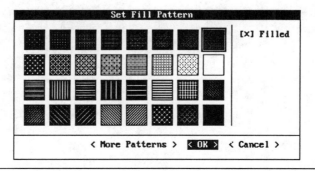

3. If you wish to change the fill pattern of the selected object, click one of the fill patterns.

4. If you wish to change the fill status of the selected object, click in the Filled check box (if the box is checked the object is filled).

5. Click OK.

The object changes to reflect your selections.

If nothing happens

There are two reasons why no visible change can occur when you go through the above procedure.

- If you choose a fill type but do not turn on the Filled option using the check box, the fill you choose does not take effect. Make sure that there is an X in the Filled check box.

- If you choose white as the fill type it can not be obvious that anything has happened. However, if you move the white object over another object you will notice that it is now opaque.

Changing the pattern palette

There are several pattern palettes included with Express Publisher. By using the More Patterns option in the Set Fill Pattern dialog box, you can choose between the various pattern palettes. Pattern palettes are stored on disk as ordinary files. The pattern palettes include groups of patterns suited for different purposes. GREY.PAT contains several degrees of even grey patterns. LINES.PAT includes different types of simple line patterns. MAC.PAT offers more complex patterns familiar to those who've used Macintosh applications.

LINES.PAT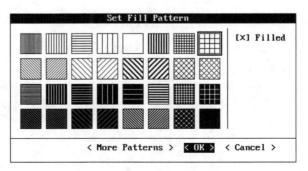

GREY.PAT

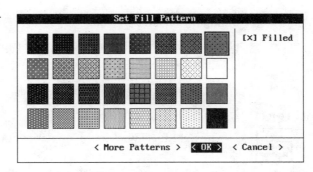

MAC.PAT

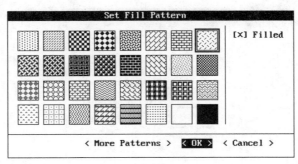

Follow these steps to choose a new Pattern palette:

The Set Fill tool

1. Click the Set Fill tool.

2. Click the More Patterns button at the bottom of the Set Fill Pattern dialog box.

   The Open a Pattern dialog box appears, displaying the available pattern palettes. It is identical in function to the Open a Document dialog box.

3. Double-click the desired pattern palette.

   The Set Fill Pattern dialog box reappears, displaying the pattern palette that you selected.

Lines   The Set Line tool lets you define the type of line to be used for drawing straight lines and rectangles. The Set Line tool invokes the Set Line Type dialog box. From this dialog box, you can choose a line thickness and set the color of the line to black or white. You can also choose to draw *non-printing* lines. Non-printing lines appear on the screen as dotted or shaded lines, but do not show up when the document is printed. They are useful for creating visual guidelines.

Changing selected objects

Follow these steps to change the line type of a selected square-edged box, or line:

1. Select a square-edged box or a line.

The Set Line tool

2. Click the Set Line tool.

   The Set Line Type dialog box appears.

The Set Line Type dialog box

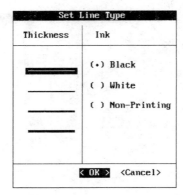

3. Select a line thickness and choose either Black, White, or Non-printing for the line color.

4. Click OK.

   The object changes to reflect your selection.

Changing the default line type

If you change the default line type, all applicable objects will be drawn with the line type until you choose a new default.

- To change the default line type, make sure that no objects are selected and use the Set Line tool to specify a new line type.

Using white and non-printing lines

Use white lines over black or shaded backgrounds, or if you don't want a line to appear on the screen. This is helpful for creating shaded areas with no borders. Non-printing lines give you the same final result, but white lines create a screen display that more closely resembles the final results.

Moving objects

All objects can be moved in the same way.

1. Select an object.

2. Move the pointer onto the object, then press and hold down the mouse button.

   The pointer shape changes to a four-headed arrow.

3. Drag the pointer to where you want the object placed.

Moving an object

The object's outline moves with the pointer. Notice that tick marks appear on the ruler displaying the position of the object's edges. The tick marks on the ruler are very useful for moving an object to a certain location.

4. When the object is in the desired location, release the mouse.

   Express Publisher redraws the object in its new location.

You can select and start moving an object at the same time. Just position the pointer on the object you want to move, press and hold down the mouse button, and immediately start dragging the pointer.

Moving lines   To move a line you have to drag the center handle. You cannot move lines by dragging the body of the line.

Moving a line

Note   When moving an object, a copy of the object can remain on screen in its original position. To correct this, press CTRL-F1 and Express Publisher will refresh the screen.

Moving grouped objects   To move grouped objects, hold down SHIFT as you drag the mouse. Once you release SHIFT, only one object can be selected. See "Grouping objects" in this chapter for information on selecting more than one object.

Using the grid   Express Publisher can automatically align objects to grid markers. This is helpful for moving objects to a certain location; it's also very useful for making straight lines. The grid is explained later in this chapter under the heading, "Using the grid."

Aligning objects

The Align tool can align any two objects to each other according to your specifications. It saves you the trouble of moving the objects manually. The Align tool works by aligning a secondary object to one or more areas of an anchor object. For instance, if you wanted to align the top of a picture to the top of a column of text, the column of text is the anchor object, and the picture is the secondary object. There are many alignment options, each of which are visually represented in the Align Two Objects dialog box.

To align objects, follow these instructions:

The Align tool   1. Click the Align tool in the toolbox.

   The pointer changes to the align shape.

   2. Move the pointer onto the anchor object and click the mouse.

   The anchor object is the object to which you align a secondary object. The anchor object is not moved during this procedure.

   3. Move the pointer to the object that you want to move and click the mouse.

   The Align Two Objects dialog box appears.

The Align Two Objects
dialog box

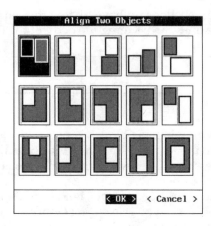

Each of the icons stands for a different alignment option. The light-colored box represents the object that will be moved. The darker box is the anchor object. The dotted lines show the sides that will be aligned.

4. Click the desired alignment option.

5. Choose OK to finish the operation.

The second object is aligned to the first according to your selection.

You can use SHIFT along with the Align tool to align several secondary objects to a single anchor object without having to repeatedly select the Align tool. Click the Align tool, select an anchor object, and then hold down the SHIFT key as you select a secondary object. Select an alignment option in the dialog box. When the dialog box disappears, notice that the Align tool is still active. You can now select an additional secondary object. The tool stays active as long as you press SHIFT while selecting secondary objects.

Changing the size of objects

You can change the size and shape of objects in a number of ways. All of the methods discussed below work on every type of object.

Changing one dimension

Express Publisher allows you to change the width of an object without changing its height, or vice versa.

1. Select the object.

2. Move the pointer to the middle handle in any of the object's sides.

3. Hold down the mouse button and drag the handle.

Notice that the object's outline moves with the pointer and that you can only change the single dimension.

Sizing one dimension

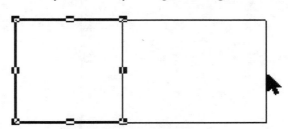

4. When the object is the right size, release the mouse button.

Express Publisher redraws the object in the new shape.

Changing two dimensions These steps tell you how to change both the height and width of an object at the same time:

1. Select the object.

2. Move the pointer to one of the corner handles.

3. Hold down the mouse button and drag the handle in any direction.

   The object's outline moves with the pointer to show you the changing size of the object.

Sizing two dimensions

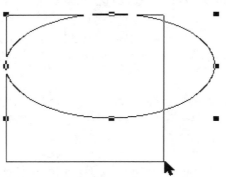

4. When the object is the right size, release the mouse button.

   Express Publisher redraws the object in the new size.

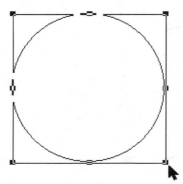

Scaling proportionally

The Scale Object command allows you to change the size of any object by an exact scaling factor. This ensures that the object's original proportions are preserved. This is especially important when scaling imported pictures. You can scale any object.

Express Publisher uses percentages to express scaling factors: 100% is the object's original size, 200% is twice the object's original size, 50% is half the object's original size, and so on. You can use any scaling factor between 1% and 999%, provided that the object's height or width does not reduce below 0.125" or expand beyond the page.

Note   Scaling factors apply to dimensions, not area. If you were to scale a 1" by 2" box by 200%, the result would be a 2" by 4" box.

To use the Scale Object command, follow these instructions:

1. Select the object that you want to scale.

2. Choose Scale Object from the Objects menu, or press F9.

   The Scale Object dialog box appears.

The Scale Object dialog box

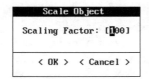

3. Type the desired scaling factor. Click OK to proceed.

Making two objects the same size

You can make two objects the same size with the Equate tool. The Equate tool works with two objects, even if they are of different types. The Equate tool equates the size of a secondary object to that of a primary object. The upper left corner of the secondary object stays in the same place as the object is re-sized.

Note   The Equate tool will only equate vertical and horizontal lines to other vertical and horizontal lines.

To make two objects the same size, follow these steps:

The Equate tool

1. Click the Equate tool.

   The pointer shape changes to the equal sign (=).

2. Select the first object.

3. Click a second object that you want to change to the same size as the first object.

The second object is made the same size as the first object.

If you want to equate several objects at the same time, hold down the SHIFT key after you select the primary object and as you select the secondary and other objects. The Equate tool remains active as long as you hold down SHIFT; the pointer remains in the equal shape (=). When you release SHIFT, the Alignment dialog box appears.

Using the grid

The grid is an optional layout feature that displays grid markers at fixed locations in the document window. Using the grid you can easily move or draw objects at exact locations or make them a certain size. Express Publisher can also automatically "snap" objects that you are drawing, moving, or resizing to the nearest grid marker. You can turn this function on and off with the Snap to Grid command. Using the Set Grid command, you can specify the intervals at which the grid markers appear, and turn grid display on or off.

The Set Grids command

The Set Grids command determines the placement of the grid markers and whether or not the grid is displayed on the screen. You can place grid markers at any interval over .25", .635 centimeters, or 1.495 picas depending on the current units of measure.

1. Select Set Grids from the Options menu.

   The Set Grid Size dialog box appears.

The Set Grid Size dialog box

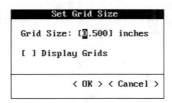

```
    Set Grid Size

Grid Size: [0.500] inches

[ ] Display Grids

      < OK > < Cancel >
```

2. If you want to change the intervals at which the grid markers appear, type a new number in the Grid Size text box.

3. Click in the Display Grid check box to make the grid markers appear.

4. Click OK.

Snap to Grid When Snap to Grid is on, Express Publisher "snaps" all objects that you move, draw, or resize to the nearest grid marker. The Snap to Grid command turns the function on or off. A dot appears next to the command when the option is on. You can turn Snap to Grid on even when the grid markers are not displayed.

- To turn Snap to Grid on or off, select the Snap to Grid command on the Options menu, or press SHIFT-F7.

Moving objects

When you move objects while Snap to Grid is on, Express Publisher always places the upper left corner of the object at the nearest grid marker. The following picture illustrates this point.

Moving an object with
Snap to Grid on

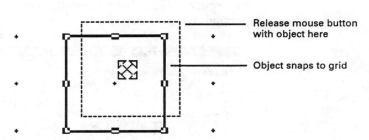

Release mouse button
with object here

Object snaps to grid

Resizing objects

If you resize an object while Snap to Grid is on, Express Publisher moves the edges of the object that you are changing to the nearest grid markers. The edges of the object that you are not changing stay where they are. The picture below makes this more clear.

Resizing an object with
Snap to Grid on

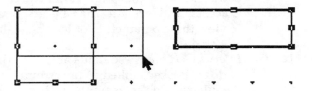

Drawing objects

When you draw an object while Snap to Grid is on, Express Publisher snaps the anchor and end points of the object you are drawing to the nearest grid markers.

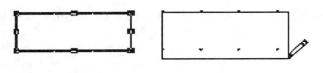

The Scale Object and Object Specs commands are not affected by
Snap to Grid. Object Specs is explained next.

Object specifications

The Object Specs command controls several specialized options
relating to objects. It allows you to control the exact size and
location of an object and tells you if text wrap has been applied.
It also lets you specify if an object is printable, selectable, hidden,
locked, or filled. You can specify pictures as transparent and text
frames for auto-import.

The Object Specifications
dialog box

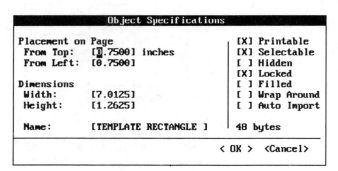

```
                    Object Specifications
Placement on Page                        [X] Printable
  From Top:    [0.7500] inches            [X] Selectable
  From Left:   [0.7500]                   [ ] Hidden
                                          [X] Locked
Dimensions                                [ ] Filled
  Width:       [7.0125]                   [ ] Wrap Around
  Height:      [1.2625]                   [ ] Auto Import

Name:      [TEMPLATE RECTANGLE ]     48 bytes

                                   < OK >   <Cancel>
```

Size and location   Remember that all Express Publisher objects are bounded by
rectangles. By defining the placement of the object's upper left
corner, and its height and width, you can control the object's
exact size and location. The Object Specs command can be used
to view these parameters, or to change them.

Object status   Every object has these status options: Printable, Selectable,
Hidden, Locked, Filled, Wrap Around, and Auto Import. By
default every object is printable, selectable, not hidden, and
unlocked. For normal use, you don't need to change any of the
status options. As you become more familiar with Express
Publisher, you may find it useful to change them.

- **Printable:** If you turn off the Printable option, the object will
  not be printed, but it remains visible on the screen. This is
  useful for posting non-printing comments on a document.

- **Selectable:** With the Selectable option off, the object is no longer selectable. This is useful if you are working with a complex document and you don't want to accidentally select and change an object. This option can be overridden by the Make All Objects Selectable option in the Display Settings dialog box (see "Display settings" in Chapter 3).

- **Hidden:** If you turn on this option, the object becomes invisible. This option can be used to temporarily hide an object within a document. This option can be overridden by the Display Hidden Objects option in the Display Settings dialog box.

- **Locked:** Turn on the Locked status option if you want to lock an object in place. Locked objects can be selected, but cannot be moved or sized. The text frames in templates or documents created with the New command are locked.

*If you select an imported picture and use the Object Specs command, Filled is replaced by the **Transparent** option. The Transparent option makes the white dots in a picture transparent; only the black dots show up.*

- **Filled:** With this option on, the object is filled, or opaque. With the option off, the object is unfilled, or transparent.

- **Wrap Around:** With this option on, text will wrap around the object. For more information on text wrap, see "Wrapping text around pictures" in Chapter 5.

- **Auto Import:** If you select this option and save the file as a template, Express Publisher opens the Import Text dialog box as soon as the template is selected. You can use this to set up Express Publisher for use by other people or to simplify laying out a frequently produced document.

  1. After designing and creating a document, select the desired empty text frame with the arrow tool.

  2. Pull down the Objects menu and select Object Specs.

  3. Click the Auto Import check box and click OK. This designates the selected frame as the auto-load text frame.

  4. Save the document as a template.

  When you (or anyone) open that template with the Open Template command, Express Publisher will select the auto-load text frame and activate the Import Text command. All you have to do is select the desired word-processing file from the Import Text dialog box and Express Publisher imports it into the selected text frame. The text will flow into linked text frames if applicable.

Using Object Specs

1. Select an object.

2. Choose the Object Specs command from the Objects menu.

The Object Specifications dialog box appears. It contains four text fields — From Top, From Left, Width, and Height — and several check boxes controlling the object status options. If you only want to view Object Specifications, click Cancel or press ESCAPE. You can alter the Object Specs values by changing the numbers in the text boxes and clicking the various check boxes.

3. Change the numbers in the From Top or From Left text boxes if you want to move the object.

   The units of measure are the same as currently displayed on the rulers and specified by the Units command. Note that the location parameters are based on measurements from the upper left corner of the document page.

4. Change the numbers in the Width or Height text boxes if you want to size the object.

   If you change only the size of an object, the upper left corner stays in the same place.

5. Click the check boxes to change the object status options.

6. Choose OK.

   The object changes to reflect your selections.

Cut, Copy, Paste, and the clipboard

Express Publisher supports the popular Cut, Copy, and Paste editing commands. You can already be familiar with them from using other programs. Cut, Copy, and Paste are very useful for moving objects from one page to another in a document.

The clipboard   The clipboard in Express Publisher is very much like a real clipboard. It is used to store information temporarily. Every time you cut or copy an object, it is stored temporarily on the clipboard. It remains on the clipboard until you cut or copy another object, use TextEffects, or quit Express Publisher. Only one object can be on the clipboard at a time.

These steps tell you how to see what is on the clipboard:

1. Choose Show Clipboard from the Edit menu.

   A window appears displaying the contents of the clipboard. Unless you have cut or copied something to the clipboard, you will get a message that the clipboard is empty.

2. Click OK when you are done looking at the clipboard.

The clipboard window disappears.

Cut and Copy   Cutting an object removes it from the document and places it on the clipboard. Copying an object places a copy of the object on the clipboard and leaves the original in the document. Both of these commands overwrite the previous contents of the clipboard.

To cut or copy an object, follow these steps:

1. Select the object.

2. Choose Cut or Copy from the Edit menu.

The object is cut or copied to the clipboard. (See above.)

Note   If you cut a text frame to the clipboard, only the box ends up on the clipboard. The text that was inside the box is redistributed to other text frames in the same story. If there are no linked text frames, a dialog box appears warning you that you are about to lose the text.

Paste   Pasting an object places a copy of the object currently on the clipboard into your document. The Paste command does not work if there is nothing on the clipboard.

1. Cut or Copy an object to the clipboard, or use Show Clipboard to see what is on the clipboard first.

2. Pull down the Edit menu and select Paste.

The object is pasted in your document.

Clear Clipboard   To erase the contents of the clipboard, pull down the Edit menu and select Clear Clipboard.

Grouped objects   You can cut, copy, and paste more than one object at a time.

1. Group objects by pressing SHIFT as you select all the objects you want to cut or copy.

2. Choose Cut or Copy from the Edit menu.

3. To paste the grouped objects back into your document, follow the steps above for pasting a single object.

Flipping and rotating objects

Rotating objects

You can rotate text with TextEffects. See Chapter 6 for more information.

Express Publisher can rotate objects left, right, and upside down. When objects are rotated, the upper left corner of the object stays in place. The only exception to this rule is when a rotation would move part of the object off the page. In this case the entire object is moved to fit within the page. Express Publisher always remembers which way an object was oriented originally. The Normal rotation option returns objects to their original orientation (pressing CTRL as you select a rotated object has the same effect).

These instructions tell you how to rotate an object:

1. Select the object to rotate.

2. Choose Rotate Object from the Objects menu.

   The Rotate Object dialog box appears.

The Rotate Object dialog box

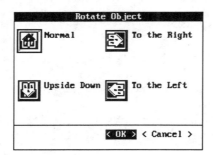

3. Select the rotate option you want and click OK, or double-click the desired option.

The object is rotated. If you select a previously rotated object and use Rotate Object again, the dialog box shows the rotate option that was applied earlier.

Flipping objects

You can flip pictures left to right and top to bottom with the Flip Object command. You cannot flip other types of objects. It can be difficult at first to understand the difference between rotating and flipping. Rotating an object is simply turning it on the page, while flipping an object is like lifting it off the page and turning it over to create a mirror image. Express Publisher remembers if an object has been flipped. The Normal option returns objects to their original orientation (hold down CTRL as you select a flipped object for the same effect).

```
┌─────────────────────┐
│     Flip Object      │
│ ┌──┐                 │
│ │🏠│   Normal         │
│ └──┘                 │
│ ┌──┐                 │
│ │🏠│   Right to Left  │
│ └──┘                 │
│ ┌──┐                 │
│ │🏠│   Top to Bottom  │
│ └──┘                 │
│                      │
│  < OK >  < Cancel >  │
└─────────────────────┘
```

To flip an object, follow these instructions:

1. Select the object.

2. Choose Flip Object from the Objects menu.

   The Flip Object dialog box appears.

3. Select the flip option you want and click OK, or simply double-click the desired option.

   The object is flipped accordingly. If you select a previously flipped object and use Flip Object again, the dialog box shows the flip option that was applied earlier.

Note   When you use the Rotate Object or Flip Object commands, Express Publisher rotates or flips the selected object relative to its original position. For example, if you rotate an object 90 degrees to the right and want to rotate it another 90 degrees to the right, you need to select the Upside Down option, not the To The Right option. Express Publisher remembers an object's original orientation and will return a rotated or flipped object to its original orientation if you hold down the CTRL key while selecting the object and press Y at the prompt.

Control-clicking objects

Control-clicking (CTRL-click) serves as a shortcut for a few similar functions relating to moving, sizing, and rotating objects.

Boxes   As mentioned earlier, all Express Publisher objects are enclosed within boxes. You can change any object's bounding rectangle to a square by holding down the Control key (CTRL) as you select it. The square is based on the original box's shortest side. If you hold down CTRL as you select a 2" x 4" box, it would immediately change to a 2" x 2" square.

Imported pictures   If you hold down CTRL as you select an imported picture, the image reverts to its original size, orientation, and colors (assuming you changed them earlier). Express Publisher asks you to confirm this action before making the change.

Lines   You can CTRL-click an angled line and it will become vertical or horizontal, depending on which axis it is closer to. The left end of the line becomes the anchor point.

Rotated objects   CTRL-clicking an object that has been rotated or flipped returns the object to its original orientation.

Duplicating objects

Duplicate   The Duplicate command makes a copy of the currently selected text or object and places it slightly below and to the right of the original object.

1. Select the object.

2. Pull down the Edit menu and select Duplicate.

   The new copy is placed slightly lower and to the right of the original object. This newly created object is then selected.

Duplicate Many   The Duplicate Many command makes several copies of a selected object and changes the location of each copy according to your specifications. This function can be used to create grids or other special effects. There are four possible variations with the Duplicate Many command: across, down, fill, and custom. Each is documented below.

The Duplicate Many dialog box

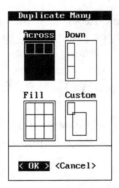

The Across and Down icons   *Across and Down*

The Across and Down options place copies in either a horizontal or vertical row. They also let you specify the amount of space between each copy.

1. Select the object you want to duplicate.

2. Choose Duplicate Many from the Edit menu.

3. Select either the Across or the Down option and click OK.

   A dialog appears that contains two text boxes: Number of Copies and Spacing Between.

4. Enter the number of copies you want.

5. Enter the amount of space between each copy.

If you leave the space value blank or enter zero, the objects are placed flush with each other. If you enter a negative number (by putting a "-" before the number) the copies will overlap.

6. Click OK.

Express Publisher places the new copies according to your selections. The original object remains selected.

The Fill icon *Fill*

The Fill option creates copies both across and down the page. You can specify how many copies you would like in each horizontal row, and how many rows you want to go down the page. You can also specify how far apart you would like each object to be. The fill option is especially useful for creating forms and grids.

1. Select the object you want to duplicate.

2. Choose Duplicate Many from the Edit menu.

3. Choose the Fill option and click OK.

   A dialog box appears containing fields for number of copies across and down, and spacing between.

4. Enter the number of objects you want in each column.

5. Enter the number of rows you want to go down the page.

6. Enter the amount of space between each copy.

   If you leave the space value blank or enter zero, the objects are placed flush with each other. If you enter a negative number (by putting a "-" before the number) the copies will overlap.

7. Click OK.

Express Publisher duplicates the original object according to your specifications. The original object is still selected.

The Custom icon *Custom*

The Custom option lets you change the size and location of each successive copy. It can be used to create geometric patterns and other special effects.

1. Select the object you want to duplicate.

2. Choose Duplicate Many from the Edit menu.

3. Choose the Custom option and click OK.

4. Enter the number of copies you want.

---

5. Enter the amount you want each copy moved horizontally and vertically.

Positive numbers in the Across field move each copy to the right, negative numbers move them to the left. Similarly, positive numbers in the Down field move the copies down, negative numbers move them up.

6. Enter the amount you want each copy resized horizontally and vertically.

Positive numbers make the objects progressively larger, negative numbers make them progressively smaller.

7. Choose OK to continue.

Express Publisher places new copies on your document. The original object stays selected.

If you're not sure what to do with this command, try using it on a one inch square. Enter 5 for Number of Copies, 0.2 inches as the Across offset, and -0.1 as the Down offset, 0.2 as the Width sizing, and 0.1 as the Height sizing. You should come up with the figure shown below.

Custom Duplicate objects

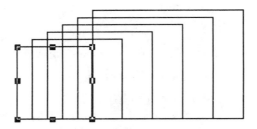

Importing pictures

Express Publisher can import pictures created by most of the popular graphics programs. This section explains the basic importing procedure. It goes on to discuss issues specific to certain types of pictures. It also offers advice on how to get the best printed results from imported pictures.

Clip art collection

See Appendix E, "Included clip art," for print-outs of all the pictures.

To help get you started in using pictures, your Express Publisher package includes a large collection of high quality clip art. All of the clip art, except for one or two PCX images, is in the TIFF format, 150 and 300 dpi (*dpi* and *TIFF* are explained below). You can copy all or part of the clip art collection onto your hard disk using the setup program. The setup program copies clip art into the \EXPRESS\ART directory. Don't try to copy the clip art directly to your hard disk without using the setup program: to fit more pictures on each disk, the pictures were compressed. The setup program decompresses them automatically as it copies them to your hard disk.

Additional clip art

If you want more clip art to work with, we offer several clip art collections. See Appendix F, "Additional clip art," for print-outs of all the collections and ordering information.

Compatible picture formats

If you're not sure if a certain picture will work with Express Publisher, try to import it anyway; Express Publisher will tell you if it doesn't recognize the picture format.

There are several formats for storing pictures. Express Publisher can import pictures that adhere to one of the following standards: PCX, MAC, ART, NAM, IMG, TIFF, GIF, and EPS. You can also import CGM files after using the CGM utility to convert them into TIFF files. Most graphics programs are capable of saving pictures in at least one of these formats. Each format has different characteristics. In most cases Express Publisher takes care of these differences so that you can treat them all the same way. Differences are explained later in this chapter under the heading "About picture formats."

Note

Certain graphics programs are able to create multi-plane color images. Express Publisher cannot import these images. It can import two-color, single-plane color images, converting every color to black. Basically, a multi-plane color image is one that uses more than two colors laid over each other to create the proper hues and tints. If you are having trouble importing an image into Express Publisher, consult your graphics program's documentation for information on how its images are created and saved.

Import Picture command

Follow these steps to import a picture file:

1. Choose the Import Picture command from the File menu, or press SHIFT-F4.

   The Import A Picture dialog box appears. It displays all of the files in the \EXPRESS\ART directory.

The Import A Picture dialog box

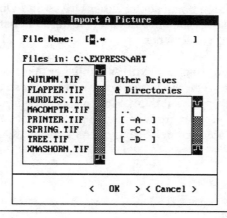

2. If necessary, change directories or disks to find the desired picture file.

3. Double-click the desired picture file.

   The picture is opened and placed in the middle of the document window. Express Publisher takes longer to import the higher resolution picture formats.

Note You can import headlines created with TextEffects into a document with the Import Picture command. See Chapter 6 for details on using TextEffects.

Insufficient memory

If your computer is low on memory (not disk space), Express Publisher will import the picture but will not display it on your screen. In its place will be a gray rectangle the actual size of your picture. The picture will, however, print accurately, unless you are really short on memory. Appendix C, "Trouble shooting," provides additional information about memory.

To view the actual picture, try placing it in a separate, empty file. If you still cannot view the picture, it is simply too large to display using your computer's current memory.

After importing a picture, you can find that it is taking longer for Express Publisher to refresh the screen. To speed up screen refresh, Choose Display Settings under the Options menu and turn off Display Bitmap Images.

Changing the default picture directory

When you use the Import Picture command, Express Publisher always looks first in the \EXPRESS\ART directory. If you want to change the default picture directory, run the setup program over again and specify a new path. Or, in the Import A Picture dialog box, use the Other Drives and Directories option to change the Files In path. Express Publisher will display the last path used when you next open that dialog box.

About picture formats In most cases Express Publisher takes care of all the differences between the various picture formats so that you don't have to worry about them. However, not every function works with every picture type. Some picture types also have different display or performance characteristics.

PCX, IMG, and ART

You won't run into any limitations when using PCX, IMG, or ART pictures. All of Express Publisher's features and characteristics will be normal.

The only problem you can run into is with color PCX pictures that have more than four colors and one plane. Color PCX images will be converted to two-color images. PCX images that were originally more than two colors may not convert very well (most of the picture's definition will be lost). Whenever possible, create and save PCX images as two-color (or black and white) images. To find out whether your picture will be usable or not, import it and see what you get.

Print Shop

Several Print Shop pictures are stored within each NAM file. When you choose to open a NAM file, a new dialog box appears listing all of the pictures stored within the file. Double-click the picture that you want to open and Express Publisher places it in the middle of the document window. (PNM files are also compatible.)

MacPaint

Express Publisher can import MacPaint pictures without any special conversion process, but this doesn't mean you can put a Macintosh disk in your IBM drive and expect Express Publisher to open the file. You must first move your MacPaint file onto an MS-DOS formatted disk. You can do this with a telecommunications program, a special Macintosh to PC conversion program such as Traveling Software's MacLink®, or a network that supports both MS-DOS and Macintosh computers.

MacPaint pictures are always a full page in size. In most cases you will only want to use a small portion of the original picture. Use the Crop Image command (documented below) to cut out the portion of the picture you want. If you leave the picture uncropped, the program will run out of memory more quickly. White (or clear) dots take up just as much memory as black dots. An 8.5" by 11" picture with a tiny image in the middle uses the same amount of memory as a detailed picture of the same size.

EPS

Encapsulated Postscript pictures (EPS) are very different from the other picture file types. Instead of storing information on the location of every dot in the picture, they store a condensed version of the Postscript commands needed to print the picture on a Postscript compatible printer. EPS pictures print at the resolution of the Postscript printer. Express Publisher cannot display EPS pictures on the screen. They appear only as grey boxes. EPS pictures can be flipped or rotated, but the Crop command and the Edit Bit Image command won't work with them. *You must have a Postscript compatible printer to print EPS pictures.*

TIFF

Scanned pictures (TIFF) usually vary in resolution from roughly 75 to 1200 dpi. Express Publisher displays them on the screen at 80 dpi but prints them at their original resolution. You cannot use the Edit Bit Image command to modify TIFF pictures. You can Flip, Rotate, or crop a TIFF picture, but if the picture is large, or of very high resolution, doing so will take up a lot of time and disk space. Express Publisher does not support RGB, palette color, or grey scaled TIFF pictures. If you're not sure what type of TIFF picture you have, try to import it anyway. Express Publisher tells you if the file is incompatible. You can import most standard black-and-white TIFF images, regardless of the compression technique used when the image was scanned. Color and grey scale images cannot be imported.

You should scan at 300 dpi to maintain the image's original size in Express Publisher. Scanning at higher or lower resolutions will cause the images to increase and decrease in size respectively when you import the image into Express Publisher.

TIFF images created by some presentation graphics or draw and paint programs appear in reversed colors when imported into Express Publisher. You can correct this problem by selecting the object and choosing Reverse Colors from the Objects menu. The image will display and print properly.

GIF

Express Publisher supports all types of GIF (CompuServe Graphics Interchange Format) pictures. It converts color pictures to monochrome black and white. The method used works well with 16 color pictures. It can distort pictures with more colors. You cannot modify GIF pictures with the Edit Bit image command (see "Editing pictures"). You can Flip or Rotate a GIF picture; doing so can take up a lot of time and disk space.

How TIFF, GIF, and EPS files are stored

Express Publisher does not save TIFF, GIF, and EPS pictures as part of the document. It remembers the name of the picture file and where it was loaded from. Every time you open a document that has one of these types of picture, Express Publisher re-loads the picture file from disk. To copy a document to a different system, you must also move the graphics files.

Large pictures
There are two limitations to importing large pictures: the physical size of your document, and memory.

- You cannot place a picture 9" wide on an 8.5" wide page. When you import a picture too large to fit on your page, Express Publisher applies whatever scaling factor is necessary to fit the entire picture on the page or tells you large PCX images are not supported (too many pixels across a page). The scaling factor is applied to both dimensions, so the original proportions of the picture are preserved.

- Express Publisher can import IMG, PCX, MAC, and ART files that take up less than 64K of memory. TIFF, GIF, and EPS pictures can be larger. There is no simple way to tell how much memory a picture uses; the file size on disk is not an indication. You can figure out how many pixels your page width will take: If you have an 8.5" wide page and the screen resolution is 80 dpi, the maximum pixel width for images is 680 (80 x 8.5). If you get an error message stating that the picture is too large to import, make it smaller using the program that generated it.

What is a picture?
A picture, as the term is used in this manual, is a collection of dots that form an image. Graphics programs that create these images work by turning dots off or on. These programs are frequently called *paint* programs. Your computer stores these pictures by saving a map in which dots are on (black) and dots are off (white); so pictures are sometimes called *bit maps*.

It is important to understand the difference between the objects you create by using Express Publisher's own drawing tools, and pictures that you import from paint programs. If you were to import a picture of a box from a paint program, and draw a box of exactly the same size with the box tool, it can be hard to tell the difference between the two boxes on the screen. The real difference is in how the program creates and stores the information needed to present the two images.

When you draw a box using the Box tool, Express Publisher keeps track of this information by remembering the characteristic of a box, where the upper left corner of the box is, and what its dimensions are. To display an imported picture of a box, on the other hand, Express Publisher has to remember where to place every single dot that makes up the image. Obviously this uses a lot more memory. By using this method, however, it is possible to present much more detailed and irregular images.

A box drawn in Express Publisher (left), and a bit mapped box

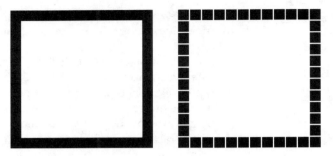

Resolution and print quality

The number of dots per inch (dpi) that compose a picture determines its resolution. The more dots per inch, the higher the resolution and the better the print quality.

Express Publisher imports PCX, ART, MAC, IMG, GIF, and NAM (or PNM) pictures at 80 dpi; it imports TIFF pictures at any resolution. The TIFF pictures in our clip art collection are either 150 dpi or 300 dpi. (EPS pictures have no set resolution.)

You can change the resolution of a picture by scaling it. Making a picture larger decreases the resolution, shrinking it increases the resolution. For example, if you import a 150 dpi TIFF picture that is 2″ by 2″, scaling the picture by 50% makes the picture 1″ by 1″, and increases the resolution from 150 to 300 dpi. Express Publisher never adds or removes dots from a scaled picture; it simply redistributes the existing dots to fit the new size.

The print quality of your pictures also depends on the resolution of your printer. You can get bad results if you try to print 300 dpi pictures on a printer that can only print at 120 dpi. To get the best results, make the picture's resolution an even multiple of your printer's resolution. (Use Choose Printer to find the resolution that Express Publisher prints on your printer.)

When your printer's resolution is higher than the resolution of your pictures, make the pictures smaller to improve quality. If your printer can print at 300 dpi you don't have to settle for 80 dpi quality, even if you are working with a PCX file that is 80 dpi. Reducing an 80 dpi PCX picture to 27% of its original size increases its resolution to approximately 300 dpi. Divide the resolution of the picture by the resolution of the printer to determine the best scaling factor (80/300 = .2666).

If your printer's resolution is lower than the resolution of your picture, make the pictures larger. When printing a 300 dpi picture on a 150 dpi printer, you get the best results by scaling the picture by a factor of 200% (300/150 = 2).

Changing pictures

Moving and sizing imported pictures

An imported picture is treated as a single object by Express Publisher. It can be modified just like any other Express Publisher object. You can move it around by dragging it, and change its size by dragging its handles. Pictures can be duplicated, rotated, flipped, aligned, or equated just like any other object.

Editing pictures

Use the Scale Object command to change the size of pictures. The Scale Object command resizes a picture while maintaining its original proportions. This ensures that it will not be distorted.

As explained in "Resolution and print quality," the printed quality of your pictures can vary depending on the scaling factor you select and how it relates to the resolution of your printer.

Every picture is made up of tiny dots. The Edit Bit Image command enlarges pictures so that you can change these dots very precisely. This makes it very easy to touch up pictures. You can also use the Edit Bit Image command to draw completely new images within existing pictures.

Always use the Edit Bit Image command before you change the size of a picture. If you resize a picture and then use Edit Bit Image, Express Publisher edits the resized copy, not the original. This drastically reduces the printed quality of the picture.

Note

The Edit Bit Image command does not work with EPS, TIFF, or GIF pictures. One PCX image (FISH.PCX) was installed in your \EXPRESS\ART directory by the set up program. Use this image to experiment with the Edit Bit Image command.

To change a picture with the Edit Bit Image command, follow these instructions:

1. Select an imported picture.
2. Pull down the Objects menu and select Edit Bit Image.

A portion of the picture is enlarged to fill the whole document window. Each dot is clearly visible. If you click a black dot, the pointer acts like an eraser; if you click a white dot, it acts like a marker. You can click dots one at a time, or hold down the mouse button and drag the pointer. At the upper left corner of the window, a small window shows the portion of picture you are working on in its normal size. Scroll bars appear to the right and bottom of the window so you can move the area that you are working on.

Using the Edit Bit Image command

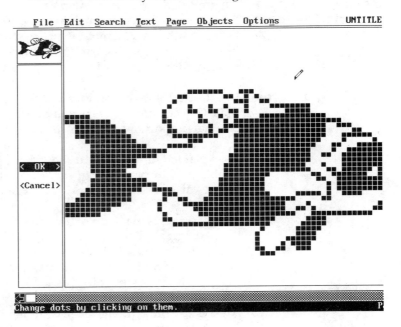

3. Click OK when you are done to carry out the changes or Cancel to abandon them.

Cropping pictures

The Crop Image command cuts out unwanted portions of pictures. Many graphics programs save a picture the size of the whole screen every time they save a file, even if the image itself is much smaller. Since Express Publisher treats an imported picture file as a single object, you will frequently want to use only a small portion of the picture in your document. While cropping a picture, you can measure the exact dimensions of the area you are cropping to make sure it fits in the space provided in your document.

Note   The Crop Image command does not work with EPS pictures.

These steps tell you how to crop a picture:

1. Pull down the Objects menu and select Crop Image.

   The pointer changes to the cropping pointer.

The Cropping pointer

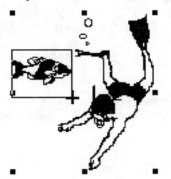

2. Move the pointer within a picture, and click the mouse button.

   The pointer changes to a cross hair.

3. Press and hold down the mouse button as you drag the pointer to draw a box defining the crop area.

Defining the crop area

Notice that while you draw the cropping box, its height and width are displayed in the message line at the bottom of the document window. This can be very helpful if you want your picture to fit in a certain area.

4. Release the mouse when the cropping box is the right size.

   The Cropping dialog box appears, asking you to confirm the action. After you have cut out part of a picture, import the picture again to restore it to its original condition.

5. Choose OK to complete the operation.

   The cropped portion of the picture remains in the document and the rest disappears.

Try this cropping trick: Use the Crop Image command as usual, but after defining the crop area inside the picture, instead of releasing the mouse button to finish drawing the cropping box, press the SHIFT key. You are then able to drag the entire cropping box around within the picture. When you release the mouse button, the Crop dialog box appears as usual.

Reversing colors

The Reverse Colors command on the Objects menu creates a negative image of any picture. It changes black to white and white to black.

Note Reverse Colors does not work with EPS pictures.

1. Select a picture.
2. Pull down the Objects menu and select Reverse Colors.

Original picture and picture with colors reversed

Making a picture solid or transparent

Ordinarily when you import pictures they are transparent. You can see objects that are within their boundaries in places where there are no black dots.

Transparent and solid pictures

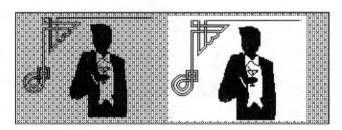

You can use the Object Specs command to make pictures solid, so that they obscure all objects behind them, or to change a solid picture back to being transparent.

1. Select a picture and choose Object Specs.

    Notice that the Filled option now says Transparent.

2. Click in the Transparent check box to change the setting and click OK.

Saving as a picture   The Save As Picture command allows you to save all or part of the document window as a PCX picture file. You can then load the picture file into any paint program that can read PCX files and work with it there, or reload it into Express Publisher. It also can be used to convert or combine pictures from different programs that will not load each other's files directly, such as The Print Shop and Microsoft Paintbrush.

To save a picture file:

1. Choose the Save As Picture command from the File menu.

   The pointer changes to a cross hair.

2. Draw a box around the area that you want to save as a picture.

   The Save Picture dialog box appears.

3. Type a name for the picture file. If necessary, change drives or directories.

   Express Publisher adds the PCX extension automatically.

4. Click OK to save the picture.

   The picture is saved to the file name and location you specified.

5

Text

This chapter details all of Express Publisher's text-handling abilities. You can create all the needed text for your documents inside of Express Publisher, or import documents from other word processors. Using Express Publisher's formatting abilities, you can specify the size and font of any text, change the justification of every paragraph, and flow text around pictures.

Express Publisher can keep track of up to 64 separate stories in one document, allowing them to flow from column to column and skip pages automatically. There are also many editing and formatting shortcuts that make your work go faster and look better.

This chapter describes the following topics:

- About stories and text frames
- Entering text
- Editing text
- Linking text frames
- Importing text
- Fonts
- Basic text formatting
- Advanced text frame formatting
- Headers and footers
- Using styles
- Text and pictures

About stories and text frames

Express Publisher groups and stores text in a way that allows you to choose exactly how much of the text is affected by the formatting command you give. By using a dialog box, many command options allow you to apply the command to a text frame, to a story, or to the entire document. The following paragraphs explain how these formatting levels work together to produce the final page.

Documents The most comprehensive formatting level is the *document* level. When you apply a command to the document, all text in the file will be affected by the command.

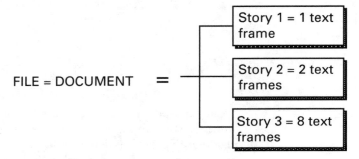

FILE = DOCUMENT =

Story 1 = 1 text frame

Story 2 = 2 text frames

Story 3 = 8 text frames

Stories Whenever you work with a conventional word processor, each document you create is a single body of text, or a *story* as referred to in this manual. When you add characters to the middle of the story, all the following characters are pushed down the page. If you delete a whole paragraph, the rest of the text is pulled back up the page.

Most word processors can only handle one body of text per document, but an Express Publisher document can contain several stories, each one completely independent from the others.

Express Publisher lets you put different parts of a story in different places in a document. When creating a document with several stories, you can link a story that starts in a text frame on page one to a text frame on page four. The text will flow between the linked frames automatically. If you add more text to the story on the first page, the rest of the text moves down, flowing from page one directly to page four. If you delete a paragraph on page one, text is pulled back from page four to fill the gap in page one. Other pages in the document may contain different stories that remain completely unaffected by the changes in the first story.

Story capacity

Express Publisher only allows stories up to 64K and can handle up to 64 stories per document. The program tells you if your story has reached this limit. If you want to continue adding to the story, you will have to divide it into two separate stories. This 64K limit can hold a lot of text (20 to 30 pages worth), so you are not likely to run into it. However, you may run up against this limitation when you import a word processing document using the Import Text command. If you want to import a large file, you will have to split it into several smaller files first, using your word processing software.

Text frames

All text in Express Publisher is contained within *text frames*. A text frame is simply a box in which you have placed text. A text frame can be selected, moved, and sized just like any other object. Anything that you do to the text frame as an object (such as moving it around in the document) does not change the story within the text frame. Think of the text frame as a window through which you are viewing the story. Express Publisher always tries to fit as much of the story in the text frame as possible, but if the frame is too small, it stores the rest of the story out of sight. If you make the text frame larger, Express Publisher adds the text that wouldn't fit earlier.

If your page layout does not allow you to make the frame large enough to display the entire story, you can display the remainder of the text in a *linked* frame. You may need to create several linked frames to display all of the text. Additional information about linking text frames can be found in "Linking text frames" later in this chapter.

Sample document showing types of text frames

Non-linked text frames

Linked text frames

Linked text frames

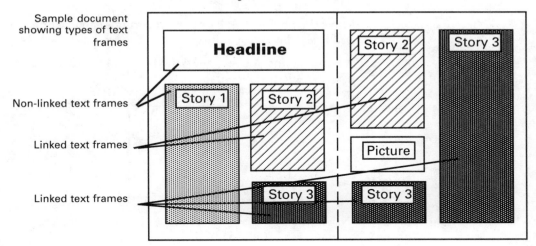

Applying commands

If you apply a command to a text frame, the command affects only the text showing in that frame, and not text in linked frames.

If you apply a command to a story, the command affects all the frames that are part of that story, but does not affect unlinked frames or other stories in the document.

The following sections explain each text-related function in detail.

Entering text

All text in Express Publisher must be entered in a text frame. A text frame is no different from any other type of box in Express Publisher. You can select, move, and scale, and otherwise change a text frame exactly as if it were a regular box.

Express Publisher creates text frames for you when you use the New command to create a document. You can also create your own text frames by drawing them with the Text Frame tool.

When clicked from within a text frame, the Text tool allows you to work with text. You are able to select and modify text, but you cannot do anything to objects. When the Text tool is active the pointer looks like an I-beam.

Follow these steps to enter text:

The Text tool

1. Click the Text tool.

   The pointer changes to an I-beam shape.

The I-beam pointer

2. Move the pointer to the upper left corner of an existing box and press the mouse button.

   A blinking line appears, marking the text insertion point; it is usually called a text cursor.

The text cursor

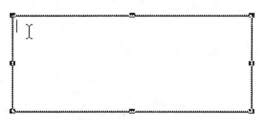

3. Type This is easier than I thought it would be, or whatever comes to mind.

The box is now a text frame. You can move the pointer to a new position in the text, or within a different box, and press the mouse button to place a new text cursor.

Text editing keys Express Publisher recognizes the standard text editing keys.

- BACKSPACE deletes the character to the left of the cursor.
- DELETE deletes the character to the right of the cursor.
- INSERT tells Express Publisher to switch back and forth between insert and overstrike text entry. Insert means that new

characters push existing characters to the right; overstrike means that new characters replace existing characters.

- LEFT and RIGHT arrows move the cursor in the direction of the arrow by one character.
- UP and DOWN arrows move the cursor up or down one line of text.
- HOME and END move the cursor to the beginning or end of a line, respectively.
- CTRL-HOME and CTRL-END move the cursor to the beginning or end of the current story.
- CTRL-PGUP and CTRL-PGDN move the cursor to the beginning or end of the text in the current frame.
- F6 moves the cursor to the next text frame in the story.
- SHIFT-F6 moves the cursor to the previous text frame in the story.

There are other keystrokes useful for various text functions. They are explained in the sections relating to those functions. The quick-reference card lists all of the text function keys.

Alternate characters

In Express Publisher you can enter a number of special characters not found on standard keyboards. These characters include mathematical and scientific symbols, foreign language characters, uncommon punctuation marks, and symbols such as ® and ©. Consult Appendix H for a complete list of these characters and instructions on how to enter them.

Selecting objects

While you are working with text you cannot select and change objects. When you want to stop working with text, you need to put away the Text tool in order to work with objects again.

The Arrow tool

- To put away the text tool, click the Arrow tool.
- Or, click the I-beam pointer outside of a box.

The pointer changes back to the arrow, and you are able to select objects again.

Editing text

Selecting text

In order to use many of Express Publisher's text formatting commands, you must first select the text that you wish to change. Selected text is always highlighted.

Warning: if you select text and then type something, the selected text is deleted.

It is important to understand the difference between selecting text and selecting the text frame as an object. When you click a text frame with the arrow pointer, you are selecting the text frame as an object. You may manipulate a selected text frame like any other box, but you can't change the text within the frame. (Review "About stories and text frames" earlier in this chapter if you are confused.) To select a block of text you must activate the Text tool (the pointer looks like an I-beam when the Text tool is active). Once you have selected text you can delete it, cut it, copy it to the clipboard, or change its size and font.

You can select text with the mouse and the I-beam pointer or with the keyboard.

With the mouse   There are several techniques for using the mouse to select text.

Dragging

You can drag the mouse across text in order to select it.

The Text tool   1. Click the Text tool, unless it is already active.

2. Move the pointer to the beginning of a body of text you want to select and hold down the mouse button.

   This marks an anchor point for the area you are selecting.

3. Still holding down the mouse button, drag the mouse in any direction.

Selecting text

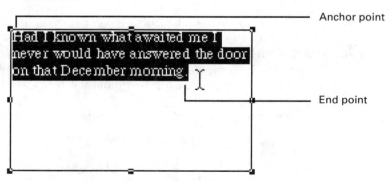

Anchor point

Had I known what awaited me I never would have answered the door on that December morning.

End point

Notice that the highlighted area moves with the pointer.

4. Release the mouse button when all the text you want selected is highlighted.

Double-clicking

You can double-click a word to select it.

- Move the I-beam pointer onto a word you want to select and double-click the mouse button to select it.

Shift-clicking

SHIFT-clicking is useful for selecting very large bodies of text within a single text frame.

1. Move the I-beam pointer to the exact beginning of the body of text you want to select and click the mouse to place a text cursor.

2. Without holding down the mouse button, move the pointer to the end of the body of text you want to select.

3. Hold down SHIFT as you click the mouse button again.

   All the text between the text cursor and the place where you SHIFT-clicked is selected.

With the keyboard If you don't want to reach for the mouse to select some text while you are typing, you can select text from the keyboard using the F8 key.

1. Move the text cursor to the beginning of the area you want to select and press F8.

2. Use the arrow keys, or any other keys that move the cursor, to extend the selection.

3. When the text you want is selected, press F8 again to close the selection. Or, you can press ESCAPE to cancel the selection.

Select entire story When you apply a command to text, the command affects only the text within that text frame. If you want to apply a command to an entire story, you must select the story:

1. Click in any of the story's text frames.

2. Choose Select Entire Story from the Edit menu.

   The entire story will become highlighted.

3. Activate any command that can be applied to highlighted text (Choose Font, Choose Style, and so on).

Replacing text You can replace a block of text by selecting it and typing. The selected text is deleted and replaced with whatever you type.

If you ever remove text accidentally this way, you can retrieve it from the clipboard by using the Paste command described below.

Moving text The Cut and Paste commands make it easy to move text from one place to another in a document.

Note   Express Publisher does not retain font attributes when you use the Cut and Paste commands.

1. Select the text that you want to place on the clipboard.

2. Choose either the Cut or Copy command from the Edit menu.

   If you chose Cut, Express Publisher removes the selected text from the document and places it on the clipboard. If you chose Copy, it places a copy of the selected text on the clipboard.

3. Use the mouse to move the cursor to where you want to place the text.

   Remember that you can only put text inside of a text frame.

4. Choose Paste from the Edit menu.

   The text on the clipboard is inserted at the current cursor location.

Correcting text display

Sometimes the screen display cannot keep up with the cut and paste operations. You may cut a part of a line and find that the remaining text does not close up properly, or that the piece you cut still seems to appear on the screen. This may also happen if you are typing very fast. You need to tell Express Publisher to refresh the screen, that is, to redisplay it with the changes you have just made. Click the Screen Refresh/Text Rewrap button or press CTRL-F1.

Moving a text frame

You can also cut and copy text frames.

Cutting a text frame

When you cut a text frame, only the frame moves to the clipboard. The text moves to the next linked frame. If there is none, the text may be deleted.

1. Click the Arrow tool.

2. Click the frame.

3. Pull down the Edit menu and choose the Cut command.

If there is another text frame linked to this one, the text moves to it, and the frame itself moves to the clipboard.

If there is no other text frame linked to this one, a dialog box warns you that the text will be lost if you continue. At this point, you can choose to cut the frame and lose the text, or cancel. If you still want to remove the frame, click the Text tool, select the text, cut it, and, for safety's sake, paste it in a new location. Then return to the empty frame and follow the steps above to cut it.

4. To paste the frame, choose Paste from the Edit menu.

Clear clipboard

To clear the clipboard, pull down the Edit menu and select Clear Clipboard.

Duplicating a text frame

You can duplicate a text frame and the text inside it.

1. Click the Arrow tool.

2. Click the frame.

3. Pull down the Edit menu and choose the Duplicate command.

   The duplicated frame is drawn on top of the original.

Search/Replace

The Search/Replace command finds a character or group of characters (a string) of up to twelve characters and replaces it with a new character string. When using the Search/Replace command you have the option of searching through the current text frame, the current story, or the whole document.

Search criteria

When you select Search/Replace from the Edit menu, a dialog box appears with a text field labeled Search For.

The Search/Replace dialog box

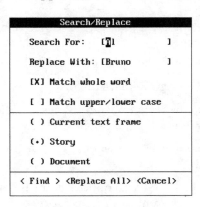

```
         Search/Replace
 Search For:   [B]          ]

 Replace With: [Bruno        ]

 [X] Match whole word

 [ ] Match upper/lower case

 ( ) Current text frame

 (•) Story

 ( ) Document
< Find > <Replace All> <Cancel>
```

Express Publisher searches for the text you type in the Search For field. It looks through the current story starting at the current cursor position and continuing to the end. If you want to look through the entire story, make sure that you place the cursor at the very beginning of the story. If you want to search the entire document, place the cursor on page One.

There are two check boxes in the Search/Replace dialog box that affect the way Express Publisher searches for text.

- **Whole Words Only** tells Express Publisher to match the text you enter in the Search For with only whole words. With this option on, Express Publisher will not find the characters "link" in the word "linkage."
- **Check Upper/Lower Case** makes Express Publisher case sensitive. With this option on, Express Publisher will not find the characters "ramp" if you type "Ramp" in the Search For field. By default, Express Publisher is not case sensitive.

Replace options

There are two buttons that affect the way text is replaced.

- **Find:** If you choose Find, Express Publisher asks you to confirm each replacement.
- **Replace All:** When you choose Replace All, Express Publisher replaces every occurrence of the search text without confirmation and also without checking to see if the replacement makes sense. Check the Search For and Replace With strings carefully before you use this option.

Find and replace text

Follow these steps to use the Search/Replace command:

1. Place a text cursor at the beginning of the story you wish to search.

2. Pull down the Edit menu and select Search/Replace.

   The Search/Replace dialog appears.

3. Type the text you want Express Publisher to look for in the Search For field, it can be up to twelve characters long.

4. Type the text you want to replace it with in the Replace With field.

5. Set the two search options according to your need, and check either Current text frame, Story, or Document.

6. Click the Find or Replace All button.

   If you click the Replace All button, Express Publisher immediately makes all the replacements without confirmation.

Clicking on the Find button causes Express Publisher to look for the search characters. When a match is found, the Search/Replace Context Window appears. It contains four buttons, Find Next, Replace, OK, and cancel.

The Search/Replace Context Window

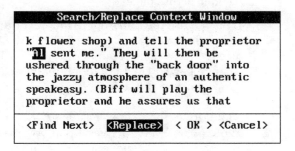

```
      Search/Replace Context Window

k flower shop) and tell the proprietor
"█l sent me." They will then be
ushered through the "back door" into
the jazzy atmosphere of an authentic
speakeasy. (Biff will play the
proprietor and he assures us that

<Find Next>  <Replace>  < OK > <Cancel>
```

- Click the Find Next button if you don't want Express Publisher to make the replacement, but to continue the search.
- Click the Replace button if you want Express Publisher to make the replacement and continue searching.
- Clicking OK closes the Search/Replace Context Window and changes the cursor position in your document so that the search text is visible and places a text cursor before the first character.
- Click Cancel to stop the procedure at any time.
- To search again using the same search string, press F7.

Linking text frames

Using the Link and Unlink tools, you can establish the manner in which stories flow between the various text frames in your document. Remember that stories are completely independent from text frames. In linking and unlinking text frames you are merely establishing a path for a story to follow. When you create a document with either the one, two, or three column preset options, all the text frames are linked together (except for the headlines).

Linking text frames   Follow these steps to link text frames:

The Link tool

1. Select the Link tool in the toolbox. The pointer changes to the link pointer.

2. Move the link pointer to the text frame that you want to be the source frame in the linkage and click the mouse button.

3. Move the pointer to the text frame you want to be the destination frame and click the mouse button.

After you click the second text frame, the pointer changes back to the arrow. Now if you fill up the first frame with text, text flows automatically to the next frame.

Linking across pages

You can use the Link tool to link text frames on different pages. After clicking the source frame with the link pointer, you may use the Next Page command, or the Go To Page command to change pages. The Link tool remains active as you change pages. Once you are at the desired page, click the destination frame.

Hold down the SHIFT key as you click the destination frame and the Link tool stays active so that you may link several frames together at once. The following example illustrates this point.

The Link tool

The Link tool is active as long as you hold down SHIFT. You don't have to select the Link tool between each frame.

1. Click the Link tool.

2. Click a text frame with the link pointer to indicate it as the source frame in the story.

3. Hold down the SHIFT key and click a destination frame.

   Text flows into the destination frame. The pointer remains in the linking shape to indicate that the Link tool is still active.

4. Still holding down the SHIFT key, click an additional destination frame.

Text flows into the third frame.

Principles of linking

- Each text frame can contain only one story.
- You can link or unlink text frames, but the story itself is not affected.
- You can link boxes together before adding text, and then as you add text, the text will flow from one frame to the next automatically.
- Text flows between the frames in the order that they were linked.
- You can link text frames across as many pages as you wish, but you cannot link a text frame to a frame on a preceding page so that text flows to the earlier page.

The More Text marker

When there is more text in a story than fits in the current frame, Express Publisher places a crooked arrow at the lower right corner of frame. It is called the More Text marker.

You can tell that all the text in a story has been placed if the More Text marker does not appear in the lower right corner.

Moving between linked frames

While you are entering text, you may want to move quickly between the frames in the story.

- Press F6 to move the text cursor to the next frame in the story.
- Press SHIFT-F6 to move the text cursor to the previous frame in the story.

These commands are also useful for determining how frames have been linked.

Unlinking text frames

When you unlink a text frame Express Publisher removes the text and redistributes it to the other linked frames that hold the story. The text frame reverts to a plain box.

The Unlink tool

1. Select the Unlink tool from the toolbox.

   The pointer changes to the unlink pointer.

2. Move the pointer to the frame that you want to unlink and click the mouse button.

As soon as you click the frame with the Unlink tool, Express Publisher unlinks the text frame, and the text disappears. Remember, the story itself has not been changed at all, so you have not lost any text. Unlinking a text frame simply removes one of your windows from the story. If you link the two frames together again, Express Publisher again displays the story text in the frame.

A quick way to unlink a text frame is to delete it as an object. Just select it with the arrow pointer and press DELETE, or choose the Cut command from the Edit menu. The text is redistributed to any other frames in the story.

Note   If you try to unlink the only text frame in your document that is displaying a certain story, a dialog box appears asking you if you really want to do this. A story is lost if it is not displayed somewhere in the document.

Unlinking in a long story

If you have linked several text frames together, unlinking one of the frames somewhere in the middle changes the sequence of the other frames in the chain. When you remove a frame, Express

Publisher links the frame that preceded it to the one that came after it. The following example makes this more clear:

1. If necessary, link together three text frames according to the instructions above and fill them with text. (It will help you to understand the example if all the frames are on one page.)

2. Unlink the text frame in the middle of the story.

   All of the text disappears from the middle text frame and is sent to the third text frame. Text now flows directly from the first text frame to the third text frame.

As long as you hold down the SHIFT key the Unlink tool remains active. You can unlink several frames at once by holding down the SHIFT key as you click text frames with the unlink pointer.

Importing text

Express Publisher can import text from all of the word processors listed below. It preserves bold, italic, and underlined status from the following programs:

- Microsoft Works and Word (version 4.0 and later)
- MicroPro WordStar and WordStar 2000 (version 3.0 and later)
- WordPerfect (version 4.0 and later)

*Save your **DisplayWrite** file in RFT/DCA format before you import it into Express Publisher.*

Express Publisher also recognizes DCA and IBM DisplayWrite 4.0 files, but cannot preserve bold, italic, or underlining for these types of files.

If your word processor is not supported, you should be able to convert your word processing documents to ASCII text files and then load them into Express Publisher. (ASCII stands for American Standard Code for Information Interchange. Almost every word processor is capable of loading and saving ASCII text files.) No text formatting is preserved when ASCII text is imported.

Once text has been imported, you can use any of Express Publisher's text handling abilities to manipulate the imported text.

Use the Import Text command to import a document from another word processor.

1. Select a box for the imported text to flow into.

2. Select Import Text from the File menu.

   The Import Text dialog box appears displaying all the files in the current disk or directory. If necessary click a new drive or directory in the Other Drives and Directories list box until the directory you want is displayed. (Click " . . " to move toward the directory."

The Import Text dialog box

3. Double-click the document you wish to import.

When you import a document that contains many styles, it may take a while to import the text. Don't worry; Express Publisher is simply making sure it imports the styles correctly.

Assuming that Express Publisher recognizes the document as one of the compatible formats, the text from the imported document flows into the text frame. If the frame is linked to other frames, the text flows through each of the linked frames until all the text is visible. If a More Text marker appears in the lower right corner of the last frame in the story, then there is more text in the story. To display it, add and link new frames to the story or make the existing frames larger.

You don't have to create a text frame ahead of time if you don't want to. Go through the import routine as documented above without first selecting a text frame. When Express Publisher imports the file it creates a text frame to contain the new story.

Unrecognizable documents

In some cases Express Publisher may not be able to determine the type of file you are trying to import. This can occur when importing ASCII text, WordPerfect, and WordStar files. When this happens, Express Publisher presents the Specify Import Format dialog box.

```
      Specify Import Format
 ┌─────────────────────────────────┐
 │ Express Publisher is not able to│
 │ determine the type of file.     │
 │ Please select one from below.   │
 ├─────────────────────────────────┤
 │ (•) ASCII text                  │
 │                                 │
 │ ( ) Word Perfect                │
 │                                 │
 │ ( ) Word Star                   │
 ├─────────────────────────────────┤
 │         < OK >   < Cancel >     │
 └─────────────────────────────────┘
```

- Click the appropriate file type in the Specify Import Format dialog box, and click OK.

As long as you choose the correct option, Express Publisher imports the file. If you choose the wrong file type, an error message appears.

You can use the Import Text command to append new text to an existing story, or to completely replace it.

- If you choose to append, Express Publisher adds the new text to the end of the existing story. The new text does not always appear right away. There may not be enough room to display the new text in the currently linked text frames, or the story may end on another page.
- If you choose to replace an existing story, Express Publisher removes the old story from the document. The new story flows into all the text frames that were linked in the old story.

Importing to existing stories

Follow these steps to import text to an existing story:

1. Select the first text frame in an existing story.

2. Choose Import Text from the File menu, select a word processing document from the Import Text dialog box, and click OK.

   The Place Story Text dialog box appears. In addition to the options discussed above, you may choose to create a new text frame for the imported text.

```
┌─────────────────────────────────────┐
│         Place Story Text            │
├─────────────────────────────────────┤
│ The text frame selected contains a  │
│ story. Select appropriate action.   │
│                                     │
│                                     │
│  (•) Append text to the story       │
│                                     │
│  ( ) Replace old text in the story  │
│                                     │
│  ( ) Create a new text frame        │
│                                     │
├─────────────────────────────────────┤
│          < OK >   < Cancel >        │
└─────────────────────────────────────┘
```

3. Choose the desired placement option and click OK.

Express Publisher imports text using the default font. To change the default font before importing, make sure that no objects are selected, and that no text cursor has been placed, and then use the Choose Font command. Your choice becomes the new default font.

Note You can place text from more than one word processor into one text frame.

Fonts

About fonts A font is a complete set of characters, comprising the alphabet, numbers, and punctuation, that has a unique design. If you're not familiar with what fonts are, notice the difference between the characters in the body text of this manual, and the characters in the headings. The headings and body text are set in two different fonts to make them more distinct from each other.

Express Publisher can print characters in several fonts and sizes. It also changes fonts by adding *attributes* such as bold and italic. The Choose Font command allows you to choose the typeface, size, and attributes of any text in your document.

Express Publisher works with three types of fonts: Express Publisher fonts, soft fonts, and printer fonts. Express Publisher fonts work on most types of printers. Printer fonts are specific to each different type of printer. Appendix I explains soft fonts.

The Express Publisher fonts are licensed from Agfa Compugraphic®, a leader in the professional typesetting field. You can scale them from 6 to 144 points, and print them on almost every printer supported by Express Publisher. There are eight Express Publisher fonts included in your package: CG Triumvirate™, CG Times™, Univers™, Cooper Black™, Garamond Antiqua™, Microstyle Bold Extended™, CG Bodoni Bold™, and Futura Bold II™.

CG Times, CG Bodoni Bold, Garamond Antiqua, and Cooper Black are serif fonts, effective for both body text and headings. A *serif* is a short, light line projecting from the top or bottom of a main stroke of a letter. Serif fonts originally developed from handwriting. CG Triumvirate is a sans serif font (without serif), similar to the popular Helvetica. Sans serif fonts such as CG Triumvirate, Univers, Futura Bold II, and Microstyle Bold Extended look more plain and modern than serif fonts. Most designers use sans serif fonts for display type such as headings and titles.

CG Times · 'Twas brillig and the slithy toves...

CG Triumvirate · 'Twas brillig and the slithy toves...

Univers · 'Twas brillig and the slithy toves...

CG Bodoni Bold · **'Twas brillig and the slithy toves...**

Cooper Black · **'Twas brillig and the slithy toves...**

Futura Bold II · **'Twas brillig and the slithy toves...**

Garamond Antiqua · 'Twas brillig and the slithy toves...

Microstyle Bold Extended · **'Twas brillig and the slithy toves...**

Additional Express Publisher fonts

Power Up Software offers additional font packages called Express Fonts. Express Publisher also works with HP Type Director Fonts and fonts sold by Agfa Compugraphic. You can install all of these fonts with the setup program and use them just like the fonts that come in the original package. See Appendix G, "Additional fonts," for more information.

Printer fonts

Express Publisher supports many printer fonts. Unless you have installed additional fonts, any fonts other than CG Times, CG Triumvirate, and Univers appearing in the Choose Font dialog box are printer fonts. A printer font is a font that is built into your printer. Each printer provides a different set of fonts. This means that Express Publisher can print different fonts on an HP LaserJet than it can on an Epson RX. Most programs, especially word processors, do not have their own fonts and use only printer fonts.

The software that controls printer fonts is not part of Express Publisher. Printer fonts are usually programmed into your printer, but they may also be controlled by extra software or hardware. For example, you can add fonts to an HP LaserJet using font cartridges that plug into the printer, or software that "downloads" fonts to the printer. When printing a character in an Express Publisher font, Express Publisher must tell the printer exactly what the character looks like. When printing with a printer font, Express Publisher only has to tell the printer what character is being printed, and what font to use; the printer then determines the exact shape of the character according to its own font information.

When using printer fonts, Express Publisher is limited by your printer's abilities. In most cases your printer can print its own fonts in only a few sizes and with a few attributes. Printer fonts, however, usually print well, since they were designed specifically for your printer.

Express Publisher cannot display printer fonts on the screen. If you select a printer font, Express Publisher substitutes a correctly scaled version of CG Triumvirate or CG Times for screen display. In spite of the substitution, each screen character occupies the correct amount of space, and the correct number of characters appear on each line. When you print the document, Express Publisher uses the printer font you specified. Express Publisher does not support printer fonts in landscape mode.

There is more information about printer fonts in Chapter 7, "Printing," under the heading "Printing issues."

PostScript printers

Express Publisher supports PostScript printers. All PostScript printers include a number of high quality scalable fonts. Express Publisher treats PostScript fonts exactly like other printer fonts. For screen display it substitutes PostScript fonts with correctly scaled versions of CG Times and CG Triumvirate.

Potential problem

Remember that printer fonts are specific to each type of printer. Express Publisher allows you to choose the printer fonts available for the printer that you chose in the setup program. If you create a document using Epson printer fonts, and then try to print the same document on an HP LaserJet, the program substitutes Express Publisher fonts for the Epson fonts. This may substantially change the design of your document. The font substitution is not permanent. The next time you print the document on an Epson printer, the correct fonts will appear.

If you installed more than one printer when you went through the setup program, use the Choose Printer command to select the printer that you want to use. Express Publisher changes the available printer fonts when you choose a new printer with the Choose Printer command. The Choose Printer command is discussed in Chapter 7, "Printing."

Font attributes
In addition to choosing a font, you may apply several style attributes to text characters. These attributes include bold, italic, underline, monospace, small caps, subscript, and superscript. These attributes are not mutually exclusive, you may apply all of them at once if you wish (superscript and subscript cancel each other out). Not all of these attributes are available for printer fonts. Pica, for example, is available on most Epson dot-matrix printers, but when you select this font the Small caps option is not available.

All of the font attributes work with the Express Publisher fonts, CG Triumvirate, CG Times, and Univers. All of the attributes also work with all Postscript fonts. (*Note: when you select CG Times italic, you are actually selecting a separate typeface that was specifically designed for italics.*)

By default all characters are set to plain, meaning that no attributes have been applied. You may select plain to remove any attributes that were applied earlier.

- **Bold**, *Italic*, and <u>Underline</u> are all useful for emphasis.
- The Monospace attribute makes each character take up the same amount of space horizontally, like a typewriter. Ordinarily, Express Publisher spaces text proportionally. When monospaced, the letter "i" takes up the same amount of horizontal space as the letter "w."
- The SMALL CAPS attribute makes all the characters uppercase, but only slightly larger than lower case characters.
- The Superscript and Subscript attributes make the characters smaller, and move them above or below the current line of text.
This is normal, this is Subscript, and this is Superscript.

Superscript and Subscript are useful for equations like $E = MC^2$, or chemical formulas like CO_2.

Using fonts
The Choose Font command allows you to change fonts and apply font attributes. You can use the Choose Font command to change existing text or to specify a font before you start typing.

Changing existing text

The basic procedure for changing the font or attribute of text already in your document is as follows:

1. Use the Text tool to select the text that you want to change.

2. Select the Choose Font command from the Text menu. (There are two shortcuts you can use to activate the Choose Font command: press SHIFT-F8, or CTRL-click a text frame while in text mode.)

   The Choose Font dialog box appears. It displays the current settings of the selected text.

Note The printer fonts that appear in the list box vary depending on the type of printer you are using.

The Choose Font dialog box

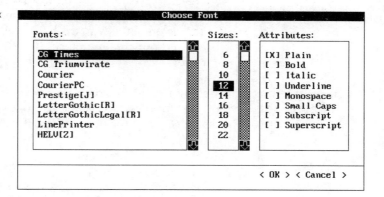

3. Click a font in the Typefaces list box.

   If you choose a printer font, some of the attributes may disappear from the Attributes list box. This is explained above under the heading "Printer fonts."

4. Click a size in the Size list box.

   The sizes are listed in points. A point is approximately 1/72".

5. If you wish to apply any character attributes, click the appropriate check boxes.

6. Click OK.

   The selected text is changed according to your specifications.

To activate the Choose Font command without selecting it from the menu, hold down CTRL as you click the text cursor inside a text frame.

Choosing a font before entering text

You can use the Choose Font command to select a font or attribute before you start typing.

1. Without selecting any text, place a text cursor in a text frame, or click the Text Frame tool to open a new text frame.

2. Select the Choose Font command from the Text menu and click a font in the Fonts list box.

   The new font appears when you start typing in that frame. If you want to import text into a specific font, follow the steps to change the default font.

Principles of character formatting

- When you select some text and then change the font or attribute, only the selected text is changed.
- When you place a text cursor in a body of text, the new characters you type will have the same font and attributes as the characters directly to the left of the cursor.
- Spaces and punctuation marks have fonts just like other characters.

Changing the default font

The default font is the one that appears when you enter or import text in a new text frame without specifying a new font. Unless you change the default font, it is 12 point CG Times.

To change the default font,

1. Make sure that no objects or text are selected, and that there is no text cursor in any frame.

   If you are working with large text frames or background objects, it is sometimes difficult to see if there are any objects selected. If you aren't sure, try pulling down the Edit menu and selecting Zoom Out to see the entire page. Click near the edge of the page, outside all frames.

2. Select a font.

Note   The default font only affects text that you are typing or importing into a new text frame. If you place a text cursor in an existing body of text, the characters that you enter will be in the same font as the characters to the left of the cursor. You cannot change the default font for the predefined, letter, 2-column, and 3-column page templates because the font is already specified as 12-point CG Times. To change the font, you must first choose Select Entire Story from the Edit menu.

Basic text formatting

The following commands—justification, hyphenation, text frame margins, and tabs—allow you to control how the text appears in a frame as opposed to individual characters or paragraphs. You may apply these commands to a single frame, every frame in the current story, or every frame in the document.

Justification

Justification controls where lines of text are placed in a text frame. Express Publisher can justify the text within a text frame both vertically and horizontally. Horizontal justification determines how lines of text will relate to the right and left margins: left, right, centered, or full. Vertically, you may justify text to the top, middle, or bottom of a text frame. You may apply both kinds of justification to a text frame.

The Justify Text command affects all of the text in a text frame. Later you will learn how to change the justification of individual paragraphs using Styles. This is covered later under the heading "Using styles."

To change the text justification of a text frame, follow these steps:

1. Place a text cursor in the frame you want to modify, or select it with the arrow pointer.

2. Pull down the Text menu and select Justify Text.

   The Text Justification dialog box appears displaying all the justification options. Each icon shows you what it will do to the text frame.

The Text Justification dialog box

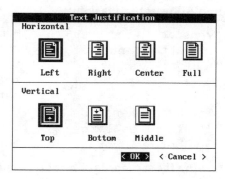

3. Click a horizontal and/or vertical justification option.

4. Click OK.

The Apply Formatting dialog box appears.

5. Decide if you want the change to affect the current frame only, every frame in the story, or the whole document, and click OK.

All the text in the frame is justified according to your selection.

Using Middle Justification

When you select Middle justification, Express Publisher centers the line between the top and bottom margins of the frame. However, because Express Publisher automatically adds a carriage return at the end of every line, Middle justification places the line just above the center of the frame. If you want the text in the exact center, first move the cursor to the end of the line and press DELETE to remove the carriage return. Then select the line and follow the steps for Middle justification.

Using full justification

When you select full justification, Express Publisher lines up all the lines of text on both the left and right margins of the text frames. Most books and newspapers are still justified in this manner, but recently many publications have begun switching to left justified. This is only a design trend, and you can make your own choice. However, if you use full justified text frames, you should also use hyphenation to compensate for the large gaps between words that may result.

Hyphenation

Hyphenation improves the appearance of your documents by smoothing out ragged right margins, or narrowing the spaces between words that result from full justification. The following example illustrates this point.

```
Hyphenation improves          Hyphenation improves
the  appearance  of           the  appearance  of
fully    justified            fully    justified
text.        Full             text. Full justifi-
justification                 cation without hy-
without hyphenation           phenation    often
often causes large            causes  large  gaps
gaps between words.           between words.
```

Note   Following the standards of most typesetting systems, Express Publisher does not hyphenate words that contain capital letters. You can override this for individual words by inserting your own optional hyphen (see "Optional hyphen" below).

You can hyphenate text manually, or use the hyphenation command to turn on automatic hyphenation.

1. Place a text cursor in the frame you want to modify, or select it with the arrow pointer.

2. Select Text Frame Margins on the Text menu.

   The Text Frame Margins dialog box appears. It displays all of the current margin settings.

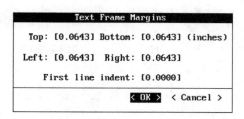

```
┌──────────────────────────────────────────────┐
│           Text Frame Margins                  │
├──────────────────────────────────────────────┤
│  Top: [0.0643] Bottom: [0.0643] (inches)      │
│                                                │
│  Left: [0.0643]  Right: [0.0643]              │
│                                                │
│      First line indent: [0.0000]              │
│                                                │
│                  < OK >  < Cancel >           │
└──────────────────────────────────────────────┘
```

3. Enter the desired top, bottom, left, and right margins in the appropriate text boxes. If you don't want to change a certain margin, don't change the number.

4. Enter a first line indent/outdent to control the placement of the first line in each paragraph relative to the frame margins.

   A negative number, such as -.5, causes an outdent. The value of the negative number cannot exceed the left margin.

5. Click OK when you finish.

   The Apply Formatting dialog box appears.

6. Decide if you want the change to affect the current frame only, every frame in the story, or the whole document, and click OK.

If there is no response, and the Apply Formatting box doesn't appear, check the numbers you entered. If an entry is too large for the frame, Express Publisher ignores the command.

Setting tabs

The Set Tabs command controls tab stops for each text frame. A tab stop places the cursor at an exact distance from the left edge of the frame. Entering tabs on successive lines creates a column of text, with the lines all indented the same distance. You should always use tab stops instead of spaces when you want to create a column of text or numbers, since inserting spaces does not always produce a straight vertical alignment.

By default, Express Publisher assigns tab stops every half inch, but you can set custom tab stops for individual text frames using the Set Tabs command. Also, existing tabs can be moved if you want to change an indent or a column.

Express Publisher supports standard left-aligned tabs and decimal tabs.

- **Left tabs** are the most common type of tab stop. They align the left side of a character to a certain horizontal position as shown below:

> one
> two
> three
> etc...

- **Decimal tabs** align characters vertically around a decimal point like this:

> 1.2324
> 123.42
> .234
> 854.45

To use the Set Tabs command, follow these steps:

1. Place a text cursor in a text frame.

2. Select the Set Tabs command from the Text menu.

   The Set Tabs dialog box appears. The dialog box displays a ruler of the same width as the current text frame. If the text frame is wider than the screen, a scroll bar allows you to move the ruler. Markers appear on the ruler displaying the current tab stops. As you move the pointer, your exact position is displayed below the ruler.

The Set Tabs dialog box

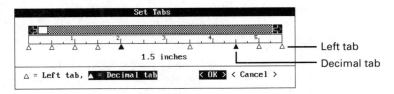

Once you have activated this dialog box, you may do a number of things. You don't have to specify all of the options if you are concerned with only a few.

3. To create new tabs, select the type of tab you want to create by clicking on Left Tab or Decimal Tab. Then move the pointer to where you want to place the new tab and click the mouse. You can set up to 16 tab stops.

4. Drag existing tab stops to move them. Any text that is aligned to an existing tab stop is moved along with the tab.

5. Drag existing tabs all the way off the ruler to remove them.

6. Once all the options are set, click OK, or cancel the operation.

   The Apply Formatting dialog box appears.

7. Decide if you want the change to affect the current frame only, every frame in the story, or the whole document, and click OK.

Advanced text frame formatting

Kerning, Line Spacing, Character Spacing, and Paragraph Spacing give you a great deal of control over the spacing of individual characters, lines, and paragraphs. They are all under the Text menu. All of these commands change entire text frames as opposed to individual characters or paragraphs. Each may be applied to one frame at a time, every frame in the current story, or every frame in the document.

These functions are optional. You don't need to worry about them when creating basic documents. As you become more familiar with Express Publisher, you may want to learn about them to gain complete control of your page designs. Be sure to read about TextEffects in Chapter 6.

Kerning Kerning is the process of adjusting the amount of space between certain characters. Even with proportional spacing, certain characters may look too far apart when placed next to each other, for example, an uppercase "W" and an uppercase "A" (WA). These letters may look better if they are placed a bit closer together.

Express Publisher is able to kern troublesome pairs of letters. The Kerning command slows down text handling and uses a lot of memory, so by default the command is turned off. You can turn it on for selected text frames. However, don't bother kerning standard body text; the results are not very noticeable on smaller fonts. In most cases you should only kern headlines and other prominent text. Since kerning is more noticeable in larger type sizes, you can specify a minimum type size to be kerned.

1. Place a text cursor in a text frame, or select the frame with the arrow pointer.

2. Pull down the Text menu and select Kerning.

   The Kerning dialog box appears.

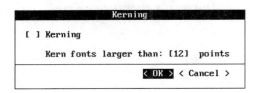

```
                    Kerning
[ ] Kerning
    Kern fonts larger than: [12]  points
                         < OK >  < Cancel >
```

3. Click the check box to turn on kerning; remove the check for no kerning.

4. Enter a number in the Kern Fonts Larger Than field.

5. Click OK.

   The Apply Formatting dialog box appears.

6. Decide if you want the change to affect the current frame only, every frame in the story, or the whole document, and click OK.

Kerning is not always visible on the screen. It is more noticeable in printed documents.

Paragraph spacing

Express Publisher automatically sets the paragraph spacing for the fonts you select. If you want your paragraphs further apart, the Paragraph Spacing command lets you specify an amount of space to be added between every paragraph in the current frame, story, or document.

1. Place a text cursor in a text frame, or select it with the arrow pointer.

2. Choose Paragraph Spacing from the Text menu.

   The Paragraph Spacing dialog box appears.

The Paragraph Spacing dialog box

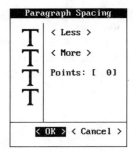

```
Paragraph Spacing
T     < Less >
T     < More >
T     Points: [  0]
T
    < OK >  < Cancel >
```

The space between the T's shown in the dialog box reflects the current paragraph spacing. You can change the spacing by clicking the More or Less buttons. The current amount of spacing is displayed in the Points text box. If you know the amount of spacing you want, you can enter the number of points (from -18 to 72 points) directly in the Points text box.

3. Click the More or Less buttons to change the amount of space between paragraphs, or enter the desired number of points in the Points text box.

   If you click More or Less, the letter T characters on the side of the dialog box shift to indicate the change in spacing.

4. Click OK.

   The Apply Formatting dialog box appears.

5. Decide if you want the change to affect the current frame only, every frame in the story, or the whole document, and click OK.

   The text in the frame is reformatted to reflect your choice.

Line spacing   Express Publisher lets you set the exact amount of space you want between each line of text. In typesetting this is called adjusting the *leading*. Express Publisher doesn't limit you to single, double, or triple space. You define the exact amount of space you want on a continuum.

Note   Don't confuse Line Spacing with Paragraph Spacing. Line Spacing controls the amount of space between every line of text. Paragraph Spacing only affects the distance between lines that are separated by a carriage return (a carriage return is placed when you press ENTER). Paragraph spacing supplements line spacing.

These steps tell you how to use the Line Spacing command:

1. Place a text cursor in a text frame, or select it with the arrow pointer.

2. Choose Line Spacing from the Text menu.

   The Line Spacing dialog box appears.

The Line Spacing dialog box

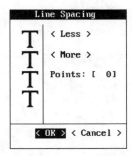

The distance between the T's shown in the dialog box reflects the current line spacing. You can change the spacing by clicking on the More or Less buttons. The current amount of spacing is displayed in the Points text box. If you know the amount of spacing you want, you can enter the number of points (from -18 to 72) directly in the Points text box.

3. Click the More or Less buttons to change the amount of space between lines, or enter the desired number of points in the Points text box.

   If you click More or Less, the letter T characters on the side of the dialog box shift to indicate the change in spacing.

4. Click OK.

   The Apply Formatting dialog box appears.

5. Decide if you want the change to affect the current frame only, every frame in the story, or the whole document, and click OK.

   The text in the frame is reformatted to reflect your choice.

Character spacing

Express Publisher automatically sets the character spacing for each font, but you can increase or decrease the amount of space between all the characters in a text frame with the Character Spacing command.

Do not confuse character spacing with kerning. Kerning applies only to certain combinations of characters. Character spacing changes the amount of space between every character as shown in the following paragraph.

Increasing the character spacing can make your page designs look more sparse and modern (and difficult to read).

The following steps document the Character Spacing command:

1. Place a text cursor in the text frame you want to modify, or select it with the arrow pointer.

2. Choose Character Spacing from the Text menu.

   The Character Spacing dialog box appears.

The Character Spacing
dialog box

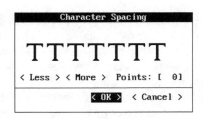

Character Spacing

< Less > < More >   Points: [0]

< OK >   < Cancel >

The space between the characters in the dialog box changes as you click the More or Less buttons. The number of additional points to be added between each character appears in the text box on the right.

3. Click the More or Less buttons to adjust the amount of space between the characters, or enter the desired number of points in the text box.

4. When the right amount of space is between the characters in the dialog box, click OK.

   The Apply Formatting dialog box appears.

5. Decide if you want the change to affect the current frame only, every frame in the story, or the whole document, and click OK.

   Express Publisher reformats the text frame according to your selection.

Headers and footers

A *header* is a line of text printed at the top of every page of a document that carries information about that document, such as the title, chapter number, and page number. A *footer* is a similar line printed at the bottom of the page. For an example, look at the footer at the bottom of this page.

You can use Express Publisher's Headers and Footers command to add one-line headers and footers to your own documents. This is also the way to add page numbers. Here are the rules governing headers and footers:

- You may have both a header and a footer on the same page.
- Each header or footer contains one line of text.
- You can place the text against the left frame margin, in the center, or against the right margin. You may choose more than one location, for example, a title and a page number.
- You can use options to automatically insert the time, date, and/or number of pages.

- You can edit the text and change the font of a header and footer like any other text. See "Editing headers and footers."
- You can choose how you want the page number displayed (see "Page numbers") and the number you want to start counting from.
- Page numbers adjust as you add or remove pages from the document so the count is always correct.
- Headers and Footers are locked. You can change their position by unlocking them with Object Specs command and dragging with the mouse.

There are two commands that control headers and footers. The Headers and Footers command defines the text, and the Insert Headers and Footers command places the header and/or footer in the document.

Defining headers and footers

Follow these steps to define a header or footer.

1. Select Header and Footers from the Page menu.

   The Headers and Footers dialog box appears.

Headers and Footers dialog box

```
┌──────────────────── Headers and Footers ────────────────────┐
│ Header:                                                      │
│   Left Text    [█                                         ]  │
│   Center Text  [                                          ]  │
│   Right Text   [                                          ]  │
├──────────────────────────────────────────────────────────────┤
│ Footer:                                                      │
│   Left Text    [                                          ]  │
│   Center Text  [                                          ]  │
│   Right Text   [                                          ]  │
├──────────────────────────────────────────────────────────────┤
│ Use the # symbol to place a page number in text.            │
│                                                              │
│ Page Number Style:  (•) 1, 2, 3    ( ) I, II, III           │
│                     ( ) A, B, C    ( ) i, ii, iii           │
│                     ( ) a, b, c    ( ) one, two, three      │
│ Starting Page: [  1]                                        │
├──────────────────────────────────────────────────────────────┤
│                                        < OK >  < Cancel >    │
└──────────────────────────────────────────────────────────────┘
```

2. Enter the text you want to appear in the header or footer in the Header or Footer position fields. You can define headers and footer simultaneously.

   There are three text fields in both the Header and Footer portions of the dialog box which correspond to the position of text in the header or footer. Text entered in the Left Text field is left justified and aligned with the left margin of your document, text in the Center Text field is aligned evenly in the center of the document, and text in the Right Text field is right justified and aligned with the right margin of your document.

While the three fields are separate in the dialog box, the text of the header or footer appears on one line. You can enter text in all three positions, but be careful not to enter too many characters in any position or it may run into text in another position.

See "Page numbers" below for instructions on entering page numbers.

3. Click OK to return to your document.

Page numbers

1. To indicate a page number, type # in the header or footer field at the location where you want the page number to be. The # symbol will be replaced by sequential numbers in your document. Do not type an actual number; this will result in the same number appearing on every page.

2. Click a page number style option if you want the numbers to appear as something other than arabic numerals (1, 2, 3).

There are six different styles of page numbering:

- numeric (1, 2, 3)
- uppercase roman (I, II, III)
- lowercase roman (i, ii, iii)
- uppercase alphabetical (A, B, C)
- lowercase alphabetical (a, b, c)
- English (one, two, three)

3. Enter the starting page number.

Express Publisher assumes that you always want to start numbering your document with page 1. However, if the document is just one piece of a longer work, you may want the first page to start with another number.

Special options

To automatically insert the time, date, and/or number of pages into a header or footer, enter the following options in the desired Header or Footer position text box in the Headers and Footers dialog box:

&T	for the time
&D	for the date
&P of &N	for the number of pages

Inserting a header or footer

In order for the header or footer to appear on a page of the document, you must use the Insert Header and Footer command.

1. Pull down the Page menu and select Insert Header and Footer.

The Insert Headers and Footers dialog box appears.

The Insert Headers and
Footers dialog box

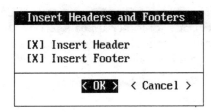

Insert Headers and Footers

[X] Insert Header
[X] Insert Footer

< OK > < Cancel >

2. Click the header and/or footer option.

3. Click OK.

The header or footer appears in your document. You must repeat these steps for every page where you want the header or footer to appear.

Removing a header or footer

- To remove a header or footer select it and press DELETE.

Editing a header or footer

You can edit the text of a header or footer as well as change its font, size, and attributes.

Changing the text of a header or footer

1. Pull down the Page menu and select Headers and Footers.

2. Make the changes you want in the respective text fields and click OK.

   Express Publisher changes every header and/or footer in your document according to the edits you made.

Formatting the text of a header or footer

You can use the Choose Font command to format the text of a header or footer.

1. Select the header or footer you want to change with the arrow pointer.

2. Pull down the Text menu and select Choose Font.

3. Select the font, size, and attribute you want, and click OK.

   Express Publisher changes the header or footer according to your selection.

Note   If no text appears you may have chosen a font size that was too large. To remedy the situation, either select a smaller font size with the Choose Font command, or enlarge the header or footer text frame. You may have to unlock the text frame with the Object Specs command before being able to resize it.

Using styles

A style is a group of formatting instructions identified by a single name. Styles allow you to instantly apply several formatting instructions to a body of text—either to a paragraph or paragraphs, or to an entire story. For example, a single style might contain instructions telling Express Publisher to make a selected body of text bold, centered, and italic.

When to use styles

Styles can be an enormous time saver. Once you have formatted some text, you can use the Create Style command to record all the settings as a new style. You can then instantly format other text in the same way by simply applying the style. It *will* take Express Publisher slightly longer to process your document, depending on the number of styles you have applied, but the results are well worth the effort.

Styles also give you dynamic control of text formatting. Once you have applied a style, you can change the style and all the text in the document controlled by that style will reformat automatically.

Formatting Paragraphs with styles

Ordinarily, you can apply the formatting commands found under the Text menu to text frames only. To apply certain types of formatting to a specific paragraph, create a style that includes the desired formatting. The types of formatting that you can include in the style that otherwise could not have been applied on a paragraph level are as follows:

- Text justification
- Character spacing
- Line spacing
- Paragraph spacing
- Margins
- 1st line indent
- Tabs

Default styles

The following styles have been created for you and are included in Express Publisher

Style Name	Attributes
Banner	Triumvirate, 70 pt. Bold, Centered, 20 points extra spacing
Bulleted 1	Times, 12 pt., .3″ left margin, –.175″ 1st indent, tabs
Bulleted 2	Times, 12 pt., .5″ left margin, –.2″ 1st indent, tabs

Bulleted 3	Times, 12 pt., .7" left margin, −.2" 1st indent, tabs
Caption	Times, 10 pt., Italic
Headline	Triumvirate, 36 pt., Bold
Mouse Type	Times, 8 pt.
Pullout	Times, 14 pt., Centered
Quotation	Times, 12 pt., Plain, .0625" left margin, .625" right margin
Subhead	Triumvirate, 18 pt., bold
Text	Times, 12 pt.

We've tried to make the titles of these styles descriptive, but you should try them to see exactly what they are.

You can use the default styles as they are, or modify the styles to suit your needs (described in "Changing existing styles" later in this chapter).

Bullets Three of the styles included with Express Publisher are Bulleted styles. Use Bulleted styles to draw the reader's attention to a specific item or to briefly list important points.

Example of bulleted styles

- This style is bulleted 1. The font is Times 12 point. It has a .3-inch left margin and a -.75 inch first indent. To get the bullet, press SHIFT-F10 (to get into alternate character mode) and then press 4. Press TAB after placing the bullet and all of your text will line up correctly.

  - This style is Bulleted 2. It is similar to bulleted 1, but it has a .5-inch left margin and a -.2 inch first indent. To get this bullet, press SHIFT-F10 and then 5. Don't forget to insert the tab space after the bullet.

    ○ This is an example of Bulleted 3. It has a -.7-inch left margin and a -.2 inch first indent. To get the bullet, press SHIFT-F10 and then 6. You can use any of these bullets with any of the bulleted styles.

Applying styles You can apply a style to a single paragraph or a series of selected paragraphs by first selecting the paragraph(s) you want to change. You can also apply styles to a whole story using the Select Entire Story command found under the Edit menu.

Applying a style to a paragraph

The steps below tell you how to apply a style to a paragraph:

1. Place the text cursor in the paragraph you want to change.

2. Select Choose Style from the Text menu, or press SHIFT-F9.

   The Choose Style dialog box appears.

The Choose Style dialog box

3. Double-click the style you wish to apply.

Express Publisher reformats the document according to the style that you selected. Styles always affect entire paragraphs. This is true even when only some of the text in a paragraph is selected, or if a paragraph continues in another frame.

Note   If you apply a style that sets justification, spacing, or margins, the corresponding frame-level formatting commands found under the Text menu no longer change that text. These commands include Justify Text, Set Tabs, Character Spacing, Line Spacing, Paragraph Spacing, First Line Indent, and Text Frame Margins. If you want to use one of these commands on a paragraph that you previously applied a style to, you can remove styles by selecting No Style in the Choose Style dialog box.

Applying a style to a range of paragraphs

You can apply a style to several paragraphs at once.

- Highlight the paragraphs that you wish to modify and use the Choose Style command.

The style changes all of the selected paragraphs.

Applying a style to a story

1. Select one of the text frames in the story with the arrow pointer.

2. Choose Select Entire Story from the Edit menu.

   Any portion of the story that is visible on the screen will become highlighted. If you move to another portion of the screen or to a different page that contains part of the story, those sections of the story will also be highlighted. Even if your screen contains a More Text arrow indicating that not all of the text is showing on the screen, you can consider the hidden portion of the story selected as well.

3. Select Choose Style from the Text menu, or press SHIFT-F9.

   The Choose Style dialog box appears.

4. Double-click the style you wish to apply.

   Express Publisher reformats the story.

Removing styles from a paragraph

If you no longer want a style applied to a specific paragraph or story, select the paragraph or story and select No Style from the Choose Style dialog box to remove any style that was applied earlier. You can apply No Style as if it were a style, using any of the methods discussed earlier.

Creating styles

With the Create Style command, you can create a new style based on the formatting characteristics of an existing paragraph. You format a paragraph using any of Express Publisher's formatting abilities, and then specify which of these parameters should be included in the new style.

For example, you could format a paragraph so that the text is all bold and the character spacing has been increased by three points. When you decide to use the paragraph as an example for a new style, you could record only the bold attribute as part of the style, leaving out the extra character spacing. When you later apply the style, it does not change the character spacing; it only applies the bold attribute.

The Create Style command is also very useful for viewing a paragraph's current formatting settings and the name of the style. You don't have to create a new style every time you use the command.

Styles are stored separately with each document. Changing the style named "headline" in one document has no effect on other documents that also have a style named headline.

Follow these steps to create a style for a document:

1. Format an existing paragraph using any of Express Publisher's formatting abilities.

2. Making sure the text cursor is in the paragraph that you wish to use as an example, select Create Style from the Text menu.

   The Create Style dialog box appears. It displays all of the current formatting parameters of the paragraph. It also shows the name of the style that was previously applied to the selected text (if any).

The Create Style dialog box

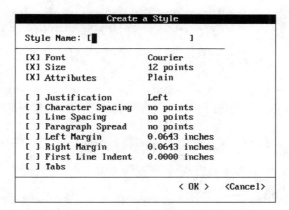

3. Enter a name of up to 19 characters for the new style.

4. Select the formatting parameters that you want recorded as part of the style by clicking in the appropriate check boxes. If you don't make any changes, Font, Size, and Attributes are selected.

5. Click OK to record the new style in that document.

Using Create Style makes no visible change in your document, but if you select Choose Style, you'll notice that the new style has been added to the list.

Changing existing styles

Use the Create Styles command to change existing styles or to use one style as the basis for another. To change an existing style, you must replace it with a new style that has the exact same name. Use the following steps to perform this procedure:

1. Use the Choose Style command to apply a style to a paragraph.

2. Select the paragraph (or story) you want to change.

3. Make any desired formatting changes.

4. Select Create Style from the Text menu

   The name of the last style applied appears in the Style Name field.

5. Type a name for the style.

   Type a new name if you want to create a new style, or leave the existing name if you wish to change that style.

6. Check the parameters that you wish to record with the style, and click OK.

   If you entered the name of an existing style a dialog box appears asking you to confirm that you wish to replace the existing style.

7. Click the Replace button.

   All the text controlled by the style you changed is reformatted.

Deleting styles

When you delete a style, all the text that was controlled by that style reverts to all of the default formatting options.

Follow these steps to delete a style:

1. Select Delete Style from the Text menu.

2. Double-click the style that you want to delete.

   A warning dialog box appears.

3. Click OK to confirm, or choose Cancel to abort the operation.

Styles are stored separately with each document. Changing the style named "Headline" in one document has no effect on other documents that also have a style named Headline.

Every new document that you create contains all of the default styles. You can add styles by using the Create Style command. It is not possible to copy styles from one document to another, but Express Publisher saves all the current styles when you save a document as a template. When you open the template to create a new document, all the styles you saved with the template are still present.

Tips on using styles

- Use the Create Style command to find out the name of the style that was applied to a paragraph. The Create Style command also displays all of the paragraph's formatting parameters.
- Select No Style from the Choose Style dialog box to remove all the styles that were previously applied to a paragraph.
- To apply justification, tabs, margins, or spacing to a paragraph, create a style that includes the desired formatting attributes and then apply the style only to the paragraph.
- If you apply a style that contains justification, spacing, or margin parameters, the corresponding frame-level formatting commands no longer change that text. These commands include Justify Text, Set Tabs, Character Spacing, Line Spacing, Paragraph Spacing, first line indent, and Text Frame Margins. If you want to use one of these commands on a paragraph that you previously applied a style to, remove the style by selecting No Style from the Choose Style dialog box.

Text and pictures

Wrapping text around pictures

Express Publisher can wrap text around pictures. The Text Wrap tool changes the left or right margins of a text frame so that the text follows the contour of the picture.

The procedure for text wrapping is very simple.

The Text Wrap tool

1. Click the Text Wrap tool.

2. Click the text frame that you want to wrap.

3. Click the picture that you want the text to wrap around.

Text wrapped around a picture

There's something new under the sun, and it's called Express Publisher from Power Up. It's the first desktop publishing program to offer high-end performance at a low-end price.

Express Publisher wraps the text around the picture. If you have difficulty selecting the right objects, make sure that the picture is in front of the text frame. If necessary, use the Bring to Front or Send to Back tools.

If you do any text formatting within a text frame that has text wrap applied, your text wrap will be lost. To rewrap text, click the Rewrap Text button in the lower right corner of the screen.

Note   The Text Wrap tool can wrap text around any object, not just pictures. For objects drawn in Express Publisher, text is wrapped around the bounding rectangle of the object. To get text wrap to follow the contour of an ellipse, use the Save As Picture command to save the ellipse as a picture, Import it, and apply text wrap. See "Saving as a picture" in Chapter 4, "Objects", for more info.

Principles of text wrapping

- Generally, you should wrap text around pictures after you have completed most of your text formatting and layout.
- If you move either the text frame or the picture after wrapping, the wrapping is completely undone.
- Click the Rewrap Text button, or press CTRL-F1 to rewrap the text around the object.
- The distance between the wrapped text and the picture is determined by the settings in the Text Frame Margins command (documented below).
- To wrap text more closely around an object than it does by default, draw another non-printing box or line to delineate the existing object, and wrap the text around that new object. This is especially useful for doing drop-caps.
- You may add or remove characters from the text frame, but if you use any formatting commands on the Text menu that change the spacing or justification of the text lines, you will probably have to re-wrap the text.
- Express Publisher cannot wrap text around both sides of a picture (if you place the picture in the middle of a text frame).
- If a text frame is too narrow, or if there is not enough space between the edge of a frame and a text wrap object, words may be split. In such a case you should widen the frame or make other adjustments so that there is more space.
- If you are wrapping a single story around more than one picture, wrap the first picture in the story first, and proceed in order.

Splitting text frames

The Split Text Frame command splits text frames either vertically or horizontally. It creates two separate frames that occupy the same space as the original frame. It also links the split frames together so that text still flows through them in the original order. You can use it to clear space for a picture, or as a layout shortcut.

Original text frame

> Members dust off your dancing shoes and brush up on your Charleston! This year's annual Spring Gala is dedicated to the celebration of the Roaring Twenties and RMCC. Director JoBeth Williams promises a fun filled evening complete with bathtub gin and plenty of surprises.

Split text frames

> Members dust off your dancing shoes and brush up on your Charleston!

> This year's annual Spring Gala is dedicated to the celebration of the ↳

To use the Split Text Frame command, follow these steps:

1. Select the text frame that you want to split.

2. Choose the Split Text Frame command from the Objects menu.

   The Split Text Frame dialog box appears.

The Split Text Frame dialog box

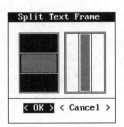

The icons represent the horizontal and vertical splitting options. The gray box represents the area that will be cleared.

3. Click the desired splitting option and click OK.

The text frame is split according to your choice.

6

TextEffects

With Express Publisher's TextEffects™ you can create distinctive, unusual, and eye-catching headlines or logos for newsletters, advertisements, or brochures. TextEffects gives you advanced typesetting effects usually found in high-end art programs. You can have text fill a polygon, bend along a curve, grow or shrink in size from one character to the next, or run along an angled line. Additional effects include giving text a shadow, making it slant, or distorting its proportions.

This chapter details all of TextEffects's features.

- About TextEffects
- Opening TextEffects
- Choosing a shape
- Entering text
- Formatting text
- Changing lines and fill patterns
- Altering headlines and moving objects
- Saving your work
- Resuming work on existing headlines
- Closing and quitting
- Importing headlines
- TextEffects principles

About TextEffects

The TextEffects tool

You can think of TextEffects as Express Publisher's special-effects typesetting work area. All you have to do to use TextEffects is click the TextEffects tool in the Express Publisher toolbox. When you're done with TextEffects, you are returned to the document you were working on in Express Publisher.

When the TextEffects screen appears, you'll notice that it bears a strong resemblance to the Express Publisher screen. A menu bar at the top of the screen lists the drop-down menus where you can find all of TextEffects's commands. Below it is the

TextEffects's toolbox. Wherever possible, TextEffects shares commands and tools with Express Publisher. For instance, if you know how to cut, copy, and paste, or align two objects in Express Publisher, then you can do the same in TextEffects. If you don't, don't worry. Every command and tool in TextEffects is documented in this chapter so you don't have to go through the rest of the manual to find the information you need.

TextEffects headlines

TextEffects headlines are the special text images you create with TextEffects. Of course, they don't have to be headlines at all, but can be used as logos on brochures or stationery, or as a special touch on announcements or invitations. Throughout this chapter, a headline is any object shape which is combined with text created by TextEffects.The following pictures illustrates some of TextEffects's typesetting effects.

Sample effects

TextEffects headlines are the combination of two elements: shape and text. Shape is simply the object the text of your headline fills. TextEffects allows you to place text in polygons, curves, lines, and distortion fields. A distortion field causes text to increase or decrease in size from one character to the next. Once you have created an object, you can place text in it. At any time you can change the shape of an object and the text of your headline is reformatted.

Any headline you create can be saved to disk as a separate file and used as often as you like. You can use Express Publisher's Import Picture command to place TextEffects headlines in your documents. When you finish working on a headline in TextEffects, Express Publisher automatically imports the last saved version of that headline into your open document.

Using Help   TextEffects has its own separate on-line help. You can find most of the information in this chapter, as well as information on using the mouse, menus, and possible shortcuts.

1. Pull down the Help menu and select Getting Started, or press F1.

   The Help Index dialog box appears. Use the scroll bar to get to the desired topic, or press the first letter of the topic you want.

2. Double-click the topic that you want help with in the list box.

3. Click Cancel when you're done.

Opening TextEffects

With a box selected   If you want to create a headline for a newsletter that is to fit within a predefined space, like the headline created with TextEffects in the Tutorial, then you can select the box that occupies that space in your Express Publisher document.

The TextEffects tool   1. Select the box where the headline is to fit.

2. Click the TextEffects tool. TextEffects opens.

With nothing selected   If you open TextEffects with nothing selected, TextEffects draws a simple horizontal line 5.5" long across the screen.

Choosing a shape

The essence of TextEffects is the ability to make text conform to a particular shape. TextEffects provides five different tools to create various object shapes: the Polygon tool, the Curve Down tool, the Curve Up tool, the Distortion tool, and the Line tool. They are similar to the drawing tools in Express Publisher. Each object tool, except for the Line tool, creates a bounding rectangle into which the final object fits.

The object tools

Using the object tools There are two different ways you can use an object tool to create an object shape. You can change an existing object shape, or draw a new one.

Change an existing object shape

When you change an existing object into another, for instance a box into a curve, TextEffects uses the dimensions of the object's bounding rectangle to create the new object. It fills the bounding rectangle with the new object.

If the existing object already contains text, TextEffects refits the text into the new object.

To change an existing object into another, follow these steps:

1. Select the object you want to change.

2. Click the tool of the new object.

   If you select the Polygon, Curve Down, Curve Up, or Distortion tools, their corresponding dimension control dialog boxes appear. Each of these dialog boxes are discussed below in the section corresponding to the particular tool. If you select the Line tool, no dialog box appears, and TextEffects changes the selected object into a line. The line lies on an angle as if drawn diagonally from the upper left corner to the lower right corner of the original object's bounding rectangle.

3. Set the options according to your needs.

4. Click OK.

   TextEffects changes the selected object into the new shape.

Note The headline text changes to fit into the new object. If a message appears warning you that the font size is too large, click OK.

Your selected object appears empty. Don't worry, your text hasn't been deleted. You need to use the Choose Font command to select a smaller font, or enlarge the object until the text reappears. See "Formatting text" later in this chapter for information on the Choose Font command.

Draw a new object

Drawing a new object is similar to drawing an object in Express Publisher.

1. Make sure no other object is selected by clicking the Pointer tool.

2. Click one of the object tools.

    If you selected the Polygon, Curve, or Distortion tool, a corresponding dimension control dialog box appears. The Line tool does not have a dimension control dialog box.

3. Set the options according to your needs.

4. Click OK.

    The arrow pointer changes to a pencil.

5. Move the pointer to where you want to place the upper left corner of your object and hold down the mouse button.

6. Drag the pointer down and to the right.

    The tick marks on the rulers move as you move the mouse. You can use these to create an object with specific measurements.

7. When the object is the desired size, release the mouse button.

    The pointer changes back to an arrow. The object you have drawn remains selected.

Polygons   Polygons are many sided objects. Triangles, squares, and octagons are all polygons. When you use a polygon shape in a headline, TextEffects places the headline text on a single line in the center of the polygon. The picture below illustrates this.

A polygon shape in a
headline

When you change an existing object into a polygon, or use the Polygon tool to draw a new polygon, you have to specify the number of sides in the Polygon Sides dialog box.

The Polygon Sides dialog box

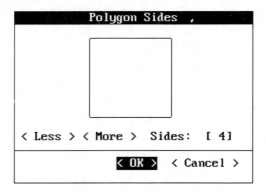

Polygon Sides

< Less >   < More >   Sides: [4]

< OK >   < Cancel >

- Click the More or Less buttons to change the number of sides in the polygon, or enter the desired number of sides in the text box. The sides of the polygon in the dialog box change as you click the More or Less buttons. When you reach the desired number of sides, click OK.

A polygon can have has few as three or as many as thirty sides.

Note   The Contour text option in the Text Input dialog box does not apply to polygons.

Curves

With the Curve tools you can determine the angle in a curve, up to 360°, make text run clockwise or counter-clockwise, and decide if the curve should bend up or down. When you draw a new curve, the curve's width reflects the selected font size in the Choose Font dialog box.

When you create curves, the bounding rectangle around any curve allows for a complete 360 degree curve angle. For example, a 180 degree curve only occupies half of the bounding rectangle.

The curve down tool   **Curve Down**

The Curve Down tool creates curves that bend down and make text run clockwise. When you use the Curve Down tool to change an existing object into a curve or draw a new curve, you must specify the curve angle in the Curve Angle dialog box.

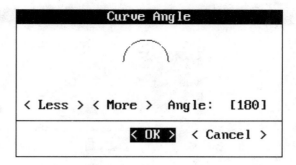

- Set the angle of the curve by clicking the More or Less buttons, or entering the angle directly in the curve angle text box. The angle of the curve in the dialog box changes when you click the More or Less buttons by five degrees. Click OK when you are finished.

The curve up tool **Curve Up**

The Curve Up tool allows you to create curves that bend up and make text run counter-clockwise. As with the Curve Down tool, you must determine the curve angle in the Curve Angle dialog box.

- Set the angle of the curve by clicking the More or Less buttons, or entering the angle directly in the curve angle text box. The angle of the curve in the dialog box changes when you click the More or Less buttons by five degrees. When you have set the desired angle, click OK.

Distortions

The Distortion tool allows you to create a shape that makes text get larger or smaller character by character. The smallest character's size is the size selected in the Choose Font dialog box.

Distorted text

INCREASE YOUR SALES!

The Distortion tool

When you change an existing object into a distortion field, or use the Distortion tool to draw a new object, you have to specify an increasing or decreasing distortion. When you draw a new distortion, the width of the smaller end is determined by the font size selected in the Choose Font dialog box.

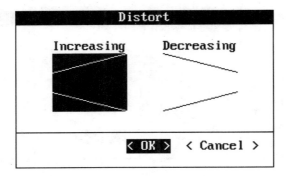

- To make text increase in size in the distortion, select Increasing. To have text decrease in size from character to character, choose Decreasing. Click OK.

Lines Lines are the simplest objects to use in TextEffects. When you change an existing object into a line, a line is drawn from the upper left corner to the lower right corner of the current object's bounding rectangle. To move a line, drag it from its center handle.

Entering text

The Text tool

TextEffects allows you to enter text into any object shape (curves, polygons, distortion fields, or on lines). To enter text you first select the object you want to place text in, then click the Text tool. The Text Input dialog box opens. This is where you enter the text you want in your headline.

The Text Input dialog box also allows you to create certain typesetting effects. You can have the baseline of the text conform to the contour of a shape, or not. The Text Input dialog box also allows you to create and control headline shadows, shear text, or distort text.

The following steps detail text entry in TextEffects.

1. Create an object with one of the object shape tools, or select an object that appears on the screen.

2. Click the Text tool.

   The Text Input dialog box appears.

The Text Input dialog box

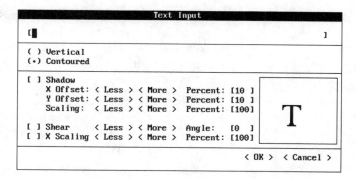

3. Type the text you want in your headline.

   You can type as many as 60 characters, but are limited to a single line of text.

4. If you want the baseline of the text to conform to the contour of the selected object, click the Contoured option box. If not, click the Vertical option box.

   The difference between contoured text and vertical text is most apparent with curves, angled lines, and distortions. Contour does not apply to polygons. The following picture illustrates the difference between contoured and vertical text in a 180° curve and along an angled line.

Contoured and vertical text

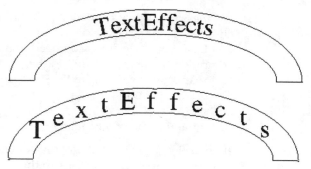

5. If you want the headline to have a gray-shaded shadow, click the Shadow check box. You can enter X Offset, Y Offset, and Scaling factors directly in the appropriate text boxes or click the More or Less buttons. The character in the lower right of the dialog box changes as you click the More or Less buttons.

   The X Offset determines how far to the left or right of the headline the shadow is. Positive numbers move the shadow to the right, negative numbers move it left. The Y Offset controls how far above or below the headline the shadow is. Positive numbers move the shadow down, negative numbers move it up. The Scaling option enlarges or shrinks the size of the shadow relative to the headline. A number above 100 makes the shadow larger than the headline text, a number below 100 makes the shadow smaller. The More and Less buttons increase or decrease respective values one percentage point for every click.

6. If you want the headline text to slant, click the Shear check box. You can set the angle the text slants by entering a value from -75 to 75 in the Shear Angle text box, or clicking the More or Less buttons.

   A positive number makes the text slant right, a negative number makes it slant left. The larger the number, the greater the angle at which the text slants.

7. If you want to distort the proportions of the text, click the X Scaling check box.

   A 100 percent X Scaling factor keeps the text's original height to width proportions. To make the text wider, enter a value above 100 in the X Scaling text box. A number below 100 makes text narrow.

8. Click OK.

   TextEffects places the text you entered in or on the selected shape. The text and shape are now joined as a headline.

Note   If a message appears warning you that the font size is too large, click OK. Your selected object appears empty. Don't worry, your text hasn't been deleted. You need to use the Choose Font command to select a smaller font, or enlarge the object until the text reappears. See "Formatting text" for information on the Choose Font command.

Changing the text of a headline

If you select a shape that already contains text and click the Text tool, that shape's text appears in the Text Input dialog box. This allows you to change the text of the headline.

Formatting text

A number of text formatting commands that are available in Express Publisher are also available in TextEffects. TextEffects allows you to choose a headline's font, determine its justification, control kerning, and set character spacing. You select text in TextEffects by selecting a headline that contains text with the arrow pointer.

The Choose Font command

The Choose Font command allows you to choose a headline's font, size, and attributes. You can use the Choose Font command to change a headline's font, or specify a font before entering text.

Changing an existing headline

To change the font of an existing headline, follow these steps:

1. Select the headline whose font you want to change.

2. Pull down the Text menu and select Choose Font.

   The Choose Font dialog box appears. It displays the current settings of the selected headline's text.

3. Click a font in the Typefaces list box.

4. Click a size in the Sizes list box.

5. If you want to apply any character attributes, click in the appropriate check boxes.

6. Click OK.

   The text in the headline changes according to your specifications.

Note   TextEffects warns you if the font size you picked is too large for the selected object. If this occurs, follow the preceding instructions and select a smaller size. Or, enlarge the selected object by dragging one of its handles.

Choosing a font before entering text

You can use the Choose Font command to select a font or attribute before you enter text.

- Without selecting an object, use the Choose Font command as described above.

Text in the new font appears when you create a new headline. When you draw a curve, the curve's width accounts for the selected font size. Similarly, the small end of a drawn distortion also accounts for the selected font size.

Justification

Justification refers to the manner in which the text of a headline is aligned within a object. The Justify Text command offers four justification options: left, right, center, and full.

To change the text justification of a headline, follow these steps:

1. Select a headline you want to modify.

2. Pull down the Text menu and select Justify Text.

   The Text Justification dialog box appears. Each option has a corresponding icon showing you what it does to the headline.

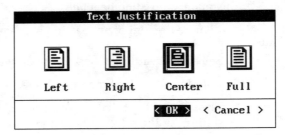

3. Click the justification option you want.

4. Click OK.

   TextEffects justifies the headline according to your selection.

Using full justification

If you use full justification on a one-word headline, TextEffects increases the space between the characters until the word is aligned to both the right and left edges of the object. If full justification is used on a headline with more than one word, space is inserted between the words until the text is aligned to both left and right edges of the object. The following picture illustrates this.

Two fully justified headlines

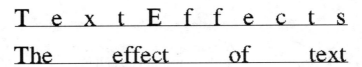

Kerning

Kerning is the process of adjusting the amount of space between certain characters. Even with proportional spacing, some characters may seem too far apart placed next to each other: an upper-case "W" next to an upper case "A," for example (WA). TextEffects kerns text in headlines automatically if you turn the kerning option on. It refers to an internal kerning table to determine which combinations of characters should be kerned.

1. Select the headline you want kerned.

2. Pull down the Text menu and select Kerning.

   The Kerning dialog box appears.

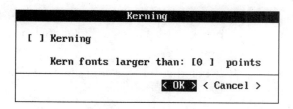

3. Click the check box to turn on kerning; remove the check for no kerning. Then enter a value in the Kern Fonts Larger Than field.

4. Click OK.

Character spacing

You can increase or decrease the amount of space between all the characters in a headline with the Character Spacing command. Do not confuse character spacing with kerning. Kerning decreases the amount of space between specific pairs of characters. Character spacing changes the amount of space between every character. Character spacing can be a very effective technique in headline design. For example, you can reduce the amount of space between large font sizes without losing legibility, or increase the space between characters for that sparse, modern look.

To change the character spacing of a headline, follow these steps:

1. Select the headline you want to modify.

2. Pull down the Text menu and choose Character Spacing.

   The Character Spacing dialog box appears.

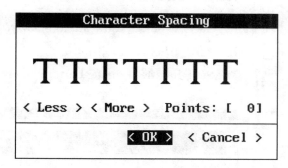

The space between the characters in the dialog box changes as you click the More or Less buttons. The number of additional points to be added or subtracted between each character appears in the text box on the right.

3. Click the More or Less buttons to adjust the amount of space between the characters, or enter the desired number of points in the text box.

4. When the right amount of space is between the characters in the dialog box, click OK.

TextEffects reformats the headline according to your selection.

Changing lines and fill patterns

You can change the line and fill type of any object in TextEffects. TextEffects also lets you to change the fill type of a headline's text, shadow, and object shape. You can use this feature to create special type effects, like reverse type, as shown below.

Reverse type effect
produced with TextEffects

Fills   Polygons, curves, and text created with TextEffects can be either filled or unfilled. The Set Fill tool allows you to specify whether an object, text, or text shadow is filled or unfilled. It also lets you choose between the available fill patterns and change the pattern palette itself.

Filling objects

To change the fill pattern of an object, follow these steps:

1. Select the object you want to modify.

The Set Fill tool   2. Click the Set Fill tool.

The Set Fill Pattern dialog box appears.

The Set Fill Pattern dialog
box

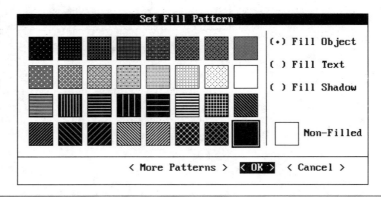

3. If you wish to change the fill pattern of the selected object, click the Fill Object check box, then select a fill pattern.

4. If you wish to change the fill status of the selected object, making it transparent, click the Fill Object check box, then click the Non-Filled icon.

5. Click OK. TextEffects changes the selected object according to your selection.

Filling text

To change the fill pattern for the text in a headline, select the headline you want to modify. Then follow the preceding instructions and click the Fill Text check box in step number 3.

Filling shadows

To change the fill pattern of a headline's shadow, select the headline you want to modify. Then follow the preceding instructions and click the Fill Shadow check box in step number 3.

Changing the pattern palette

The various pattern palettes that are available in Express Publisher are also available in TextEffects. Each palette is illustrated in Chapter 4, "Objects."

To change the pattern palette in TextEffects, follow these steps:

1. Select an object.

2. Click the Set Fill tool.

3. Click the More Patterns button at the bottom of the Set Fill Pattern dialog box.

   The Open a Pattern dialog box appears, displaying the available pattern palettes. It is identical in function to the Open a Document dialog box.

4. Double-click the desired pattern palette.

   The Set Fill Pattern dialog box reappears, displaying the pattern palette that you selected.

Lines   You can change the line type of any object in TextEffects. You can choose the color, black or white, for the lines of polygons, distortions, and lines. You can also choose non-printing lines. Non-printing lines are lines that show on the screen as dotted or shaded lines, but that do not show up when a document is printed. You can set the thickness of lines for regular and distorted objects, but not curves or polygons.

These steps describe changing the line type for an existing object.

1. Select the object you want to modify.

The Set Line tool

2. Click the Set Line tool.

   The Set Line Type dialog box appears.

The Set Line Type dialog box

Set Line Type	
Thickness	**Ink**
▬▬▬▬	(•) Black
────	( ) White
────	( ) Non-Printing
────	
	‹ OK › ‹Cancel›

3. Select a line thickness (if the object is a line) and choose either Black, White, or Non-Printing for the line color.

4. Click OK.

   The object changes according to your selections.

Altering headlines and moving objects

TextEffects provides a number of commands that allow you to alter headlines and move objects.

Rotating   You can rotate a headline in TextEffects two ways. You can use either the Rotate tool or the Rotate Object command from the Objects menu.

Using the Rotate tool

To use the Rotate tool, follow these steps:

The Rotate tool

1. Click the Rotate tool.

   The pointer changes to the rotate shape.

2. Select the object you want to rotate and continue to hold down the mouse button.

3. With the mouse button held down, push the mouse up to rotate the object counter-clockwise. To move the object clockwise, move the mouse down. Notice that the angle of rotation appears along the command line in the lower left of the screen.

4. When the object is rotated to the desired angle, let go of the mouse button.

   The pointer changes back to an arrow and the object remains selected.

Using the Rotate Objects command

1. Select the object you want to rotate.

2. Pull down the Objects menu and select Rotate Objects.

   The Rotate Objects dialog box appears.

The Rotate Objects dialog box

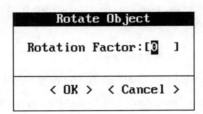

3. Enter the angle of rotation in the text box.

4. Click OK.

   TextEffects rotates the selected object according to your selection.

Scaling The Scale Object command allows you to scale any object by an exact scaling factor. This ensures that the object's original proportions are preserved.

Note The Scale Object command does not scale text. If you scale an object that is filled with text, the text remains its original size.

To use the Scale Object command, follow these instructions:

1. Select the object that you want to scale.

2. Choose Scale Object from the Objects menu, or press F9.

   The Scale Object dialog box appears.

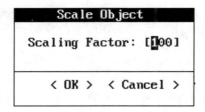

3. Type the desired scaling factor. Click OK.

   The object is scaled according to the scaling factor you selected.

Aligning   The Align tool can align two objects to each other according to
your specifications. This can be helpful if you are creating a
headline that uses more than one shape. For instance, if you
wanted to create a circle logo by combining two half circles, or
180° curves, you can use the Align tool to align the curves so that
they form a perfect circle.

The Align tool   1. Click the Align tool.

   The pointer changes to the align shape.

2. Move the pointer onto the primary object and click the mouse.

   The primary object is the one to which the secondary object is
   aligned. The primary object does not move during this
   procedure.

3. Move the pointer onto the object you want to move and click
   the mouse.

   The Align Two Objects dialog box appears.

The Align Two Objects
dialog box

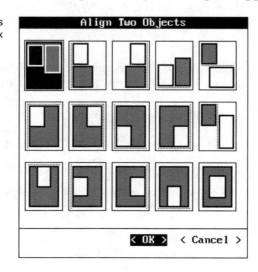

Each of the icons represents an alignment option. The light-colored box represents the object that will be moved. The darker box is the primary object. The dotted lines show the sides that will be aligned.

4. Click the desired alignment option.

5. Click OK.

The second object is aligned to the first object according to your selection.

Equating You can make two objects the same size with the equate tool. The Equate tool works with two objects, even if they are of different types. It makes a secondary object the same size as a primary object.

Objects are equated based on the sizes of their bounding rectangles. If one of the objects you want to equate is a rotated object, click it to check the size of its bounding rectangle.

Note The Equate tool only equates object sizes; it has no effect upon text. You can only equate vertical and horizontal lines to other vertical and horizontal lines.

The Equate tool 1. Click the Equate tool.

The pointer changes to the equal sign (=).

2. Select the first object.

3. Click the second object that you want to change to the same size as the first object.

The second object is made the same size as the first object. As TextEffects resizes the second object, its upper left corner remains in place.

Duplicating The Duplicate command makes a copy of the currently selected object. It duplicates text as well as objects.

1. Select an object.

2. Pull down the Edit menu and choose Duplicate.

The new copy is placed slightly below and to the right of the original object

Cut, Copy, and Paste Every time you cut or copy an object, it is stored temporarily on the clipboard. It remains on the clipboard until you cut or copy another object, or quit TextEffects. Only one object may be on the clipboard at a time.

Cut and Copy

Cutting an object removes it from your headline and places it on the clipboard. Copying an object places a copy of the object on the clipboard and leaves the original in the headline. Both of these commands overwrite the previous contents of the clipboard.

To cut or copy an object, follow these steps:

1. Select the object.

2. Choose Cut or Copy from the Edit menu.

   The object is cut or copied to the clipboard.

Pasting

Pasting an object places a copy of the object currently on the clipboard into your headline. The Paste command does not work if there is nothing on the clipboard.

1. Cut or Copy an object to the clipboard.

2. Pull down the File menu and select Paste.

   The object is pasted into your headline.

Changing the stacking order

The Bring to Front, Send to Back, Shuffle Up, and Shuffle Down commands on the Objects menu help you to rearrange the stacking order of objects in your document. Remember that objects are stacked chronologically in your headline. The first object you create is at the bottom of the stack, and the last is at the top.

- The Bring to Front command brings any selected object all the way to the top of the stack.
- The Send to Back command sends a selected object all the way to the bottom of the stack.
- The Shuffle Up command moves a selected object one layer up in the stack.
- The Shuffle Down command moves a selected object one layer down in the stack.

Bring to Front/Send to Back

To bring an object to the front of the object stack, or send it to the back, follow these steps:

1. Select the object you want to bring to the front or send to the back.

2. Pull down the Objects menu and select either Bring to Front or Send to Back.

Shuffle Up/Shuffle Down

These steps tell you how to use the Shuffle Up or Shuffle Down commands:

1. Select the Object you want to change.

2. Pull down the Objects menu and choose either Shuffle Up or Shuffle Down.

3. Repeat step 2 until the object is in the desired position.

Undoing   The Undo Move command allows you to undo the following actions: changing an object's shape, moving an object, rotating an object, and deleting an object.

- To use the Undo Move command, pull down the Edit menu and select Undo Move.

Your last action is undone, or a dialog box appears informing you that your last action cannot be undone.

Note   If you change an object from one type effect to another, you cannot use the Undo command to restore it to its previous type. Instead, just choose the new effect you want, even if it is one you've used before.

Saving your work

When you are making changes, you should save frequently. Don't wait until you are completely finished with a headline before you save it. It only takes a second for a power failure or computer malfunction to destroy hours worth of work. Saving your work in TextEffects is similar to saving documents in Express Publisher.

Note   TextEffects saves your headline at the print resolution currently selected in the Choose Printer dialog box. For example, If your current printer selection is HPII (HP LaserJet Series II) at 150 dpi resolution, your headline will be saved at 150 dpi.

When placed in your document, the headline will still print at 150 dpi, even if you change your printer choice to 300 dpi.

To change the resolution of a TextEffects headline, first choose the desired printer driver and resolution in the Choose Printer dialog box. Then import or open the headline in TextEffects and use the Save or Save As command to save your headline.

The Save command   The Save command saves your headline to disk. If you are using the Save command for the first time, you have to tell TextEffects what to name the headline. After you have saved a headline once, choose Save to save an updated version of the document at the name and location you specified earlier.

These steps tell you how to save a headline for the first time:

1. Pull down the File menu and choose Save.

   The Save a TextEffects Image dialog box appears. It is similar to the Save a Document dialog box in Express Publisher. The current file name is displayed in the File Name text box. TextEffects Image files have the extension .EPI. Below the File Name text box appears the drive and directory the headline file is saved to. The default directory for TextEffects Image files is \EXPRESS\ART.

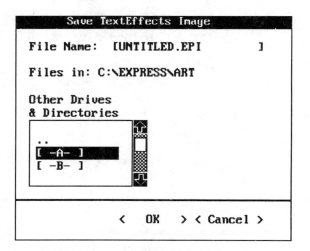

2. Enter a name for the headline file in the File Name text box. Your file name can only contain eight characters. Do not use spaces or any of the following characters: * ? / . , ; [ ] + = \ : < >. For more information, refer to "Naming files" in Chapter 3, "Fundamentals."

3. If you want to save the document to a different drive or directory, choose the desired location in the Other Drives and Directories list box. Change directories and drives by double-clicking their names.

4. When you have all the options set, click OK. If a headline file with the same name exists, you are asked if you want to cancel, or overwrite the existing file.

You can now continue working on your headline, close the file, or quit TextEffects. The name of your headline appears at the far right of the menu bar.

The Save As command

The Save As command allow you to change all the Save options of an existing headline file. There are two main reasons why you might want to change some of the Save options:

- To create a new copy of a headline with a different name, leaving the old copy unchanged.
- To save a headline file to a new location.

The Save As command activates the Save TextEffects Image dialog box. This is the same dialog box that appears when you save a headline for the first time.

1. Pull down the File menu and select Save As.

2. Follow the instructions for the Save command found in the previous section.

Resuming work on existing headlines

You can resume work on an existing headline at any time with TextEffects. The Open command closes the current headline file before opening the selected file. The Append command opens the selected file without closing the currently open file. This allows you to use the Append command to make a headline that uses elements from any number of existing headline files.

Follow these steps to open an existing headline file from within TextEffects:

1. Pull down the File menu and choose Open.

   TextEffects asks if you want to save changes to the current file. If you are saving for the first time, the Save TextEffects Image dialog box appears. Otherwise, the Open a TextEffects Image dialog box appears listing all of the headlines in the \EXPRESS\ART directory.

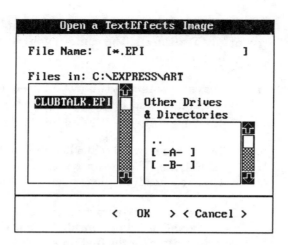

2. If necessary, change the current drive or directory by double-clicking an option in the Other Drives and Directories list box.

3. Scroll through the listing of files in the File list box. Select the headline you want by clicking it and then clicking OK, or simply by double-clicking the file you want to open.

Using the Append command

To use the Append command, pull down the File menu and select Append. The Append a TextEffects Image dialog box appears. It works exactly like the Open a TextEffects Image dialog box detailed earlier.

Closing and quitting

Closing a headline

To close a TextEffects headline file is to put the file away without quitting TextEffects. Close a headline file at any time by choosing Close from the File menu. If you made any changes to a headline without saving, TextEffects asks you if you want to save these changes.

- If you choose Yes, the headline file is saved at the current name and location. If the headline is untitled, the Save TextEffects Image dialog box appears.

- If you choose No, the headline file is closed and the changes are abandoned.

Quitting TextEffects

Quitting TextEffects closes your headline file, returns you to Express Publisher, and imports the last-saved text object. If you have made any changes without saving, TextEffects asks you if you want to save the changes.

1. Pull down the File menu and select Exit.

If you haven't made any changes to the headline file, TextEffects returns you to Express Publisher and imports the headline file. If you do not have a headline file open, you are returned to Express Publisher and no headline is imported.

2. If TextEffects asks you if you want to save any changes, select an option.

If you choose to save the changes, TextEffects saves the headline file at the current name and location. If the file is untitled, the Save a Headliner File dialog box appears.

If you choose not to save the changes, the changes are abandoned and TextEffects returns you to Express Publisher.

Importing headlines

You can use a headline or logo you created with TextEffects in more than one document. Placing a TextEffects image into a document is similar to importing a picture.

1. Pull down the File menu and select Import Picture.

The Import a Picture dialog box appears. It displays all of the files in the \EXPRESS\ART directory.

2. If necessary, change directories or disks to find the desired TextEffects file.

3. Double-click the desired file.

The headline is imported and placed in the middle of the document window. The more complex the headline, the longer it takes Express Publisher to import the file.

Changing headlines

Once you import a TextEffects image into your document, the image can be altered with certain Express Publisher commands. TextEffects images have the same properties as TIF pictures. Refer to "About picture formats" in Chapter 4, "Objects," for more information.

Editing headlines in TextEffects

You can easily move TextEffects headlines back into TextEffects to edit, and then import them into your document again.

- To move a TextEffects headline from Express Publisher into TextEffects to edit, select the headline and click the TextEffects tool. TextEffects opens and your headline appears in the center of the screen. Notice that its name appears to the right of the menu bar.

TextEffects principles

- Selecting a box before opening TextEffects creates a corresponding polygon object shape in TextEffects. Use this technique to create headlines of a desired size.

- You must select an object shape first before text can be entered into it.

- When creating headlines, keep things simple. Don't lump 15 effects into one headline. Remember that design should enhance clarity, not cloud it.

- Use the Import Picture command in Express Publisher to load TextEffects files into your documents.

- You can change the shape of a headline at any time with the object shape tools.

- When you change a polygon, distortion field, or curve into a line, the line is drawn diagonally across the bounding rectangle of the previous object. The line is drawn from the upper left corner to the lower right corner of the bounding rectangle.

- The bounding rectangle around any curve allows for a complete 360 degree circle.

- The Choose Font, Justify Text, and Character Spacing commands allow you to format a headline's text.

- The Append command allows you to have more than one headline file open at a time so you can use various elements from different headlines to create new ones.

- TextEffects can fill text and text shadows, curves and polygons.

- You can change the line color of rectangles, lines, and distortions. You can change the weight (thickness) of a line.

- Headline files are saved separately from your Express Publisher documents, just like TIF pictures, with an EPI extension.

- To enhance performance, you should save only one headline image per TextEffects file.

- Headlines are saved at the resolution that is selected in the choose printer dialog.

- Once loaded into your documents, headline files have characteristics similar to TIF files.

- TextEffects headlines can be as long as 60 characters.

- When you exit TextEffects, Express Publisher places the last saved version of the headline you had open into your current document.

Osman
to dorm
4:35pm
Ms. Oliver

7

Printing

Express Publisher offers a number of printing options that control the destination and quality of your output. This chapter addresses all of Express Publisher's printing functions and offers some advice on how to get the best results.

This chapter covers:

- Printing a document
- Printing specific pages
- Printing options
- Printing issues

Printing a document

There are two commands controlling printing with Express Publisher, Choose Printer and Print. Choose Printer lets you tell Express Publisher what printer you want to use, and the level of printing quality. The Print command prints your document and controls all of the printing options.

Using Choose Printer
Use the Choose Printer command to choose between the options available for the printers you selected when you went through the setup program. You don't have to use the Choose Printer command unless you want to change one of these options.

The Choose Printer dialog box displays the file names of the printer drivers that you installed. These are the actual files that contain all of the information about the different types of printers. Next to the driver names, a list box shows all the printer models supported by the currently selected driver. Some printer drivers support several similar printers. See Appendix D, "Supported printers," for a list of all the printers supported by each driver. On the far right, the Graphics Mode list box shows all the resolution options available for the current printer model. Resolution is expressed in dots per inch (dpi).

Choose a lower resolution, if available, when you want to print a quick draft copy. Since Express Publisher doesn't have to send so much information to the printer, printing goes a lot faster. Select the highest resolution option when printing the final copy.

Choose Printer and printer fonts

The Choose Printer command also determines which printer fonts you can use. Choosing a new printer driver usually changes the printer fonts that appear in the Fonts list box in the Choose Font dialog box. Printer fonts are discussed in Chapter 5, "Text," under the heading "About fonts." The Choose Printer command has no effect on Express Publisher fonts.

To use the Choose Printer command, follow these steps:

1. Pull down the File menu and select Choose Printer.

    The Choose Printer dialog box appears.

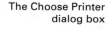
The Choose Printer dialog box

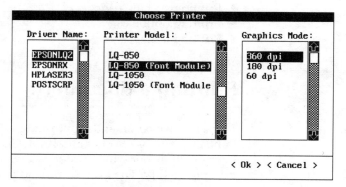

The printer drivers are listed by file name, so their names are limited to eight characters. If you selected only one printer when you went through the setup program, only one driver will appear on the list. If no printer drivers appear, or if the correct driver is not on the list, run the setup program again and install the driver for your printer.

2. Select the printer driver you want from the Driver Name list box.

    Notice that when you choose a new driver, the information in the other two list boxes change.

3. Click one of the printers in the Printer Model list box.

4. Select one of the dpi options in the Graphics Mode list box.

5. Click OK to record the changes.

Using the Print command

Before printing a document, make sure that you have selected the printer driver and resolution option you want to use with the Choose Printer command.

These instructions tell you how print a document:

1. Pull down the File menu and select Print.

   The Print dialog box appears. The title bar of the dialog box displays the currently selected printer and resolution.

The Print dialog box

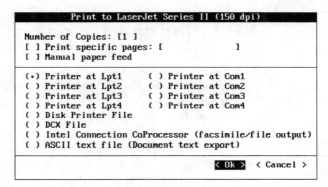

```
         Print to LaserJet Series II (150 dpi)

Number of Copies: [1 ]
[ ] Print specific pages: [                      ]
[ ] Manual paper feed

(•) Printer at Lpt1      ( ) Printer at Com1
( ) Printer at Lpt2      ( ) Printer at Com2
( ) Printer at Lpt3      ( ) Printer at Com3
( ) Printer at Lpt4      ( ) Printer at Com4
( ) Disk Printer File
( ) DCX File
( ) Intel Connection CoProcessor (facsimile/file output)
( ) ASCII text file (Document text export)

                            < Ok >   < Cancel >
```

2. Type the number of copies you want in the Number of Copies box.

3. If you want to print specific pages, click the Print Specific Pages check box and type the desired page numbers in the text box. (See "Printing specific pages" below for instructions on what to type here.)

Note If you don't check the Print Specific Pages check box, the text in the text box has no effect.

4. If necessary, check the Manual Paper Feed box. (This is not necessary on most systems.)

5. Select the printer port that your printer is connected to as the destination.

   Most parallel printers are connected to LPT1; most serial printers are connected to COM1.

6. Click OK or cancel the operation.

   After you have set all the options in the dialog box and clicked OK, the Printing Progress dialog box appears. You can press ESCAPE to cancel printing at any time.

```
Processing page #1

  5 of  11 objects have been printed.


Press ESCAPE to stop printing
```

Express Publisher displays the number of the page being printed, and how many of the total number of objects on the page have been printed. It resets the number of objects printed when a page is completed. Some objects take a lot longer to print than others. For this reason, the program may stay on a certain count for a long time as it prints a large object (especially pictures). During printing, the pointer changes to the watch.

Printing specific pages

By typing the right instructions in the Print Specific Pages text box, you can tell Express Publisher to print only certain pages or a specified range of pages in normal or reverse order. You can also combine a number of instructions.

- If you type numbers separated by commas, only the pages you specify will print. If you type 1,4,8, only pages one, four, and eight will print.

- Put hyphens between numbers to print a range of pages. Typing 1-4 would print pages one through four.

- If you type a reverse range, such as 4-1, the pages print in reverse order, starting with four and ending with one.

- You can also combine commands. Typing 1,3,6-10 would print page one, page three, and pages six through ten.

Printing options

Express Publisher can print to five different destinations: a printer, a disk printer file, an ASCII text file, a DCX file, and the Intel Connection Co-processor.

See Appendix I for information on EPCopy, which copies pictures and text.

- **Printer at...:** These options send the output to the currently selected printer at the specified location.
- **Disk printer file:** The disk printer file option sends all the information that normally would be sent to your printer to a file on disk. You can the print the file using the DOS COPY command without having to use Express Publisher. This option is useful if you do not have a printer installed on your

system. Use the Choose Printer command to select the correct driver for the printer that the document will eventually be printed on. Then print the document to a file on your hard disk, copy the file to a floppy disk, bring the floppy disk over to the other system and print out your document using the DOS COPY command. To use the DOS COPY command to print, type `COPY /B FILENAME.PRN <DESTINATION>` where FILENAME.PRN is the name of your disk printer file and <DESTINATION> is the printer port you are using. For example, `COPY /B INVITE.PRN LPT1`.

When you select the Disk Printer File option on the Print dialog box and click OK, a standard file saving dialog box appears. Type a name for the new file and specify a location using the Other Drives and Directories list box. When you click OK, the printing routine continues as usual.

- **ASCII text file:** This option prints the text in your document to a file on disk; pictures and other objects are not printed. ASCII stands for American Standard Code for Information Interchange. Almost every word processor can read ASCII text files. They are also useful for sending text via modem to be used on other types of computers.

  When you select the ASCII Text File option on the Print dialog box and click OK, a standard file saving dialog box appears. Type a name for the new file and specify a location using the Other Drives and Directories list box. When you click OK, the printing routine continues as usual.

- **DCX file:** A DCX file is almost identical to a PCX file. DCX files can be loaded by many graphics programs. Printing to a DCX file is like saving your document as a PCX picture.

  When you select the DCX file option in the Print dialog box and click OK, a standard file saving dialog box appears. Type a name for the new file and specify a location using the Other Drives and Directories list box. When you click OK, the print routine continues as usual.

- **Intel Connection Co-processor:** This is a very specialized option that allows you to send whole documents to an Intel Connection Co-Processor®. This device is essentially a FAX machine on a card. If you have an Intel Connection, you can send an Express Publisher document to any FAX machine in the world without having to print it on a printer first.

Note This feature does not work with other faxboards.

Printing issues

This section addresses some of the most common printing issues. If you have a question about printing that is not answered below, read Appendix C, "Trouble shooting," or Appendix D, "Supported printers."

Printing speed

If you've never used another desktop publishing program, it may seem like your documents take a long time to print. Express Publisher has to send about a thousand times more information to your printer than an ordinary word processor. Express Publisher's printing speed is comparable to most other publishing programs for the PC. The time it takes to print relates directly to your computer and printer's speed, the printer's print quality and the document's complexity. The best way to speed up printing is to improve the performance of your hardware; you can also avoid time-consuming printing routines.

Some printers have memory expansion options that effectively do the same thing as a computer-based print spooler. These printers can improve their print quality with additional memory. We strongly recommend adding memory to your printer if the option exists, especially if you plan to use graphics heavily.

Other suggestions

You have probably noticed the terms *high resolution* and *low resolution* used frequently in this manual. Both terms are relative, but they each apply to how many dots per inch (dpi) your printer places on the page. The more dots per inch, the higher the resolution and the better the quality. Since Express Publisher has to tell your printer exactly where to put every dot, higher resolution printing takes longer.

Use the Choose Printer command to select a lower resolution, if available, when you want to print a rough draft of your document. Switch to a higher resolution to print your final copy.

Pictures take a lot longer to print than ordinary objects and text. If you just want to see a rough layout of your document, leave out the pictures until you are ready to print the final draft, or hide them using the Object Specs command.

Printer margins

Express Publisher allows you to place objects anywhere on the page regardless of printer margins. DeskJet and laser printers are not capable of printing to the very edge of the page. They have nonprinting areas of a half-inch at the top and bottom of the page, and a quarter-inch at the left and right margins. This can cause objects to be cut off at the edges of your documents. Print a test document with a box placed at the very top left and bottom left corners. Then measure the distance between the edge of the page and where the objects are cut off to determine your printer's margins.

Note   Be sure to check Appendix D for information regarding specific printers.

8

Layout

Before desktop publishing, page layout was a tedious and demanding process that was better left to professional designers. Desktop publishing (DTP) programs have made the process much easier, but a good sense of design is still required to produce professional-looking documents. This chapter shows you how best to use Express Publisher to create a typical menu and a newsletter. It discusses some general design concepts and explains how you can use Express Publisher's automatic layout features to speed up your work.

This section does not document each procedure referred to. All of the features have been documented in previous chapters. It is intended only to help you in approaching your work if you're new to page layout and you're not sure where to start.

This chapter discusses the following topics:

- Layout overview
- Creating a menu
- Making a newsletter

Layout overview

Most graphic artists develop a routine for doing page layout. You will probably develop a system of your own as you become more familiar with Express Publisher, but this information should provide you with a good starting point.

Where to start   You should start planning your document by asking yourself two questions:

- **Who is my audience?** Who are you trying to reach with the document? What design will appeal to them? Should you challenge them, or do what they expect? Do you want to grab their attention quickly with a single thought, or intrigue them with some more complex ideas?

- **What am I saying?** This question is not as easy to answer as it sounds. We all realize that every document has at least two messages: literal and visual. The literal meaning is the meaning of the text, the visual meaning is a combination of the text's meaning and the design of the page. Often the visual meaning of the page is more important than the text. Artists have debated the importance of form versus content for centuries. But the content of your document will not get the attention it deserves if the form is confusing or cluttered. If you have a clear idea not only of what you are trying to say literally but also of the style you want to project, your document will have a more coherent look and feel.

Making decisions Decide exactly what type of document will best serve your needs: a multi-column page, a small card, a hand-out sheet, a form, a letter, or something else. Try to anticipate as many mechanical problems as you can. Are you going to reduce or enlarge the document after you create it, or create it in its final size? You should also take into account how it will be distributed. If you're going to pass the document around the office, you don't need to worry about room for an address. If it's a flyer that will be posted on walls, it should be readable from at least ten feet away. If it will be mailed, you should think about how to fold it to fit in an envelope.

Sketching your work Before you start Express Publisher, it will help you to sketch the design of your entire document on paper. This is called creating a *dummy* and you should make several. A dummy doesn't have to look exactly like your page, but is should have roughly the same proportions. Think about how many pages you will need, and what text will go where. There should be one basic design that applies to every page in the document. This will give the document a consistent appearance from page to page. Keep the dummy nearby while you create the actual document.

Follow your eyes Decide what the most important visual element of the document you are creating is and plan the design around it. In some cases it will be a catchy headline, or perhaps a picture. Look at some publications that you think are well designed, and without thinking too hard about what you're doing, notice the path that your eyes follow as they look at the page. In general, people look at a page from upper left to lower right, and they see pictures before they read text. The focus of attention is usually on the upper third of the page, but not the very top. You can add lines or draw boxes around certain items to guide the reader's eye, but be careful not to overuse this technique or your document will look cluttered and fragmented.

Hierarchy of ideas   Arrange the contents of your document in order of importance. Decide exactly how the hierarchy of ideas will be apparent in the formatting. If one idea is more important than another, make sure that it is more powerful visually.

This applies most clearly to headings in a newsletter. You may have a banner headline in 36 point type. To make that headline stand out, you shouldn't use 36 point type anywhere else in the document. Space around headlines and pictures will also make them stand out. All of the story headings should be smaller but still large enough to be headlines, 24 point type, for example. You may want to have subheadings within stories. These should be the same size as the body text or close to it, but in a different font or made bold. To distinguish specific text within the story, use italics or even uppercase letters.

Once you have established a hierarchy, stick to it. Don't put a 24 point subheading in the middle of a story; it will con-fuse the reader. At the same time, make sure that the hierarchy is clear in the formatting. The reader should be able to tell that he or she has completed one section and is now reading something new.

Use restraint   Just because you now have a program that can handle several different fonts and bit-mapped graphics doesn't mean you need to use every feature in every document. If you use too many fonts and pictures in your documents, they will look cluttered and amateurish, and your readers will think you're trying to show off your new program.

Documents with plenty of white space are always easier to read and more pleasing to the eye. Don't try to fit too much on one page.

The fonts, sizes, and styles of text you choose for your document have a big effect on your message. Some fonts look friendly and warm, while others are serious and professional. Rules are made for breaking, but the following is a list of commonly accepted guidelines for formatting text:

- The body of your text should be between 9 and 12 point type. Anything smaller is hard to read, and anything larger is too distracting.

- Don't use more than two fonts and three or four type sizes in a publication. This manual, for example, uses two fonts and five sizes. (We said rules were for breaking — the additional size is only for page footers, so we can get away with it.) If you need to make more distinctions, use bold and italic text.

- Look for some contrast in the fonts you choose, but also make sure they look good together. Use the same font for the same purpose throughout your document. Use one font for every headline, and try not to use that font in the body of the text.

- Keep your columns narrow; 24 to 50 characters is the most common range. Text columns that contain more than 50 characters are sometimes hard to read, depending on what font you use. Again, if a column seems fine to you and it's 58 characters wide, don't worry about it.

Be a critic Try to evaluate your work honestly. After you complete the first draft of your document, print it out and look at it carefully. It's much easier to judge it on paper than on the screen. If you think it looks great and does what you want it to do, don't bother with the points made below. If you're not so sure, the ideas below may help you to find the problems in your work.

Clarity

Remember your main idea. If some elements are distracting, make them smaller, or move them away from the focus of attention.

Balance

Is one side, the top, or the bottom much more interesting than the other? The page should have a focus of attention, but there should be an overall sense of balance. Center your most important idea in the upper third of the page and distribute the attention-grabbing elements equally around the rest of the page.

Clutter

Remember, white space is not boring, it helps to emphasize the few things that are on the page. Remove anything that is not serving a purpose or is redundant.

Style

There should be a coherent look to every page. If any elements stand out in the wrong way, change or remove them.

Creating a menu

Using Express Publisher, a restaurant can print a new, professional-looking menu every week that shows all the week's specials. In this example, you'll create a specials menu for Alexander's restaurant.

Alexander's motto is "only the freshest," so they like to offer many seasonal specials each week. Until recently this meant a large indecipherable chalk board. Using Express Publisher and a well designed template, the process of designing and printing a new menu now takes less than an hour, and the menu can be changed easily every week without having to start all over. The first part of this example explains how to use TextEffects to create a dramatic logo, the second covers the basic layout of the menu template.

In designing this sort of document, determine the parts that are not likely to change. These would include the name of the restaurant, the title of the menu, the address and phone number, and of course the basic design of the document. You will create a template that includes all the non- changing elements. This will make it a simple matter to add each week's special entrees.

The design of the menu is very stripped down and modern, in keeping with the restaurant's image. The entire document is set in the CG Triumvirate font. This lends consistency to the design. There is plenty of white space to make the page elements stand out.

The following picture shows you what the finished menu should look like. Refer to this picture as you follow the example.

A menu for Alexander's Restaurant created by Express Publisher

Start your work by using the Custom Page option in the New command.

- Use the Custom Page option in the New command to create a 8.5" x 11" one page document with one column of text. Make the top margin 1.5", the bottom 0.75", the left 0.75", and the right margin 0.75".

Creating a logo

Before you actually begin creating the menu, you need a strong logo to build the design around. TextEffects can be used to create the special typesetting effects you need.

1. Select the text frame at the top of the new document and click the TextEffects tool.

2. When TextEffects opens, the text frame appears selected. Click the Text tool.

3. Type ALEXANDER'S in all capital letters in the text field of the Text Input dialog box.

4. Click the Shadow box and change the X Offset to 3 and the Y Offset to -3 to create a subtle shadow effect. Click More and Less to preview the font. The T displays the effect of the Y scaling.

5. Reduce the horizontal perspective of the text by clicking the X Scaling check box and typing 50 in the X Scaling Percent text field. Be careful not to enter 500. Click the More button to preview the font. The T changes to reflect the new scaling. Click OK.

6. Pull down the Text menu and select Justify text. Change the text justification to Full.

7. Use the Choose Font command to change the type to 80 point CG Triumvirate. At this point, your logo should look like the picture below. If everything looks fine, take this time to save your headline. Use a descriptive name like ALEXLOGO.

First part of logo

ALEXANDER'S

8. Deselect the headline by selecting the arrow tool.

9. Making sure that no other object is selected, click the Polygon tool. It defaults to a 4-sided polygon; click OK. Draw a rectangle 7" wide and 0.5" high, use the tick marks on the ruler to measure the rectangle. This is as wide as the box containing "Alexander's."

want to use the Object Specs command and lock the logo into place. This assures you don't inadvertently move it when creating any of the menus.

3. Type `Specials of the week` (yes, that's all) in the main text frame. Select the text and change the font to 30 point CG Triumvirate.

You'll fill in the rest of the text when you complete the menu each week.

4. Pull down the Page menu and select Headers and Footers. Type Alexander's in the Footers Left Text box. Complete the Footer by typing in your street address in the Center Text box and your city in the Right text box.

5. Pull down the Page menu and select Insert Headers and Footers. Click OK. Scroll down to the bottom of the screen to see the Footers.

6. Select each Footer and use the Choose Font command to change the font to 12 point CG Triumvirate.

The menu template

Now you laid out all the non-changing parts of the menu. This partially completed menu will serve as a template for all other menus.

7. Pull down the File menu and choose Save As. Type a name for the template, select the Template option, and click OK.

8. Use the Open Template command to open the template you just saved. It appears as UNTITLED.EPD.

   Now all you have to do is type in the remaining text. The rest of the text is in 12 point. Each week you need only reopen the template you saved and type in the new entrees.

Making a newsletter

Producing a monthly newsletter can be very time consuming if you have to start from scratch every time. If your newsletter follows the same basic format from month to month, a simple template can do most of the work for you. In this example, you will become the editor/writer/production department of the Dolores Park Association monthly newsletter.

The Dolores Park Association publishes a newsletter called "The Park Watch" every month to keep local residents informed of issues that might affect them. Usually there is a feature story, and a community calendar. The second page is designed so that the newsletter can be folded in thirds and sent through the mail. Using Express Publisher's automated layout features and a simple template, assembling the newsletter is a half hour job.

Park Watch, the Dolores Park Neighborhood Association Newsletter

These instructions assume that the default font is 12 point CG Times. If you need to reset the default font, read "Changing the default font" in the "Changing fonts" section of Chapter 5.

1. Select the New command and choose the 3-column format in the Create a New Document dialog box to create a 2-page document.

Check your work against the picture of the completed newsletter.

2. Type the title of the newsletter in the text frame at the top of the page, but leave off the date: Put `The Park Watch` in 48 point CG Times, but leave `Dolores Park Association Newsletter` in 12 point CG Times.

3. Import the picture AUTUMN.TIF from the \EXPRESS\ART directory and place it to the right of the title, as shown in the completed template. You may have to scroll to the right with the horizontal scroll bar to reach the right side of the document.

4. To clear space for a headline, drag the top edge of the left and center text frames down with the center headline so that they are three inches from the top of the page. Use the tick marks on the vertical ruler for reference.

5. Draw a text frame for the story headline with the Text Frame tool. The upper left corner should be 2" from the top of page, and 3/4" from the left. It should by 1" high and extend over the first two text frames.

Ordinarily, the feature story takes up the first two columns on the front page, and all of the columns on the second page. The community calendar goes in the right column of the first page. To make your template more effective, you should link the text frames in the way that the stories normally flow. When you create a document with the three-column preset option, all of the text frames are linked together. You must unlink the right text frame on the first page in order to separate the community calendar from the rest of the frames.

The Unlink tool

6. Use the Unlink tool to unlink the right text frame on page one.

Now that you have unlinked this frame, the first two frames are linked directly to the frames on the second page. You won't have to do any special linking when you import the feature story.

Since the community calendar is a separate story, you should do more to separate it from the other story on the first page.

7. Use the Set Line tool to change the line type of the right text frame from Non Printing to Black.

   The community calendar has the same headline every month, so you may as well make it part of your template.

8. Type `Community Calendar` in the right text frame, and change the font to 18 point CG Times.

Adjusting the second page

Now you're ready to lay out the second page of the newsletter template. This involves making room at the bottom of the page for the necessary mailing information.

1. Press F4 to move to page two.

2. Move to the bottom of the page and drag the bottom edge of the left text frame up to the 7.5" grid marker. Then use the Equate tool to equate the center and right text frames to the left text frame.

3. Draw a line along the bottom of the text frames as shown in the finished document.

4. Create a text frame for the return address and enter the address in 12 point CG Times.

5. Press F3 to return to page one.

It's important to save the template while on page one. Express Publisher always opens documents and template to the page that was current when the file was saved.

Saving the template

You have placed all the unchanging elements of the newsletter, now you're ready to save your work as a template.

1. Select the Save As command from the File menu.

2. Type `PARKWTCH` in the File Name field.

3. Click in the Template option box, and then click OK.

 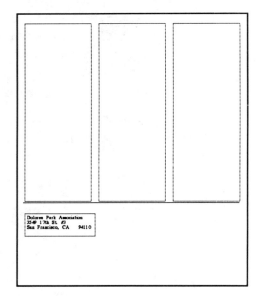

Completing the document

To make this example more useful, imagine that a month has passed and you're ready to use the template you saved last month. You've just finished writing the stories using Wordstar 2000 and you're ready to assemble the newsletter. To complete the document you need only import the stories and type in the date and the story headline.

1. Use the Open Template command to open PARKWTCH.EPT.

   The template you saved earlier appears as an untitled document. Start your work by clearing space for a picture.

2. Drag the top of the center column down so that it is 4.5" from the top of the page.

3. Import the picture HURDLES.TIF from the \EXPRESS\ART directory, and place it in the space above the center frame.

4. Select the text frame on the left and use the Import Text command to import the file FEATURE.WPS from the \EXPRESS\TEXT directory.

   The text flows through the first two frames directly to the second page. Switch to the second page to see it.

5. Type Dolores Park Festival Draws Thousands into the frame for the story headline on page one. Change the font to 30 point CG Times.

6. Import the file CALENDAR.WPS from the \EXPRESS\TEXT directory into the frame on the right side of page one. Since

the frame already contains the headline text, make sure that you append the imported text to the existing story instead of replacing it (the Place Story Text dialog offers you these choices during the import procedure).

7. Type November, 1990 in the title frame at the top of page one.

8. Use the Save command to save your work as NOV90.EPD. This name will later inform you which issue of "The Park Watch" is contained in the file.

Your newsletter is now ready for printing.

Sample documents

The following documents were created with Express Publisher . They include special typesetting effects created with TextEffects. We've annotated the pictures so you can get an idea of how they were created.

"EUR" and "OPE" are two separate TextEffects objects. Both are in 144-point Futura Bold II with 150% X scaling. To create the reverse type, fill the polygon with black and make the text transparent. The two objects were then placed over clip art that was placed in the Express Publisher document.

The "Airway..." subhead is in 44-point CG Times, and the destination/price list is in 14-point CG Times. The small print is in 8-point CG Times.

Airway travel offers the lowest fares to Europe this summer:

Paris	$678
Rome	$750
London	$684
Frankfurt	$813
Instanbul	$950
Madrid	$820

All fares are round trip, departing from San Francisco, Oakland, or San Jose. Must depart on Tuesdays and return on Wednesdays, stay for longer than two weeks, and less than 8 weeks. Deplaning in Madrid by parachute only, must be under 40 and in good health. Parachute not provided.

Airway Travel, 234 Ritch St., San Francisco, CA 90001 (415)555-4674

This document has three TextEffects objects. "Fast Forward" is in 30-point Future Bold II with a shear value of 8, 70% X scaling, and a shadow with 8% X offset and 14% Y offset. The text is filled with white; the shadow with black. It was placed over clip art.

"Advice..." is center-justified in 10-point Futura Bold II.

"Falling apart" is three TextEffects objects. "Falling" is in 30-point Futura Bold II on a line angled at 7 degrees. "Ap-" is a decreasing distortion field of 1.5" x 1.25" size, in 30-point CG Times rotated at 346 degrees. "Art" is an increasing distortion field of 2.5" x 1.75" size, in 30-point CG Times rotated at 7 degrees.

The headline is in 28-point CG Times and the body text is 12-point CG Times.

"Deep space" is four TextEffects objects: the two words and their shadows. The text is in 30-point Futura Bold II with full justification. The shadow text is the same, with a shear value of 50 and 65% X scaling.

The rest of the text is in 20-point Futura Bold II.

FAST FORWARD

| Advice for executives on the go | July 1991 |

What to do when it seems like everything is ...

falling ap- art

"Sometimes we should be happy about our failures - they are tremendous learning opportunities."

Sales topped 2.5 million units last quarter, exceeding even our most optimistic forecasts. An unexpected surge in demand fueled the growth spurt, as customers clamored for any product bearing the prestigious Esprizio label. Other labels performed well, either meeting or exceeding out projections.

New product development manager Lech Kutowski attributes the sales growth to his department's careful analysis of customer desires, "and, I must admit, a bit of plain old luck." Kutowski adds, "The market is very fickle these days. When it turns against you, you can hardly give away these products. When you're in the right place with the right product, you can practically name your price."

Ipsom loarumisjistic crealyesize quati ip cat isoems, "Wanna comma point." New sentence if it is qundom ec lipusom delorum. Ad hoc muestra dupiticus. Lo it comen dic slotfu. Didleus kridjistic is ec dome flug ic dreg. "Im so docle! I couldn't wandum do floaz!"

Id ip comum ef ic ad harum scarum. Lef mid quatatus

left efto asto opum do is ectld ip comum ef ic ad harum scarum. Lef mid quatatus midsum quorum. Sales doftof trandop quidop operatus ec spellum wrongisticly. When left efto asto opum do is ectorum. Id ip comum ef ic ad harum scarum. Lef mid quatatus midsum quorum. Sales doftof trandop quidop operatus ec spellum wrongisticly. When left efto asto opum do is ectorum. Id ip comum ef ic ad harum scarum. Lef mid quatatus midsum quorum. Sales doftof trandop quidop operatus ec spellum wrongisticly. When left efto asto opum do is ectorum.

Ipsom loarumisjistic crealyesize quati ip cat isoems, "Wanna comma point." New sentence if it is qundom ec lipusom delorum. Ad hoc muestra dupiticus. Lo it comen dic slotfu. Didleus kridjistic is ec dome flug ic dreg. "Im so docle! I couldn't wandum do floaz!" Ipsom loarumisjistic crealyesize quati ip cat isoems, "Wanna comma point." New sentence if it is qundom ec lipusom delorum. Ad hoc muestra dupiticus. Lo it comen dic slotfu. Didleus kridjistic is ec dome flug ic dreg. "Im so docle! I couldn't wandum do floaz!" Ad hoc muestra dupiticus. Lo it comen dic slotfu. Didleus kridjistic is ec dome flug ic

DEEP SPACE

come explore deep space at the Hayden planetarium

shows take place Wednesday through Sunday evenings at 6:30 and 8:30 pm

admission: $5.00 adults, $2.50 children under 12 tickets available at the box office, or call 555-2455

Basic DOS

If you are new to computers or unfamiliar with some of the DOS features referred to in this manual, this appendix is for you. It tells you what DOS is and describes

- the difference between computer memory (RAM) and disk space
- how you can tell which version of DOS you have
- what a DOS directory is and how to create one
- what a path and a pathname are
- the CONFIG.SYS file
- the AUTOEXEC.BAT file
- RAM-resident or terminate-stay-resident programs (TSRs)
- how to back up your files

Don't worry if what you see on your display isn't exactly the same as our examples.

While we strive to give you the latest and most accurate information possible, use your particular DOS manual as the final authority for any questions you may have. There are several versions of DOS on the market, which differ slightly.

Important

Any command that you type doesn't take effect until you press ENTER (also called RETURN on some keyboards).

Basic concepts

DOS stands for *disk operating system*, and it is the program that controls your computer's basic procedures and functions. It's the traffic manager between the different parts of the computer and between you and the computer. For example, DOS supervises input-output operations — how you get information into a computer from a floppy disk or telecommunications program, or send information out to a printer or modem. It keeps track of your information (stored in files on your hard or floppy disk) and implements the commands that you enter.

Disks are permanent storage media. The amount of storage you have on your hard disk (usually from 10 to 100 megabytes) and on your floppy disks has nothing to do with your *system memory* (RAM). RAM is the working area, like your desktop; disks are where you store information, like file cabinets.

When you turn on your computer, the start-up program takes DOS out of storage (floppy or hard) and puts it in RAM. You then take whatever application program you want to work with out of storage and put that in RAM: This is called *loading* the program. Before you turn off your computer, you must take whatever you've left in your temporary working space (RAM) and save it in storage (on disk).

To work with most Power Up programs, your computer should have at least 512 kilobytes of RAM (and sometimes 640 K). If you get an `Out of Memory` error message, it means the desktop doesn't have enough working space to run your program. To check how much RAM and disk space you have, type `chkdsk` from the root or DOS directory (whichever contains the CHKDSK.COM or CHKDSK.EXE program) and press ENTER.

A *program* (or application) is a series of instructions that tells the computer how to perform a specific task or tasks. The program works on top of and with DOS. A *command* is the word that starts a program, such as VER or CCPLUS. Commands are executable files that you start by typing their first name.

What version of DOS do I have?

Your DOS manual or disk will show the version number, such as Version 3.30. You can also type `ver` from the DOS prompt (see the following section), and DOS will display the version information, such as `IBM Personal Computer DOS Version 3.30`.

To check the version of COMMAND.COM (the DOS command interpreter) on your system, type `command` from the root directory of your boot drive (usually C:, but if you boot from a floppy drive, type `command` with your boot disk in the drive.) Your COMMAND.COM file should be the same version as your version of DOS.

Drives, directories, and paths

DOS displays information in uppercase, but you can normally type data in either uppercase, lowercase, or a combination of both.

The *command line* or *DOS prompt* usually shows the drive and directory that is active, such as `C:\EXPRESS\DOCS>`.

The *drive* is the unit that rotates the *disks* and lets you read information from or write information on them. A and B are the drives into which you insert floppy disks; C is usually the hard disk drive (if you have one). If you work on a network, you'll be working with F, G, and other drives as well. When you type in a drive name, you always follow it with a colon, as in

    C:

A *directory* is an area of storage on the disk, like a folder in a file cabinet. It's a way to organize your disks so that your computer can find your information easily. You can further subdivide directories into more directories.

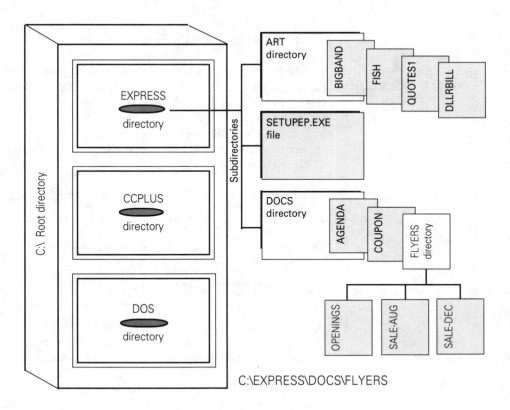

C:\EXPRESS\DOCS\FLYERS

Type cd\ *to move to the root directory of the current drive.*

To see what directories you have on a disk, move to the root and type dir. For example, type dir b: to find out what directories are on the floppy in drive B. You can also type dir from any directory to get a list of the files it contains.

The backslash (\) stands for the root directory, like the file cabinet itself. To create a directory and subdirectory named CCPLUS and DATA,

1. Type cd\ to move to the root directory.

2. Type md\ccplus. DOS creates a directory called ccplus.

3. Now, type cd ccplus to move to that directory. You'll see the DOS prompt C:\CCPLUS>. (If you don't, skip to "Displaying your location," then return to this section.)

4. From the C:\CCPLUS directory, type md data to create a directory to hold all your documents.

5. Type cd data. The DOS prompt will change to C:\CCPLUS\DATA>. Note that you don't type a backslash because this is a subdirectory off of the current directory, which isn't the root directory.

The DOS prompt is also called the command line.

The DOS prompt C:\CCPLUS\DATA> is a *path* name. It tells DOS that you are in the C drive and in the DATA directory off of the CCPLUS directory.

You can transfer files between directories. Let's say you want to transfer a file named MYFILE in the C:\CCPLUS directory to the C:\TOP directory:

1. Move to the CCPLUS directory by typing cd \ccplus

2. Type copy myfile \top

That's it. DOS copies MYFILE to the TOP directory.

The CONFIG.SYS file

When you turn on your computer, the DOS start-up program checks for your CONFIG.SYS file and then your AUTOEXEC.BAT file to see if you have special instructions.

If the CONFIG.SYS file exists, DOS executes the commands listed in the file. This file tells DOS how your computer system is set up (configured). If you need to set up special software to run such devices as printers or expanded memory, this is where you'd do it.

If this manual tells you to change your FILES=x statement to a minimum number, enter `type config.sys` at the DOS or root directory of the boot drive to see what your FILES statement says. See your DOS documentation for details.

The AUTOEXEC.BAT file

If the AUTOEXEC.BAT file exists, DOS goes ahead and performs the commands listed in that file. The .BAT extension tells you it is a batch file, which means it contains simple, one-line commands for DOS to execute. Here's a sample Autoexec file:

```
echo off
prompt=$p$g
path=c:\;c:\dos
c:\mouse\mouse.com
cls
```

The first line tells DOS not to display (echo on the screen) these commands as they are executed. The second line tells DOS to display the path ($p) and the greater-than sign or prompt ($g). Check your DOS manual for options. The Path command tells DOS where to look for the files associated with the commands you enter. The Mouse command loads the mouse driver (the program that runs the connection between the mouse and the computer). Finally, the Cls command clears the screen so that all you see is the prompt.

Make sure to use the Type command before creating a new AUTOEXEC.BAT file. The following commands will overwrite an existing AUTOEXEC.BAT file.

You should check your DOS manual for information on how to create or modify the AUTOEXEC file. If you have an AUTOEXEC file, enter `type autoexec.bat` from the root directory of your boot disk to check its contents. If you don't have one, check your DOS manual or type the following lines at the root directory's command line to create one:

When you see the word "ENTER," press the ENTER key.

```
cd \ ENTER
copy con autoexec.bat ENTER
echo off ENTER
prompt $p$g ENTER
CTRL-Z (hold down the Control key and press z) ENTER
```

The Copy Con command tells DOS to copy the text that follows to a file called AUTOEXEC.BAT. *Con* stands for console, which is another name for the keyboard and screen. The CTRL-Z ENTER sequence saves your commands as the AUTOEXEC.BAT file.

Restarting DOS is also called <u>rebooting</u>.

Your new Autoexec file won't take effect until you restart DOS by pressing CTRL-ALT-DELETE simultaneously. You can also turn your computer off and on again.

Displaying your location

You or someone else may have already set up your computer to show the directory *path* (the road to where you are, beginning from the root directory). If not, your prompt displays as C>. To display the path, type `prompt=$p$g` at the DOS prompt. DOS will display your path until you turn off your computer.

If you want DOS to show your path every time you turn on your computer, you need to add the Prompt command to your AUTOEXEC.BAT file, as explained in the preceding section.

Checking for RAM-resident software

RAM-resident programs are also called TSRs for Terminate-stay-resident.

Some RAM-resident programs you may have on your system — such as DOS menu programs (shells), print spoolers, disk cache utilities, and applications such as SideKick and Lotus Metro — use too much RAM or do not work with Power Up programs. If you have problems running one of Power Up's software products, restart your computer from DOS on a floppy disk, so that your AUTOEXEC.BAT file doesn't go into effect:

1. Insert a DOS disk into drive A and close the drive door.

2. Press CTRL-ALT-DELETE at the same time to restart your computer.

3. The computer will start up from drive A, thus circumventing any RAM-resident programs normally loaded from the AUTOEXEC.BAT file.

4. Move to the drive and directory containing your Power Up program and start it up. See if the problem has gone away. If it has, then your RAM-resident software is incompatible with the Power Up program.

5. Check each RAM-resident software you have to see which one is incompatible with the Power Up program.

Backing up your files

DOS Copy command

1. If your original data file is on a hard drive, place a formatted disk in the floppy drive. (If you aren't sure how to format a disk, consult your DOS manual.)

   If you are running your application from a dual floppy drive, place a formatted disk in the second drive.

2. To copy all the files to a disk in drive A, type

   ```
   copy *.* a:
   ```

   If you are copying to a drive with another name, substitute that name.

3. To copy all the files with the same extension to a disk in drive a, type

   ```
   copy *.ext a:
   ```

   where ext is the file extension. For example, to copy all of the files with a .doc extension, type

   ```
   copy *.doc a:
   ```

   To copy one file, type the copy command, the file name with the extension, and the drive, for example,

   ```
   copy lablcopy.lb3 a:
   ```

Restoring a file

To restore the file, repeat the process above, but change the command slightly.

1. Place your backup disk in the floppy drive.

2. To copy all your files from a disk in drive A to drive C, type

   ```
   copy a:\*.* c:
   ```

   To copy one file, type the copy command, the full path name of the backup file name and the drive from which you are running the program. For example,

   ```
   copy a:\lablcopy.lb3 c:
   ```

Some DOS commands

Here's a short list of useful DOS commands. Be sure to check your DOS documentation for updates or warnings about using these commands. In most cases, you must be in the directory that contains the file you want the DOS command to work on.

Command	What you are telling DOS to do
cd	Change from the current directory to the one specified, as in `cd \express\art`
cd..	Move one directory closer to the root
cd\	Move to the root directory
con	The console (keyboard and screen), as in `copy con autoexec.bat`
dir	List all the directories and files in the current directory; use with /p to display one screenful at a time, as in `dir /p`
md	Make a directory, as in `md \ccplus`
prn	DOS's name for the printer attached to your computer (by default, LPT1)
ren	Rename this file with this new name, as in `ren april90.txt april90.old`
>	Redirect output to another device, such as a printer, as in `dir > prn`

Sample templates

The following pages show examples of the templates that are included with Express Publisher. We've filled in the templates with artwork and suggestions for the style and pattern of the text. You can delete the text and artwork, then use the templates as they are or change them to meet your needs. "Using templates" in Chapter 3 provides information about opening and revising templates.

**Agenda Template
(AGENDA.EPT)**

The "Agenda" headline is Times 54 pt. It is the non-changing text element on this template.

This major heading is in Triumvirate 24 pt. bold text, center-justified. This typestyle shows up clearly on handouts and overhead projections.

Horizontal lines help separate major topics.

Bulleted and sub-items appear in Triumvirate 18 pt. text.

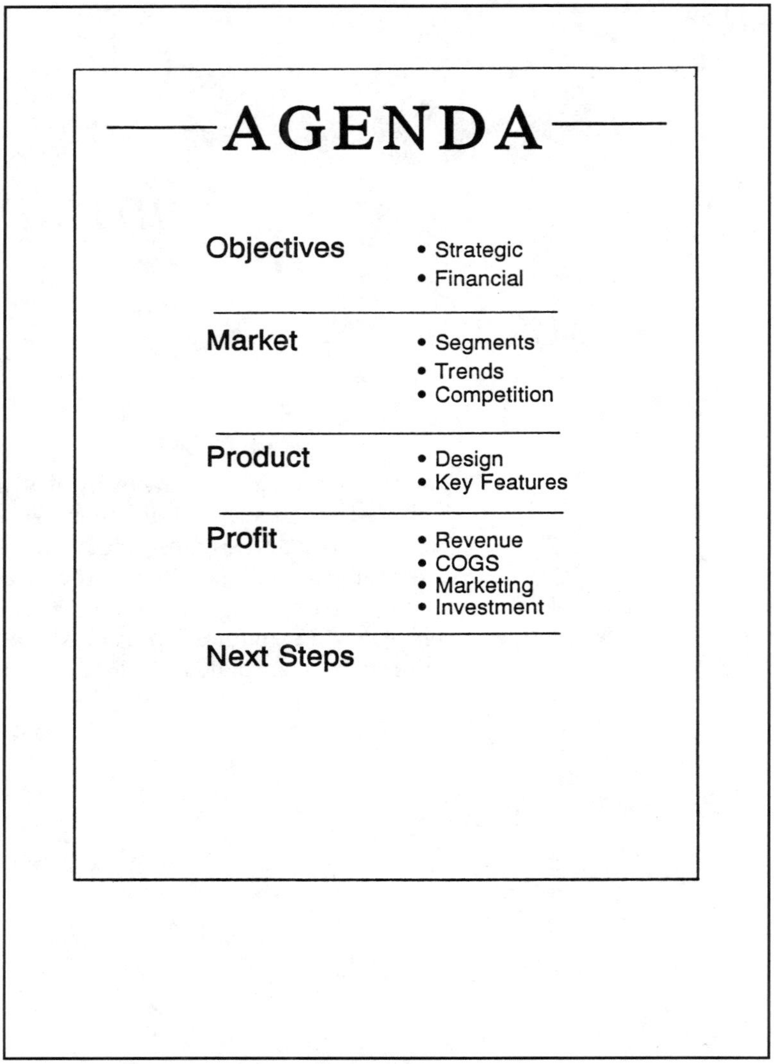

AGENDA

Objectives
- Strategic
- Financial

Market
- Segments
- Trends
- Competition

Product
- Design
- Key Features

Profit
- Revenue
- COGS
- Marketing
- Investment

Next Steps

Coupon Template
(COUPON.EPT)

The dollar amount of the coupon appears in Times 36 pt. bold text.

You can paste in, crop, or scale clip art to the correct size to create borders.

The coupon's main text is in Times 20 pt. bold text, centered.

Choose from the wide variety of available clip art to accent your coupons.

$1 — BACK TO SCHOOL COUPON — $1

One Dollar
Off School
Supplies*
at PACE

Good Through
Nov. 20, 1989
At All
PACE Stores

* $10 Minimum Purchase

$1 PACE, THE SAVINGS PLACE $1

$1 — BACK TO SCHOOL COUPON — $1

One Dollar
Off School
Supplies*
at PACE

Good Through
Nov. 20, 1989
At All
PACE Stores

* $10 Minimum Purchase

$1 PACE, THE SAVINGS PLACE $1

$1 — BACK TO SCHOOL COUPON — $1

One Dollar
Off School
Supplies*
at PACE

Good Through
Nov. 20, 1989
At All
PACE Stores

*$10 Minimum Purchase

$1 PACE, THE SAVINGS PLACE $1

Invitation Template
(INVITE.EPT)

This major heading is in Times 40 pt. bold-italic text.

Use the drawing tools or paste in clip art to add flair to your invitation.

For the invitation specifics, we suggest Times 24 pt. italic text. The text shown here is centered with extra line spacing (6 pts.) for a look that is classic, yet easy to read.

For additional invitation information, use Times 14 pt. italic text, centered with extra line spacing.

You Are
Invited

To View
New Fall Fashions
From Our
Pace Petites Dept.

Saturday, November 25, 1989
9 a.m.
In Our BayPark Mall Store

Please RSVP
by calling one of our associates in the
Pace Petites Dept.
(415) 345-5900 Ext. 408

Coffee, juice, and pastries
will be served from 9 to 10

This headline is in Triumvirate 70 pt. plain text. You may want to try centering the headline or adding additional character spacing to achieve the desired look.

We suggest a small print style such as Triumvirate 8 pt. bold for the volume number, issue number date, and so on.

Horizontal lines can add definition to headlines. Try different sizes to see which creates the best effect.

This major story heading is in Times 36 pt. bold, italic text.

Times 12 pt. plain text is a clean, easy-to-read typestyle, ideal for body text. Use Import Text to bring in new text.

Use the drawing tools or paste in clip art to add logos, bullets, and graphics to your newsletter.

NEWS EXPRESS

Volume 1, Issue 1   Premiere Edition   November 1989

Record-Breaking Christmas Expected

usiness prospects are outstanding as we move into the holiday season. The nation has enjoyed eight straight years of economic expansion with more growth forecast for next year. Technological advances in home electronics and growing "nest-building" among aging baby boomers will drive consumer purchases to record levels. So, its time to gear up and make sure all preparations are well made for the busy time of year.

First, check and streamline your inventory control systems. Once the selling season begins in earnest, your employees will be working full-tilt to serve customers. They will have little time to work the stockroom. This presents the danger of developing excess shortage due to errors or pilferage. It's not too late to carefully review your stockroom systems or even implement new technologies to streamline stock flow and accountability.

Mike Haines, an inventory systems specialist, says: "Two main techniques apply: 1) divide and conquer and 2) modernization. You can improve stock control by managing your stock room to match

For the Christmas season, you want to focus on EFFICIENT selling.

merchandise flow; establish a restocking pattern that rotates through your floor, and set up your stock room to match. Then you can quickly check your inventory just before it is moved to the floor, without running all around the stockroom. "I also recommend implementing a bar-code system whenever possible.

A bar-code reader records inventory in less than one-tenth the time required by manual methods, and permits instant analysis on inventory flow using your PC."

A second key issue is employee training. Good store employees are increasingly difficult to recruit, so you may find yourself short-staffed this Christmas. Your best precaution is to maximize the productivity of the employees you have, according to Sheila Schaeffer, a sales training specialist.

"Investing in sales training can produce dramatic returns. For the Christmas season, you want to focus on EFFICIENT selling. Your salespeople must quickly help customers zero in on a specific alternative by slicing away options that are out of the question. Next, they should identify two or three good alternatives and close by asking the customer which would make the best gift. Finally, and the most important productivity gainer, once one sale is closed, your salespeople should suggestion-sell other gifts for other family members. Too many salespeople close a sale of one item and feel they are finished – but these days people are so busy that they are often glad to finish large

continued on page 2

CONTENTS

NOTICE

- Watch your dinosaur stocks carefully. Most fads last three years, and this is the fourth year of the Dinosaur craze.

- Provide lots of positive feedback to new Christmas employees. Inadequate, harsh feedback is the most common cause of early employee turnover.

- New "next afternoon" services in the overnight delivery industry are providing opportunities to provide cost-effective, quick delivery to your customers. Check around for the best deal.

- We're overjoyed to announce the birth of Johann Sebastian Boch, son of Bob and Mary Boch. Most of you know Bob, one of our co-founders. Johann weighed 7 lbs., 11 oz. at birth; and we hear he arrived with a smile and a wink, just like

---

The table of contents can be set apart from the body text by using Triumvirate 10 pt. bold, italic text. Use extra line spacing to make the table of contents easier to find and scan.

Wrap text around objects—even other text frames—for an exciting visual effect. Use printing and non-printing lines to get the diamond effect of the call-out.

This headline is in Helvetica 84 pt. plain text.

We suggest Triumvirate 8 pt. italic for the volume number, issue number date, and other publishing details.

We've created a special underline effect under the word *Perspective* by drawing two lines, one on each side of the lowercase *p*.

Times 14 pt. italic text with extra line spacing helps set off quotes or other special information from the body text.

Times 12 pt. text provides a contemporary look for body text. Use Import Text to place new text.

A line provides a subtle break between stories, graphics, and issues.

Use the drawing tools or paste in clip art to add logos and graphics to your newsletter. Wrap text around clip art images for a smooth flow of text through your newsletter.

ABC
Company

Perspectives

November 1989 — Volume 1, Issue 1

It Shipped! Party

Ed promises good food and short speeches

Congratulations Everybody! Overcoming all obstacles, we shipped a record number of new products this past quarter — leading to the most profitable quarter in the company's history! Our catalog now contains twice as many products as this time last year, and sales are up by over 300%. We've also signed our first ever multi-million dollar OEM deal.

Best of all, our new products represent a new level of quality and market potential. Pat Brown, our National Accounts Manager, says "Surpass is already a great success at EDS and BDB, our major accounts". The new models in the base product line all leapfrog their compe- tition. In the GUI market, ABP sets a new standard for easy-to-use power. The changes we've made in the company over this past year are producing tremendous results. With such

success in hand, a celebration is in order! So, on Thursday, October 12, the company will sponsor a dinner party for everyone at the Dumpfy Hotel. Awards will be given to the key players from Product Development, Marketing, Manufacturing, and Sales who went the extra mile to make the quarter happen. Ed has promised good food and short speeches. Live entertainment is being arranged, and rumors have been heard that Ed, Harvey, Elizabeth and Julie may make a cameo appearance on stage. Come prepared to egg them on!

The party will be at the Dumpfy Hotel, (at the intersection of 101 and

Cont. page 3

Inside Perspectives

New Systems Approved

Starting Nov. 1, all new employees will receive new 286 and 386 type computers from an approved list created by MIS. MIS has also established corporate accounts with two local sources and one mail order company, and will handle system ordering and setup. System specification will still be handled by employees and their managers, with MIS acting to streamline the process and access purchase economies. "We've grown large enough to sup-

port centralized ordering" says Elizabeth, VP of MIS and Manufacturing. She explained: "Purchasing computer systems is quite complex — you have to decide on the system performance your job requires, the specific system components required to achieve that performance, the manufacturers that provide the best quality/price ratio for each system component, and then find a good vendor with good support and competitive

Cont. page 3

Trouble shooting

Setup problems

The setup program does not run, or tells you that you are done before you have started.

Solution 1: A memory resident program may be interfering with it. Memory resident programs are programs that stay in your computer's memory while other programs are running. You may not realize that you are using a memory resident program. Memory resident programs, such as SideKick, often pop up within other programs when you press certain key combinations. Others act as program selectors and reappear every time you quit another program. Disk caching and print spooling programs are also memory resident. Try removing all memory resident programs or restarting with a floppy DOS disk in drive A, and then running the setup program. See "Memory problems" in this chapter, Appendix A, or your DOS manual for more information on configuring your system's memory.

Solution 2: You may be using an old version of DOS. Express Publisher requires version 3.0 or greater of DOS.

Problems starting Express Publisher

Message "Unable to create working copy" appears.

QEMM, 386MAX, and CEMM users: If you have both expanded and extended memory, you must disable one type of memory each time you start the program. Type EP -X0 (zero) at the DOS prompt to remove extended memory, or EP -E0 for expanded.

Solution: Express Publisher needs at least 135K of free disk space to run. If there is not enough space, this message appears. (This working space has nothing to do with the amount of space needed to install Express Publisher.) The program needs this disk space to make temporary working copies of your document while you are changing it.

Express Publisher also uses additional disk space as virtual memory, so the more disk space you have free, the better the performance will be.

Graphics adapters   Express Publisher locks up at "Loading....".

All of the following conditions can be caused by compatibility problems with different types of graphic adapters:

- Cursor moves down a line and machine locks up when you try to start Express Publisher.
- Express Publisher starts up and runs, but the screen doesn't look right.
- Express Publisher starts up, but screen is not cleared. Menu bar appears and you are returned to DOS when you press a key.

Solution: Most problems with graphics adapters cause Express Publisher to crash immediately upon startup. Express Publisher works with Hercules, CGA, EGA, VGA, and MCGA graphics adapters. Unfortunately, not every graphics card that claims to adhere to one or more of these standards is fully compatible with the standard as it was originally defined. This is especially true of EGA and VGA adapters.

Fortunately, most graphic adapters support both higher and lower resolution standards. If Express Publisher will not run in VGA on your machine, it will probably run in EGA or CGA. If you have one of the problems described above, try specifying a different graphics adapter when you run Express Publisher.

You do not have to run the setup program every time you want to specify a new type of graphics adapter. You can use a special command when you start Express Publisher to override the settings you chose in the setup program. Instead of typing **EP** and pressing return, type one of the following commands:

EP/CGA	(to specify CGA)
EP/HGC	(to specify Hercules)
EP/EGA	(to specify EGA)
EP/EGABW	(to specify black-and-white EGA)
EP/VGA	(to specify VGA)
EP/MCGA	(to specify MCGA)

If none of these commands work, your graphics adapter may be too non-standard for Express Publisher to work on your system. The hardware manufacturer may be able to help you.

Note   You may encounter this problem if you have an Adaptec hard disk controller card and two physical hard disks connected to it. Contact Adaptec in San Jose, California, for a driver called ADAPTEC.SYS. At present, their telephone number is (408) 945-2550.

Express Publisher won't start on a black-and-white VGA system.

Solution: The setup program often doesn't correctly detect black-and-white VGA display adapters. The problem does not become apparent until you try to run Express Publisher. The machine freezes and nothing appears on the screen. Select MCGA if you have a black-and-white VGA system.

Express Publisher won't start, and none of the suggestions above help.

Solution 1: Check to see that you are using version 3.0 or later of DOS, and that your system meets Express Publisher's hardware requirements (listed in the introduction).

Solution 2: See the discussion of memory resident programs earlier in this chapter entitled "Memory problems."

Memory problems

The message "Low Memory. We recommend removing other applications from memory when running Express Publisher" appears.

While starting up, Express Publisher displays this warning if your available RAM is less than 520 Kilobytes (K). If you see this message you should exit and make more RAM available.

The most common problems that can arise when you use Express Publisher relate to your system's memory configuration. Your computer may have enough memory (RAM) to run Express Publisher, but some of this memory may be allocated for use by other software or hardware so that Express Publisher cannot access it.

Note   If you continue to use the program under low memory conditions, you will not be able to use TextEffects, and you will probably encounter problems while creating and printing complex documents.

Memory requirements

Express Publisher requires a minimum memory configuration to operate properly:

- 640K RAM
- 520K or more *available* RAM
- A CONFIG.SYS file with the statement FILES=20 (or greater)

Note Express Publisher requires a minimum of 520K available RAM, but it performs best when 560K or more is available.

Your computer should have 640K RAM as its base memory (also called conventional memory). To see how much conventional RAM is available on your system, type `chkdsk` at the C:\> prompt (or at the directory where your DOS files reside) and press ENTER. You will see a screen full of information about your system's memory. The last two lines display your available RAM. For example,

```
655,360 bytes total memory (640 Kilobytes)
528,384 bytes free (516 Kilobytes)
```

In this example, there is only 516K available RAM. Express Publisher will display the low memory warning upon startup.

What if I have extended/expanded memory?

Express Publisher can take advantage of extended or expanded memory, but DOS has some restrictions on how this memory can be used. Extended and expanded memory cannot make up for a lack of conventional memory.

Resolving memory problems

You can resolve most memory-related problems by changing the configuration of your system, thereby making more memory available to Express Publisher.

Configuring your system

See appendix A, "Basic DOS," for more information about the CONFIG.SYS and AUTOEXEC.BAT files. When you start your computer, DOS checks for two files in your root directory: CONFIG.SYS and AUTOEXEC.BAT. If it finds these files, it executes the commands listed in them. If you don't have as much available RAM as you think you should, it may be due to commands in these files that load unnecessary utilities, device drivers, and memory resident programs (also called TSRs).

There are two ways to configure your system to make more memory available for Express Publisher:

- Edit your CONFIG.SYS and AUTOEXEC.BAT files to prevent your system from loading any unnecessary programs.
- Create a DOS boot disk especially for Express Publisher so that you can prevent utilities, TSRs, and device drivers from loading only when you run Express Publisher.

Checking the contents of your files

To decide which solution will work best for you, you should first check the contents of your CONFIG.SYS and AUTOEXEC.BAT files for any unnecessary commands that are consuming valuable memory. To do this,

1. Check to see that your printer is plugged into LPT1, and make sure that it is on-line and has paper.

2. Move to the directory that contains Express Publisher by typing `cd\express` and pressing ENTER.

   If Express Publisher is in a different drive or directory, substitute that pathname.

3. At the C:\EXPRESS prompt, type `epsys` and press ENTER.

   This sends a file to your printer that lists the contents of your CONFIG.SYS and AUTOEXEC.BAT files, the amount of memory available, and the version of DOS that you are using.

4. Use this listing to help you determine the best memory configuration for your needs.

These are just examples. Look for commands that load TSR's and device drivers that you don't use.

First, search the listing of the CONFIG.SYS file for utilities and device drivers that are consuming memory. The left column below contains examples of lines to look for in the CONFIG.SYS file; the right column shows the approximate amount of RAM that the device uses.

Do not delete the FILES=20 or the DEVICE=MOUSE.SYS statements; they are necessary for Express Publisher to run properly.

DEVICE = ANSI.SYS	(1K)
DEVICE = DRIVER.SYS	(1K)
INSTALL=C:\DOS\FASTOPEN	(2-10K)
DEVICE=C:\CONNECT\CONNECT.SYS	(64K)
DEVICE=CPCSCAN.SYS 3e0 2 1	(3-5K)

Second, search the listing of the AUTOEXEC.BAT file for utilities, device drivers, and memory-resident programs that consume memory. The left column below contains examples of lines to look for in the AUTOEXEC.BAT file; the right column shows the approximate amount of RAM that the device uses. If you are not sure what your system needs, consult with your computer dealer or system administrator for assistance.

Do not remove your MOUSE statement. It allows your mouse to work with Express Publisher.

PRINT /D:LPT1	(5K)
APPEND /E	(5K)
APPEND C:\DOS	(10K)
GRAPHICS	(2K)
DOSSHELL	(40K)
SIDEKICK	(64-200K)
C:\CONNECT\CCAM	
C:\CONNECT\CCAM.CFG	(64K)
XT	(10-30K)
Net3 (Netware)	(55K)
NC (Norton Commander)	(3K)

Use the following system configurations to determine the minimum requirements for your type of computer. Please note that there are many variations of CONFIG.SYS and AUTOEXEC.BAT files. Your system may need additional drivers to operate properly.

Your mouse driver may appear in either file. It is usually listed as MOUSE in an AUTOEXEC.BAT file and MOUSE.SYS in a CONFIG.SYS file.

The statements DEVICE=HARDRIVE.SYS and DEVICE=DMDRVR.BIN are required for some hard disks.

640K system

| CONFIG.SYS | FILES=20 |
| | BUFFERS=20 |

AUTOEXEC.BAT	PROMPT PG
	PATH C:\; C:\DOS
	MOUSE

1MB 286/386 system (640K conventional + 384K extended memory)

CONFIG.SYS	FILES=20
	BUFFERS=20
	DEVICE=C:\EXPRESS\HIMEM.SYS
	DEVICE=SMARTDRV.SYS 256

AUTOEXEC.BAT	PROMPT PG
	PATH C:\; C:\DOS
	MOUSE
	SET TMP=[ramdrive letter]:\

2MB 286/386 system (640K conventional + 1408K extended memory)

CONFIG.SYS	FILES=20
	BUFFERS=20
	DEVICE=C:\EXPRESS\HIMEM.SYS
	DEVICE=RAMDRIVE.SYS 1024 /E
	DEVICE=SMARTDRV.SYS 256 256

AUTOEXEC.BAT	PROMPT PG
	PATH C:\; C:\DOS
	MOUSE
	SET TMP=[ramdrive letter]:\

4MB 286/386 system (640K conventional + 3456K extended memory)

CONFIG.SYS	FILES=20
	BUFFERS=20
	DEVICE=C:\EXPRESS\HIMEM.SYS
	DEVICE=RAMDRIVE.SYS 1024 /E
	DEVICE=SMARTDRV.SYS 1024 256

AUTOEXEC.BAT	PROMPT PG
	PATH C:\; C:\DOS
	MOUSE
	SET TMP=[ramdrive letter]:\

HIMEM.SYS provides an extra 64K of RAM to be accessed as conventional RAM. Express Publisher installs HIMEM.SYS if you have a 286 or 386 machine and at least 1MB RAM.

Do not use VDISK.SYS and HIMEM.SYS together; use RAMDRIVE.SYS with HIMEM.SYS instead. Do not use VDISK.SYS in conjunction with SMARTDRV.SYS in extended memory.

SMARTDRV.SYS is a disk-caching utility that comes with Windows and DOS version 4.0. It can be run in extended or expanded memory. Consult the documentation that comes with your version of SMARTDRV.SYS for more information.

RAMDRIVE.SYS is a RAM-disk utility that comes with some versions of DOS. It is used in conjunction with the SET TMP statement in the AUTOEXEC.BAT file (see below). Consult your DOS manual for instructions on using RAMDRIVE.SYS.

VDISK.SYS is a RAM-disk utility provided with some versions of DOS that is used in conjunction with the SET TMP statement in the AUTOEXEC.BAT file (see below). Consult your DOS manual for instructions on using VDISK.SYS.

SET TMP=[ramdrive letter]:\ is an environment variable. The environment is a small amount of memory that DOS sets aside to keep track of information such as the command path and the system prompt. You can use this command to specify where Express Publisher should write its temporary work files. For example, if you have set up your RAM drive to be E, place the command SET TMP=E:\ in your AUTOEXEC.BAT file.

Where to go from here

If you're not sure of which lines to delete, it's a good idea to leave the files as they are and create a boot disk.

If, after examining the contents of your CONFIG.SYS and AUTOEXEC.BAT files, you decide to modify them, follow the instructions below for doing so. You should modify these files if you find that there are unnecessary programs being loaded into your system when you start your computer.

On the other hand, if you have examined your CONFIG.SYS and AUTOEXEC.BAT files and found that all of the commands are necessary, go on to the next section entitled "Creating a boot disk."

Making backup copies of your files

Before proceeding further, you should make copies of your CONFIG.SYS and AUTOEXEC.BAT files.

1. At the C:\> prompt, type copy config.sys config.old and press ENTER. This makes a copy of your CONFIG.SYS file and names it CONFIG.OLD.

2. Then type copy autoexec.bat autoexec.old and press ENTER. This makes a copy of your AUTOEXEC.BAT file and names it AUTOEXEC.OLD.

See "Backing up your files" in Appendix A for more information on making copies of important files.

3. If you ever need to retrieve one of the original files for use, just execute the reverse of the command. For example, type `copy config.old config.sys` and press ENTER. After rebooting your computer, you will have your original CONFIG.SYS file again.

Editing the files

Follow these steps to edit your files. You may need to consult your DOS manual and documentation from other software programs that you use, so keep them nearby.

1. Use the DOS line editor, EDLIN, or your word processor to edit the CONFIG.SYS and AUTOEXEC.BAT files.

   Consult your DOS manual for instructions on using EDLIN. If you use a word processor, make sure you open and save the files as ASCII text files. If you're not sure how to do this, check your word processor's manual for the steps necessary to open and save ASCII files.

2. Remove the lines that load unnecessary utilities, device drivers, and memory-resident programs.

   Note   Some statements are required to insure that your computer runs software properly. Examples are the FILES=20 and MOUSE statements that Express Publisher requires. If you are unsure about which lines to remove, contact your computer supplier, system administrator, or Power Up Product Support for assistance.

3. After modifying and saving your CONFIG.SYS and AUTOEXEC.BAT files, reboot your computer by simultaneously holding down the CTRL and ALT keys and pressing DELETE. Then start Express Publisher.

Creating a boot disk

When you use a boot disk, you bypass your regular CONFIG.SYS and AUTOEXEC.BAT files and make more RAM available for Express Publisher. Follow these steps to create a boot disk:

1. Insert a blank disk into the A drive and close the drive door.

2. At the C:\> prompt, type `format a:/s` and press ENTER. Press ENTER again when you see the message asking you to insert a disk (you did that in step 1).

3. When prompted to format another disk, press n and then ENTER.

4. At the C:\> prompt, type `a:` and press ENTER to log on to the A drive.

5. Create a CONFIG.SYS file by typing `copy con:config.sys` and pressing ENTER.

   A blinking cursor appears on the next line.

6. Type `files=20` and press ENTER.

7. Type `buffers=20` and press ENTER.

8. Press F6 to indicate that you are done creating this file. You will see the symbol ^Z appear on the screen.

9. Press ENTER. You will see the message `one file(s) copied`. Do not remove the disk from the drive.

10. Reboot your computer by simultaneously holding down the CTRL and ALT keys and pressing DELETE. Your computer will boot from the disk in the A drive instead of the hard disk.

    After you respond to the Time and Date prompts, you will see the A> prompt.

11. Type `c:` and press ENTER to log onto the C drive.

12. Load your mouse driver by typing `mouse` and pressing ENTER.

Note   The command to load your mouse driver might be different, or it may be stored in a subdirectory. If you encounter a Bad command or file name error, check your CONFIG.SYS and AUTOEXEC.BAT files in your EPSYS printout, or your mouse manual, for the proper command(s).

13. Move to the Express Publisher directory by typing `cd\express` and pressing ENTER. Then type `ep` and press ENTER to load the program.

14. When you are done, label the disk with a memorable name such as *Express Publisher boot disk*.

When you want to use Express Publisher, simply place this disk in your A drive and follow steps 10-13.

How do I take advantage of extended and expanded memory for best performance?

- Use HIMEM.SYS. The main benefit of extra memory is speed. Using HIMEM.SYS adds another benefit, because it provides an extra 64K RAM that can be accessed as conventional RAM. Express Publisher automatically installs HIMEM.SYS on 286 and 386 machines with at least 1MB of RAM.
- Create a RAM drive or VDISK in extended/expanded RAM for the TMP variable to write to. Then type the command `SET TMP=n:\` (where n is the drive letter of the RAM disk,) at the DOS prompt before starting Express Publisher, or add this line to your AUTOEXEC.BAT file.
- Create a large SMARTDRV.SYS cache (up to 1MB).

Problems running Express Publisher

Mouse problems

Why is my mouse pointer jumpy or erratic?

Here are a few potential reasons for mouse problems and their solutions:

- Depending on the version of your mouse driver, you may encounter this problem. Many older mouse drivers, as well as generic mouse drivers, can cause this problem. Contact the manufacturer of your mouse for an update to the latest edition of the mouse driver.
- If your Microsoft mouse doesn't work properly with Express Publisher, an upgrade of the mouse driver will probably fix the problem. Express Publisher works well with version 7.04 of the Microsoft mouse driver. If you are having problems with your Microsoft mouse and have driver version 7.00, 7.01, 7.02, or 7.03, call Microsoft technical support at (206) 454-2030. They will ask you for the version number of your mouse driver and the serial number on your mouse.
- If you have version 7.01 of the Mouse Systems mouse driver, call Mouse Systems to go back to version 6.23, or to upgrade when the next version is available.
- If your mouse driver allows you to limit sensitivity and/or disable ballistic tracking, you should do so. Check your mouse's documentation or contact the mouse manufacturer for details on how to make these adjustments.

No mouse pointer appears when you start the program.

Solution 1: If you have not run the mouse driver required by your mouse prior to starting Express Publisher, no mouse pointer will appear. Follow the installation instructions that came with your mouse. This usually involves running a program named MOUSE.COM, or calling a device driver named MOUSE.SYS in your CONFIG.SYS file.

Note

Some programs include their own mouse driver. Microsoft Windows and PaintBrush are two such programs. Your mouse may work with these programs even though you have not installed the mouse driver software. This has no bearing on how your mouse will work with Express Publisher; you still must install the mouse driver software that came with your mouse.

Solution 2: If you have trouble with any mouse that we do not explicitly support, you should contact the manufacturer. In many cases the problems are due to incompatibilities in the mouse driver software. Often a newer version of the mouse driver software will solve the problem.

There are several variables that determine how much memory a character will require: the print resolution (dots per inch) of the printer, the size of the character, and any special characteristics you add to the character, such as shearing.

For example, if you create a 144-point character in a 2-inch by 2-inch frame and print it at 180 dots per inch (dpi), you will use up 16K (kilobytes) of memory. Printing the same character at 300 dpi requires 45K.

If you scale the character at 150% (to 3 inches wide), you will exceed the 64K memory-segment limitation of the 80xx processor. The character will not print.

If you shear (tilt) the character, you increase the full width of the character even more.

So, if you find missing characters in your TextEffects headline or other Express Publisher document,

- make the point size of the character smaller until it prints
- select a lower resolution for your printer

The printer's output is garbled, or contains extra characters.

Solution 1: Turn the printer off, wait five seconds, turn it on, and try to print again. Also check to make sure that you have selected the correct printer driver with the Choose Printer command. Your printer cable may also be defective.

Solution 2: If you have a dot-matrix printer and the output resembles the following sample, it may be because the default font on your printer is set to something other than 10 characters per inch (cpi). The default font can usually be controlled by a switch or a button on the front panel of your printer, or by the dip switches found inside the printer, depending on the model of your printer.

Example of a dot-matrix printing problem

To fix this problem, consult your printer manual for instructions on changing the default font to 10 cpi. After changing the default font, turn your printer off and on again and print with Express Publisher.

Express Publisher doesn't print the fonts you expected.

Solution: You may have specified printer fonts that are not available on the printer you are using. The printer driver you select with the Choose Printer command determines the printer fonts that you can use. If you use a printer font, and then switch printer drivers, the program substitutes an Express Publisher font when you print the document. See "About fonts" in Chapter 5, "Text" for more about printer fonts. (If you have an H-P printer clone, try using the HPSHADOW driver.)

Objects or characters cut off, objects not printing, and extra form feeding.

Solution: All of these problems are due to placing objects outside of your printer's print area. The print area is the part of the page that your printer is physically capable of printing on. Express Publisher allows you to put objects anywhere on the page, even if they are outside of your printer's print area. See "Printer margins" in Chapter 7, "Printing" for more information.

Objects or characters cut off using the IBM PS/1 printer.

The PS/1 printer has 1/4-inch nonprinting left and right margins. Objects and text that extend into these margins will be truncated.

Express Publisher can't find TIF, GIF, or EPS pictures during printing.

Solution: Express Publisher does not store TIF, GIF, or EPS pictures with the rest of the document. It stores only a low resolution version of these pictures for screen display. At print time, Express Publisher prints the pictures directly from the original files on disk. If you move or delete one of these picture types, or if you move a document to a different system, Express Publisher stops during printing and asks you where to find the picture file.

If you move a document file to a different system, you must copy all of the TIFF, GIF, and EPS pictures separately. For example, a document named DOC.EPD contains a TIFF picture called FLAG.TIF. To move DOC.EPD to a different computer, you must copy both DOC.EPD and FLAG.TIF onto the other system.

Unable to print overlapping objects correctly, particularly shadow boxes, on an HP LaserJet.

Solution: Most of the HP LaserJet printer drivers print all objects in their entirety, even if they are supposed to be covered by other objects. This means that solid white objects will not obscure filled objects that they cover. Reprint the document after selecting the printer driver HPSHADOW.PRD with the Choose Printer command. Read "Printing overlapping objects" in Chapter 7.

Bold fonts print plain.

Solution: Large, bold fonts may print as plain if your computer runs out of memory.

Printer not responding.

Solution: Express Publisher may tell you that your printer is not responding, even if the printer is correctly connected and on line. This can occur if your printer is connected to a parallel printing port. The problem is not unique to Express Publisher. To correct this, exit to DOS and type MODE LPT1: , , P and press ENTER. This sets the printer port to infinite retry. Consult your DOS manual for more information about the MODE command.

Error messages

Following is an alphabetical listing of all the error messages you may get while working in Express Publisher. Each message is followed by a suggested resolution, when there is one. If you get a message that doesn't appear in this list, it may be a DOS message. Check your DOS manual.

A text frame cannot be linked to itself. You have selected the same text frame twice when attempting to link two text frames.

A text frame must first be created to enter text. Before you can type in text, you must create a text frame by clicking the Text Frame tool.

An internal font error has occurred. There is not enough memory for the CompuGraphic font.

An object cannot be aligned to itself. You have selected the same object twice with the align tool. Make sure that the two objects you wish to align are selectable and try again.

Cannot wrap text around this object. You've tried to wrap text around an object that Express Publisher does not let you wrap text around, such as a page number.

Can't find setup file EP.INI. Express Cannot find this important start-up file. Re-run the Setup program and try again.

Can't load Express Publisher document (filename). Your document is corrupted. You may have to generate it again.

Color settings are for EGA and VGA color adapters. You have attempted to change colors, but don't have an EGA or VGA color video card.

Critical hardware failure. This unlikely condition probably has to do with extended or expanded memory and a memory conflict. Check your memory allocation.

Default printer driver DRIVERNAME is not located. Express Publisher can't find the default printer driver that you selected during setup. Run SETUPEP from the hard disk and select Copy Printers. Select your printer from the list of supported printers. If this message does not specify a printer driver, you may have accidentally erased or moved the file EP.INI. Rerun the SETUPEP program from your original Express Publisher disks like a first-time installation.

Disk Space Problem. Express Publisher requires a minimum of 135K of disk space while you are using it. You need to create more space on your disk by deleting files you don't need or transferring them to floppies.

Document not compatible with Express Publisher version. You may be trying to load a document created in version 2.0 into version 1.x. You must use version 2.0 with 2.0 documents; it is not downward compatible.

Excessive font size chosen for page number. Express Publisher is unable to display a page number in the selected type size. Select a smaller number and try again.

Express Publisher documents/templates cannot be imported. You have selected an Express Publisher document or template to import. You do not need to import Express Publisher documents; open them with the File I Open command.

Express Publisher requires at least 135K of free space on your hard disk in order to run. You may get this message if you try to start Express Publisher without sufficient space on your hard disk. Clear up some space on your hard disk (delete old files or transfer them to floppy disks) and start the program again.

Express Publisher supports only Monochrome GEM images! You cannot use color GEM image with Express Publisher.

Facing Pages cannot be shown for this document. Your document probably has only one page.

File "EP.INI" not located. During the setup process, a file called EP.INI is created that contains all of the selections you've specified. This includes the type of graphics adapter used, the drive and path for program files, and the printer(s) selected. If the setup process was interrupted for any reason, this file would not have been created. Then, when you first try to load Express Publisher, this error message appears. Rerun the setup program.

File Not Found. You may have specified a file at the command line by typing EP FILENAME, but Express Publisher could not find the file. Check that you spelled the file name correctly and that the file is in the directory specified in the pathname.

File saved, insufficient work space to proceed. Express Publisher has saved your current document, but you need to exit and make additional space on your hard disk before continuing.

First frame in story must be selected to replace text. You have not placed the text cursor in the first frame of the story. Press SHIFT F-6 until you reach the first frame of the story and try again.

Image loaded but there is not enough memory to display it. Express Publisher has loaded your image, but there isn't enough RAM to display it. The image appears as a grey box on the screen, but will print correctly.

Insufficient disk space! You do not have enough disk space to perform the requested action. Clear some room on your hard disk and try again.

Insufficient disk space to create a work file. Express Publisher makes temporary work files as you create each page of your document. This message means you've run out of hard disk space for the temporary work files. Save your work and exit the program. Make additional space on your hard disk before continuing.

Insufficient memory to load file. You don't have enough available RAM to load the file. Get rid of any Memory resident programs you have on your system and try again.

Insufficient room on disk to save document! There is not enough room on your hard or floppy disk to save the document. Save to a different floppy disk.

Invalid duplication values specified. You have entered duplication values that are impossible for Express Publisher to execute. Enter new values and try again.

Invalid Express Publisher document. You may be trying to open either a document that you created with version 1.*x* of Express Publisher or a corrupted file. Express Publisher cannot read this file.

Invalid grid size specified. You have specified a grid size that is too small or too large. You cannot specify a grid smaller than 0.1 inch or larger than the page size. Select another grid size and try again.

Invalid object specification. You've entered an invalid entry in the Object Specifications dialog box, such as invalid page or dimension values at those prompts.

Invalid page specification. You've made an invalid entry in the Custom Page dialog box. The faulty entry may be the number of columns, gutter width, header height, or margins.

Invalid page specified for printing. You have specified a page for printing that does not exist. Correct the specified page numbers and try printing again.

Large GEM/PAINT/PCX images not supported in Express Publisher. You cannot use GEM files that are bigger than 64 K when decompressed.

Last style in story cannot be deleted! There must always be at least one style in the list of styles. Enter a new style, then you can delete the existing one.

Line objects cannot be filled. You can only fill ovals and rectangles.

Low Memory. We reccomend removing other applications from memory when running Express Publisher. Your available RAM is less than 520 Kilobytes (K). See "Memory problems" earlier in this chapter for information on configuring your system to avoid low memory conditions.

Maximum Custom page size is 8.5 by 11 inches. You have specified a Custom page size larger than 8.5 by 11 inches. Specify a page size within these parameters and try again.

No printer drivers found. You may not have installed printers when you run the Setup program. From the DOS prompt, type SETUPEP and follow the prompts for printer installation.

No styles have been located in range. You may have tried to delete a style without selecting a style first.

Object inappropriate for linking text. You have selected a non-text object that cannot be linked to text.

Object too large to rotate. Express Publisher cannot rotate this object because it is too large to fit on the page sideways. Use the Scale Object command to make the object smaller and try again.

Only 64 stories per document are allowed. You have reached the maximum number of *stories* in your document. Review the section on stories and text frames in Chapter 5.

Only 400 objects per page are allowed. You have more than 400 objects on the current page. You must delete some objects before adding any more.

Out of disk space for Virtual Memory! Express Publisher requires a minimum of 135K. You need to create more space on your disk by deleting files you don't need or transferring them to floppies.

Picture file type not recognized. Express Publisher is having difficulty in recognizing the type of picture you are importing. Check that it is one of Express Publisher's supported formats.

Print Shop DAT file not located. NAM files must have a corresponding .DAT file for each image.

Printer driver DRIVERNAME not found, must remap fonts. The program is unable to find the printer driver that you created the document with. It will remap the document using the current default printer driver. This can happen when you print a document from a different computer. The main change to your document will be to any printer-specific fonts you selected. It will not change any CG fonts (except when remapping to PostScript).

Printshop Color/Border/Font/Panel graphics not supported! You are trying to use a graphics format that Express Publisher does not support. Choose another type of graphic image.

Save file is read-only, unable to save to it! If you are using Express Publisher on a network, someone has designated the file you are trying to save it as Read-Only. Check the attribute set to this file and change it so that you can write to the file. Also, make sure your CONFIG.SYS file shows FILES= 20 (or more).

Secondary object cannot be aligned this way. Doing so would place the object outside of the page boundaries, such as when you try to place a second object beside a primary objec that is already at the edge.

Select a text frame before using Split Text Frame. Before choosing the Split Text Frame command, you must select a text frame for the command to work on.

Select an object before using Rotate Object. You have tried to use the Rotate Object command without selecting an object first.

Startup file not located. You've loaded an Express Publisher document from the DOS command line, such as EP FILENAME.EPD, and the program is unable to locate the file due to an invalid path or filename.

Story has only this text frame. Delete entire story? This message appears if you try to Unlink or delete a single text frame. You can proceed and delete the text from the text frame, or click Cancel.

Synchronization error reading GEM paint file. Your GEM file may be corrupted. Try importing it again.

The file you are attempting to import would consume the majority of your conventional memory. Express Publisher cannot import it. You don't have enough RAM (memory) to import the file. Remove any memory-resident programs and try again.

The Intel resident scheduler must be loaded first. If you want to print your file to the Intel Connection Co-processor, make sure the connector is in memory (that is, you typed XCAM to load it). Check the Intel documentation to make sure you have loaded it correctly.

The largest possible font for this text frame is (point size). Express Publisher is unable to display any text in the frame because the font is larger than the text frame. Enlarge the text frame and try again.

The printer is not responding. Your printer is not turned on. Turn it on and print the file again.

The printer is not responding. This may be because it is out of memory, out of paper or off-line. Check your printer to make sure it has paper, is on-line, and is connected properly. See Appendix D for information about specific printers. See your printer manual for information about printer memory.

The style name cannot be blank. You have created a new Style but failed to give it a name. Type a name in the Style Name field or cancel the command.

This text frame is already part of the story. You are using preset formats where text frames are already linked and are attempting to link them again. You need to use the Unlink tool to unlink the frame(s) first. You may see this message if you try to link one text frame to two different stories.

The text frame is full. When you enter text from the keyboard, Express Publisher tries to fit as much text in the text frame as possible. Once the text frame becomes full, this message appears (unless the frame is already linked to a subsequent frame). Click OK. Make the frame larger, or link the frame to a new frame and continue typing.

The text frame is too small to display the text! Make the text frame larger or shorten the text.

The text frame must first be unlinked. You have attempted to enter text into a text frame that is linked to a different text frame. You can move to a previous frame that has text and enter text until it flows to the current frame, or Unlink the text frame.

This rectangle is too short to accommodate any text. You need to make the rectangle larger.

This type of TIFF file is not supported. You cannot import color or grayscale TIFF images.

Unable to create a work file. There is not enough space on your hard disk for Express Publisher to work in. Clear up some space by removing files.

Unable to create a working copy of document. You do not have enough disk space for Express Publisher to work in. Clear up some space on your hard disk by removing files.

Unable to equate the two objects. There are two possible problems: one of the objects is locked, or equating the objects would make them too large to fit on the page.

Unable to load document properly. The document you are trying to open may be corrupted. Generate the document again.

Unable to load this TIFF file. The TIFF image you are trying to import is too large, corrupt, or the wrong (color or grayscale) type.

Unable to locate file (filename). A critical Express Publisher program file is missing (EP.*) which you may have deleted accidentally. Re-install Express Publisher.

Unable to open Express Publisher document. Express Publisher can't find the document you specified. Make sure you typed the file name correctly and that the file is in the correct directory.

Unable to save document page to disk! There is not enough space on your hard disk for the document. If you can, use the File | Save As command to save the document to a floppy disk, then clear up some space on your hard disk.

Unable to save file FILENAME. This message appears any time you are unable to save a file, for example, your disk may be full or have a bad sector. Try to save this file with a different filename (with the DOS limitations of up to 8 characters, no spaces, and none of these characters: *?.,;{}+=\<>). Or try to save it to a formatted floppy disk.

Unable to save work file, print document! There is not enough memory on your computer to save the document or print it. Save your file to a floppy disk. Exit Express Publisher and make room in memory.

Unable to scale a line. Express Publisher can only scale pictures, rectangles, and ovals. Select one of these and try again.

Unable to scale object to specified size. There is not enough space on the page to scale the object to the specified size. Try again with a smaller scaling percentage.

Unable to Undo previous action. Express Publisher can undo anything that you delete, rotate, or move from one place to another. You probably tried to undo a different type of action.

You can only flip pictures. You have attempted to flip an object that is not a picture, such as a rectangle or a line.

You can only split text frames. You want to split a text frame vertically or horizontally but have selected an object other than a text frame. A box is not considered a text frame until you've entered text into it or placed the text (I-beam) cursor in it.

You can't crop this type of object. The cropping tool works with all picture formats except GIF, and EPS pictures.

You can't delete the only page in a document. Any Express Publisher document must have at least one page. You can delete text, text frames, or other objects on the page, but not the page itself.

You cannot invert EPS pictures. Express Publisher can only invert TIFF and bit-mapped images.

You have selected too many fonts for this printer. You can have up to 16 fonts per page on HP LaserJet, LaserJet Plus, LaserJet 2000, LaserJet 500 Plus, and most LaserJet Series II printers. The LaserJet IID and IIP allow as many fonts as defined by available memory in the printer. Note: In this context font is defined as any unique combination of typeface, style, and size. For instance, CG Times Bold 12 point and CG Times Italic 12 point count as two fonts. This is a hardware limitation.

You have used too many fonts on this page. Your document will probably not be formatted correctly. There is a limit of 14 fonts per page with the HP LaserJet Series III printer. If there are too many fonts on a page, some of the fonts may be changed during the printing process. Remember, a font is any variation of type size and style. For example, 12 point Times plain and 12 point Times italic are two different fonts.

You must select a paragraph or story first. Express Publisher cannot perform the selected action because you have not selected a paragraph or story. Select a paragraph or story and try again.

You must select a paragraph with text first. You probably tried to create a new style without selecting a paragraph first. Select the paragraph, then the command to apply to it.

You must select a text frame first. You tried to enter text without selecting a text frame first.

You must select an object first. You have selected a command such as Flip Object or Rotate Object without first selecting the object.

Directories created by the setup program

The setup program creates several directories on your hard disk. The table below displays the contents of these directories. There may be additional files if you install more fonts or clip art.

Directory of \EXPRESS
Express Publisher program files

SETUPEP.EXE	TS.ICO	92244.TYP
SETUPEP.MSG	TYPSETPS.EXE	92500.TYP
EP.PLM	TYPSETPS.INI	92501.TYP
EP.RES	CLIPART.ASC	92585.TYP
EP.PPM	PRD.ASC	94021.TYP
EPM.RES	CGA.EVD	35MM.CFG
EP.CL2	CGA400.EVD	AP.CFG
EP.CL3	EGA.EVD	CGM2TIF.CFG
EP.COM	EGABW.EVD	CGM2TIF.EXE
EP.CUR	HGC.EVD	CGM2TIF.MGR
EP.HLP	MCGA.EVD	CGM2TIF.MSG
EP.ICC	NOEXT.COM	DP.CFG
EP.ICO	TS.CUR	FL.CFG
EP.PAT	TS.HLP	HG.CFG
HQ3.TYP	TS.PAT	PLUGIN.TYQ
HQ3UPDT.TYQ	TS.RES	EP.INI
IF.FNT	VGA.EVD	SOFTFONT.EXE
IF.LST	EP.TSP	EP.PIF
IF.SS	90369.TYP	EPSYS.BAT
LINES.PAT	90460.TYP	EPSYS.NO
MAC.PAT	91545.TYP	
POSTSCRP INI	91816.TYP	

Directory of \EXPRESS\DOCS	**Directory of \EXPRESS\TEXT**	**Directory of \EXPRESS\ART**
Sample templates	*Sample text files for Tutorial and Layout*	*Clip art*
AGENDA.EPT		AIRPLANE.PCX
COUPON.EPT	AUTHOR.WPS	AUTUMN.TIF
INVITE.EPT	CALENDAR.WPS	BURST1.TIF
LEARN_EP.EPT	FEATURE.WPS	BURST2.TIF
NEWSLTR.EPT	NEWSLTTR.WPS	FLAPPER.TIF
NEWSLTR2 EPT	STORY2.WPS	HURDLES.TIF
		FISH.PCX

Supported printers

Included printer drivers

Express Publisher comes with all of the printer drivers listed below. The column on the left includes the file names of the printer drivers. These file names appear in the Driver Name list box in the Choose Printer dialog box. The column on the right lists all of the printers supported by that printer driver. This table is especially useful if you are using an HP LaserJet with font cartridges.

Driver file name	Printers supported
EPSONEX.PRD	Epson EX 800, EX 1000
EPSONFX.PRD	Epson FX 286e, FX 1050, FX 86e, FX 850, FX 286, FX 185, FX 85, FX 80, FX 100
EPSONJX.PRD	Epson JX 80
EPSONLQ.PRD	Epson LQ 1500, LQ 1500 (Font module)
EPSONLQ1.PRD	Epson LQ 800, LQ 800 (ID module), LQ 1000, LQ 1000 (ID module), Panasonic KXP1124
EPSONLQ2.PRD	Epson LQ 850, LQ 850 (Font module), LQ 1050
EPSONLQ3.PRD	Epson LQ 500, LQ 500 (Font module)
LQ2500.PRD	Epson LQ 2500
EPSONRX.PRD	Epson RX 80, RX 100
FDL2400.PRD	Fujitsu DL-2400
FDX2000F.PRD	Fujitsu DX-2300-2400 (Epson emulation)
FDX2000I.PRD	Fujitsu DX-2300-2400 (IBM emulation)
HPDESK1.PRD	HP DeskJet, internal fonts, no cartridges; DeskJet with cartridges A, B, C
HPPAINT.PRD	HP PaintJet
HP.PRD	HP LaserJet 500+, HP LaserJet+, HP LaserJet (original), Panasonic KX-P4450, with internal fonts, no cartridges.
HPQUIET.PRD	HP QuietJet
HPSHADOW.PRD	HP LaserJet Series II, LaserJet 500+, LaserJet+, LaserJet(original), LaserJet 2000, LaserJet IID, LaserJet III, Panasonic KX-P4450. For printing overlapping objects.
HP2000.PRD	HP LaserJet 2000 with internal fonts, no cartridges.
HPII.PRD	HP LaserJet Series II, with internal fonts, no cartridges.

HPIID.PRD	HP LaserJet IID, with internal fonts, no cartridges.
HPIII.PRD	HP LaserJet Series III, with internal fonts, no cartridges.
IBM4019.PRD	IBM 4019 Laser printer
IBMGRAPH.PRD	IBM Graphics printer
IBMPRO.PRD	IBM Proprinter
IBMPROXL.PRD	IBM Proprinter II & XL
IBMPRO3.PRD	IBM Proprinter III, Proprinter IIIXL
IBMPS1.PRD	IBM PS/1 printer
IBMXL24.PRD	IBM Proprinter X24, and Proprinter XL24
IBMQUIET.PRD	IBM QuietWriter I, II, and III
NECP2200.PRD	NEC P2200
NEC.PRD	NEC P5XL, P9XL, P6 , P7
NECP5200.PRD	NEC P5200 & P5300
OKI192.PRD	Okidata 192, 193
OKI192PS.PRD	Okidata 192, 193 with proportional fonts
OKI292.PRD	Okidata 292, 293
OKI393.PRD	Okidata 393
OKILASER.PRD	Okidata Laserline 6 or 8
PANA1080.PRD	Panasonic KX-P1080i, KX-P1592
PANA1092.PRD	Panasonic KX-P1091i, KX-P1092i
PANA1524.PRD	Panasonic KX-P1524
POSTSCRP.PRD	QMS PS 810, AST TurboLaser PS, DEC LN03R,Postscript Printer - single bin,Postscript printer - dual bin, NEC Silent Writer
STARNB24.PRD	Star Micronics NB24-15
STARNX15.PRD	Star Micronics NX-10 & NX-15

Other printer drivers

Your Express Publisher disks do not include drivers for some less common printers. If your printer, or a compatible printer, is not listed, a Product Support representative may be able to help.

Unlisted printers   If your printer is not listed in the setup program, select a printer that is compatible with your printer. Most unlisted dot-matrix printers are compatible with either the IBM Graphics/ Proprinter, the Epson X series, or the Epson LQ series. Most laser printers are compatible with the HP LaserJet Plus or HP LaserJet Series II. Look in your printer's manual, or call the manufacturer, to find out which standard your printer is compatible with. The chart below lists several printers and the standards that their manufacturers state they are compatible with. Power Up has not tested these printers.

Express Publisher includes several Epson X* series printer drivers. The Epson FX 80 driver should work with many X series printers. Other drivers may also work if your printer is compatible with a specific printer within the X series. If your printer is Epson LQ compatible, select the Epson LQ 1500 or Epson LQ800 (EPSONLQ2) driver.

Manufacturer	Models
ALPS	ALQ200, ALQ218, P2000, P2100, 2400C, *Epson X Series*; ALQ224, ALQ324, 2424C, *Epson LQ*
BROTHER	1109, 1209, 1409, 1509, 1709, 2518, 4018, *Epson X Series*; 1724L, 2024L *Epson LQ*
C. ITOH	C-210, C-215, C-310, C-315, C0815, Prowriter Jr. Plus, 1550EP; *Epson X Series*; C-715, C-715A, 24LQ, *Epson LQ*
CITIZEN	120D, MSP 10, 15, 20, 25, 40, 45, 50, 55, *Epson X Series*; Tribute 124, 224, *Epson LQ*
GENICOM	222, 1000, 1020, 1025, 3014, 3210, 3310, 3320, 3410, *IBM Graphics*
MANNESMANN TALLY	85, 86, 87, 88, 230, 290, 340, 490, *Epson X Series* 330, *Epson LQ*; Spirit 80, 180, 440L, *IBM Graphics*
NEC	P5, P5XL, P6, P7, P9Xl, 2200, CP7, P5200, P5300, *Epson LQ Series*
PANASONIC	1080, 1180, 1090, 1091, *Epson X Series*; 1124, 1624, *Epson LQ*
SEIKOSHA	BP-5420AI, MP1300-AI, MP-5300AI, SK-3000AI, SK-3005AI, SP-1000A, SP-1200AI, SBP-10AI, *Epson X Series*; SL-80AI, SL-130AI, *Epson LQ*
STAR MICRONICS	F-10, LV-1210, NB-10, NB-15, NL-10, NP-10, NR-15, NX-10, NX-15 SD-10, SD-15, SG-10, SG-15, SR-10, SR-15, *Epson X Series*; NB2410, NB2415, *Epson LQ*
TANDY	DMP-130, DMP-130A, DMP-132, DMP-430, DMP-440, DMP-2100P, DMP-2110, DMP-2120, DMP-2200, TRP-100, *IBM Graphics*
TEXAS INSTR.	875, 877, *Epson LQ*; 880 AT, OMNI 880, *IBM Graphics*

* Epson X Series = Epson EX/FX/LX/MX/RX

Printer specific information

IBM PS/1 printer Express Publisher cannot display the PS/1 printer fonts on the screen. If you select a printer font, Express Publisher substitutes a correctly scaled version of CG Triumvirate or CG Times for screen display. In spite of the substitution, each screen character occupies the correct amount of space, and the correct number of characters appear on each line. When you print the document, Express Publisher uses the printer font you specified. For more information, see "About fonts," in Chapter 5.

HP LaserJet The HP LaserJet is one of the most popular laser printers. Express Publisher can print on most versions of the LaserJet at 75, 150, and 300 dpi.

Running out of memory

Unlike other printers, the LaserJet stops printing and ejects the page when it runs out of memory. To print a large or complex Express Publisher document at 300 dpi on the LaserJet, you must have at least 1.5 megabytes of memory expansion installed in your printer. The HP laser driver must calculate the entire area that an object covers, even if it is mostly white space. At 300 dots per inch, a large text frame takes up quite a bit of memory. If your LaserJet displays the out of memory error message and prints an incomplete page, switch to a lower resolution.

Printing overlapping objects

Express Publisher offers two types of printer drivers for the HP Laserjet to optimize the unique abilities of this line of printers. The first type is one of the standard Laserjet drivers, whose file names start with HP, such as HPIII.PRD. You choose the specific one you use depending on the model of the Laserjet that you own. The second type is the HP Shadow driver (HPSHADOW.PRD). This works with all models of the HP Laserjet that we support.

Most of the HP LaserJet printer drivers print all solid objects in their entirety, even if they are supposed to be covered by other objects. This means that solid white objects don't obscure filled objects that they overlap, or cover. That's because each object on the page is drawn as an individual object, just the way you create it.

If you have a complicated document, you may want to use the HP Shadow driver. Overlapping objects print correctly with this driver, because it doesn't print each object separately. It prints the document as it appears. Also, the HP Shadow driver doesn't need to perform calculations for an entire object; it only needs to calculate for the printable part of the object. It can skip over the white spaces. (See the previous section "Running out of memory").

For complicated documents, the HP Shadow driver will often work more efficiently than the standard HP Laser driver. You should install this driver in addition to your standard HP printer driver. To install this driver, select the model of your printer with the line For Overlapping Objects when you go through the setup program.

HP Laserjet series III The HP LaserJet III printer has eight built-in Compugraphic outlines: Times Normal, Times Bold, Times Italic, Times Bold/ Italic, Univers Normal, Univers Bold, Univers Italic, Univers Bold/Italic. Some of these fonts are already a part of Express Publisher. If you install for the LaserJet series III, you may see

---

duplicate font names in the Choose Font dialog, with "(HPIII)" distinguishing the HPIII fonts from the CG fonts. For optimum performance, use the HPIII fonts. Using these built-in fonts can increase print speed, particularly when you use large type sizes and several type sizes and styles.

Although the CG Times and Univers fonts included with Express Publisher and on the LaserJet III are nearly identical, there is one difference: Express Publisher uses a different symbol set (alternate characters) than the LaserJet. Both symbol sets produce the same standard keyboard characters. However, they produce different alternate (extended) characters.

For example, Express Publisher's alternate-character set provides predefined bullet, dagger, copyright, and trademark symbols. If you use the LaserJet III's built-in scalable fonts, the Express Publisher character will display on screen but will be substituted with the corresponding LaserJet III character when you print. That is, all standard characters will map correctly, but any alternate characters you use in your document will not.

In addition, the LaserJet III does not support Express Publisher's superscript and subscript font styles.

Using both fonts

You can use both LaserJet III and Express Publisher fonts in one document. For example, you can use LaserJet III fonts for most of your text, then use Express Publisher fonts for such alternate characters as bullets or subscripts. Your document will then print faster than if you use all Express Publisher fonts.

To access the LaserJet III's built-in scalable CG Times and Univers fonts, go to the Text menu, click Choose Font, and choose those printer fonts from the Choose Font dialog box. They are identified as CG-Times(HPIII) and Univers(HPIII) on the typeface selection scroll box.

Other printers

DEC LN03R and AST Turbo Laser

If you install one of the PostScript printer drivers, you will see the DECLN03R and AST Turbo Laser choices in the Choose Printer dialog box. These printers have not been tested by Power Up, but assuming that they are 100% PostScript compatible, they should work.

Epson LX 800

If you have an Epson LX 800, select Epson FX 80 as your printer type in the setup program.

Color printers

Choices designated as "color" in the Choose Printer dialog box are not meant to imply that Express Publisher can print in different colors. However, if you are using a color printer and you sometimes do print in color with other programs, you should choose one of the color choices to guarantee that Express Publisher will switch your printer to black ink. Other applications may leave the printer set up for the last ink color used.

Toshiba printers

Select IBM Graphics Printer, or IBM ProPrinter to configure Express Publisher for most Toshiba dot-matrix printers. Some older model Toshibas do not emulate the IBM Graphics Printer or Proprinter and are not supported.

Older Okidata printers

Express Publisher can print with older Okidata printers (192 and 292 models) only if they are equipped with the "Plug 'n Play" option for IBM Graphics Printer emulation. Express Publisher is not compatible with Okidata printers that print in native mode.

IBM 4019 Laser printer

The IBM 4019 Laser printer must be in HP LaserJet emulation mode to work with Express Publisher. To operate in LaserJet mode, press and hold the Font button on the printer as you turn it on. Release the Font button when any panel lights come on. You can then choose either HP LaserJet or IBM 4019 as the printer driver in Express Publisher.

Included clip art

300 dpi images

All of the following images are included with your Express Publisher disks. They are stored in a compressed format. You must install them with the setup program. Do not try to copy them to your hard disk with the DOS COPY command. (The following images have been reduced to conserve a little paper.)

This software allows the user to print trademarks and service marks which are proprietary to their respective companies or organizations. The inclusion of these marks is not intended to constitute an endorsement of this software by any of these companies or organizations, neither is it intended to signify a connection between any of these companies or organizations and Power Up Software Corporation.

1STPRIZE.TIF   AMERFLAG.TIF   ATHENS.TIF

AUTUMN.TIF   BARBEQUE.TIF   BULLSEYE.TIF

BUSNESMN.TIF   CALCULTR.TIF   CHEF.TIF

COINS.TIF   COMPUTR1.TIF   COMPUTR2.TIF

COMPUTR3.TIF   CONGRATS.TIF   COWBOY.TIF

DELIVVAN.TIF

FIRSTAID.TIF

FRNCHHRN.TIF

GOLFING.TIF

GRADUATN.TIF

HLLYBELL.TIF

HLLYBRRY.TIF

HOMACCTG.TIF

HURDLES.TIF

INVITATN.TIF

LADYSEYE.TIF

LASSO.TIF

MACOMPTR.TIF

MARIGOLD.TIF

MATCH.TIF

MOVIECAM.TIF

NEWSMAN.TIF

PISA.TIF

PRINTER.TIF PROGOLFR.TIF QUOTES1.TIF

QUOTES2.TIF QUOTES3.TIF ROSES.TIF

SNOWFLAK.TIF SPRING.TIF STARTBLX.TIF

SUMMER.TIF TREE.TIF TREE3.TIF

TROPHY.TIF TULIPS.TIF TYPWRITR.TIF

WATERSKI.TIF WEDCAKE.TIF XMASHORN.TIF

150 dpi images

ALARMCLK.TIF

AMEX.TIF

ANCHOR.TIF

ARROW4.TIF

ARROW5.TIF

ARROW6.TIF

ARROW7.TIF

ARROW8.TIF

BASSDRUM.TIF

BEAGLE.TIF

BOUQUET.TIF

BULLDOG.TIF

CAUTION.TIF

CHEESES.TIF

CHKMARK.TIF

COFFEE.TIF

COUPON.TIF

COUPON2.TIF

CURVROAD.TIF

DIVROAD.TIF

DLLRBIL1.TIF

DLLRBILL.TIF

DLLRFIST.TIF

DLLRSIGN.TIF

DRMAMASK.TIF

EAGLE.TIF

FIREMAN1.TIF

FNCYDRNK.TIF

HAND1.TIF

HAND2.TIF

HANDSHAK.TIF

JACKPOT.TIF

MEMO.TIF

MSTRCARD.TIF

NOTICE.TIF

REDCARPT.TIF

ROWMACH.TIF

SIGAHEAD.TIF

SLOW.TIF

SNAKTRAY.TIF

STAR.TIF

STOP.TIF

STORK.TIF

SWIMMING.TIF

THANKS.TIF

TLKTURKY.TIF

UMPIRE.TIF

USMAP.TIF

VISA.TIF

WEDCARD.TIF

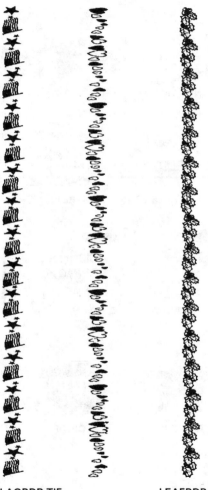

FLAGBDR.TIF

HEARTBDR.TIF

LEAFBDR.TIF

PARTYBDR.TIF

PMPKNBDR.TIF

**Food and
Travel**

AIRPLANE.TIF ANNVCAKE.TIF BUFFET.TIF

FLYGCORK.TIF DNRTOAST.TIF COFDONUT.TIF CRUISHIP.TIF

CAR.TIF VACSCENE.TIF VAN.TIF SUITCASE.TIF

**Business
Symbols**

ARROW1.TIF ARROW2.TIF ATTACHE.TIF CANDLE.TIF

CRYSBALL.TIF STACKS.TIF LITEBULB.TIF KEYS.TIF

DOLLAR2.TIF TROPHY2.TIF DART1.TIF

Business People

2BIZMEN.TIF

BUSRVEW1.TIF

LADYPHNE.TIF

MANOFFCE.TIF

MANPHONE.TIF

MEETING.TIF

VISIONRY.TIF

TRIOMEET.TIF

RATRACE.TIF

WRHSEMEN.TIF

WOMANEX2.TIF

WOMANEXC.TIF

Hands

FLIPCOIN.TIF

FNGCRSS.TIF

OKHAND.TIF

POINTING.TIF

REMNDHND.TIF

THUMBSUP.TIF

WITHCOIN.TIF

WITHPAPR.TIF

Express Publisher

Industry Images

COMMERCE.TIF

CONTSRCN.TIF

SHIPPING.TIF

TELECOMM.TIF

RADAR.TIF

OILMILL.TIF

AGRICLTR.TIF

REFINERY.TIF

TRUCKING.TIF

TRAIN.TIF

Office Supplies

SCISSORS.TIF

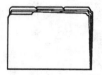

FILEFLDR.TIF

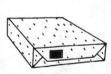

COPYPAPR.TIF

FILECART.TIF

STAPLER.TIF

INBOX.TIF

PENCILS.TIF

STPLREMV.TIF

ROLODEX.TIF

BINDER.TIF

TAPEDISP.TIF

ADMCTAPE.TIF

MEMOPAD.TIF

Industry people

BINOCULR.TIF

MICROSCP.TIF

CONWRKR.TIF

RXSYMBOL.TIF

CADUCEUS.TIF

REALTSYM.TIF

PUBLISHG.TIF

MDRESRCH.TIF

Borders and mortises

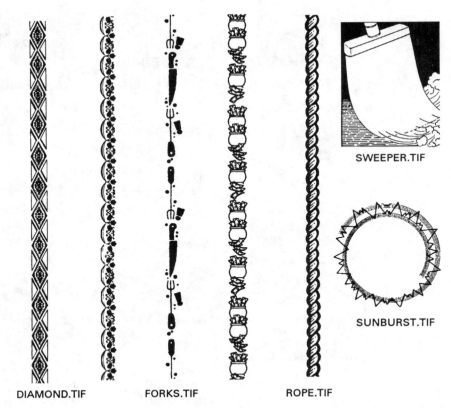

DIAMOND.TIF

FLOWER.TIF

FORKS.TIF

MONEY.TIF

ROPE.TIF

SWEEPER.TIF

SUNBURST.TIF

Business 2 portfolio

General Headings

ANNOUNCG.TIF

EXTRA!.TIF

FREE!.TIF

GRDOPEN1.TIF

WOW!.TIF

WELCOME4.TIF

THANKS2.TIF

GRDOPEN2.TIF

NEW1.TIF

WELCOME1.TIF

MOVING.TIF

THANKYOU.TIF

NOW.TIF

Seasonal Sale Headings

AUTMSALE.TIF

BLOOMBRG.TIF

WTRCLRNCE.TIF

READYSMR.TIF

HOTBUYS.TIF

HARVEST.TIF

SPRGARRV.TIF

SUMRSPEC.TIF

RAINYDAY.TIF

Real estate

AGENT.TIF

BLNKSGN1.TIF

HOMEOWNR.TIF

HOMESALE.TIF

BLNKSGN2.TIF

OPENHSE1.TIF

GATE.TIF

OPENHSE2.TIF

SOLDSIGN.TIF

Sale headings

SUPERCPN.TIF

TAGSALE.TIF

WHSESALE.TIF

READYDEA.TIF

PRCHOPPD.TIF

COUPONSV.TIF

SPECIALS.TIF

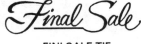

FINLSALE.TIF

SALE!.TIF

CLEARNCE.TIF

Mortises

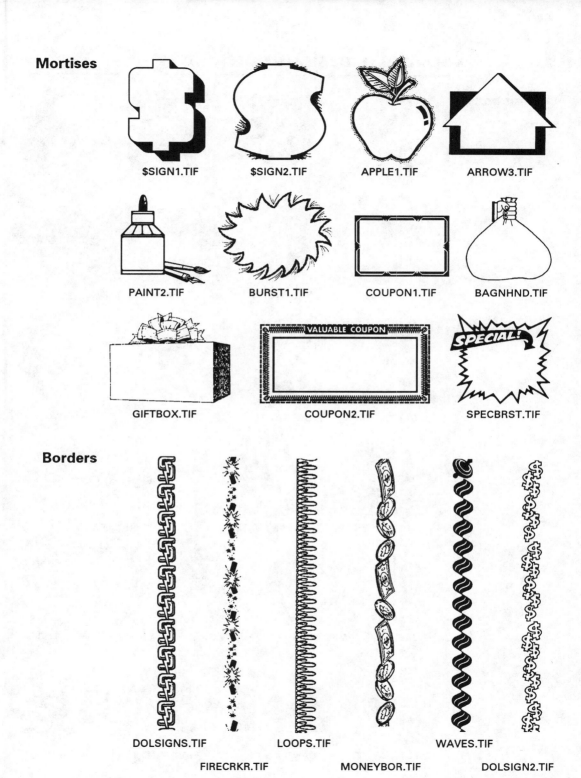

$SIGN1.TIF

$SIGN2.TIF

APPLE1.TIF

ARROW3.TIF

PAINT2.TIF

BURST1.TIF

COUPON1.TIF

BAGNHND.TIF

GIFTBOX.TIF

VALUABLE COUPON

COUPON2.TIF

SPECIAL!

SPECBRST.TIF

Borders

DOLSIGNS.TIF

FIRECRKR.TIF

LOOPS.TIF

MONEYBOR.TIF

WAVES.TIF

DOLSIGN2.TIF

Additional clip art

Special occasions portfolio

Christmas

CANDLE.TIF

SNOWMAN1.TIF

GIFTS.TIF

TREE1.TIF

TREE2.TIF

STOCKING.TIF

XMASCENE.TIF

SANTA1.TIF

SANTA2.TIF

SANTA3.TIF

SANTA4.TIF

SANTA5.TIF

SANTA6.TIF

CAROLING.TIF

Patriotic Holidays

HORSE1.TIF

WREATH.TIF

MARTKING.TIF

LABOR.TIF

LINCOLN.TIF

COLUMDAY.TIF

CANFLAG.TIF

WASHING1.TIF

WASHING2.TIF

E x p r e s s   P u b l i s h e r

New Year Thanksgiving and Halloween

NWYRBABY.TIF

CHAMPGNE.TIF

CHINENYR.TIF

PARTYHAT.TIF

NYEARELF.TIF

Halloween

GHOST.TIF

WITCH.TIF

TRICKTRE.TIF

PUMPKIN1.TIF

PUMPKIN2.TIF

SCRCROW2.TIF

Thanksgiving

CORNACOP.TIF

PILGRIM.TIF

TRKYDINR.TIF

TURKEY1.TIF

Other Holidays

APRLFOOL.TIF

CUPID.TIF

VALENTIN.TIF

FATHER1.TIF

FATHER2.TIF

MOTHER1.TIF

MOTHER2.TIF

LEPRECHN.TIF

CLOVER.TIF

Special Themes

ANTIQUE.TIF

CARNIVAL.TIF

CIRCUS.TIF

OKTBERFS.TIF

BEERBUST.TIF

MASQRADE.TIF

PARADE.TIF

CINCO.TIF

BELL.TIF

HAYRIDE.TIF

ICECREAM.TIF

CASINO.TIF

WESTERN.TIF

PICNIC.TIF

VACATION.TIF

Music and Party

CONDUCTR.TIF

ROCKGRP.TIF

BIGBAND.TIF

JAZZGRP.TIF

COCKTAIL.TIF

PARTY1.TIF

BARBRSHP.TIF

WESTNGRP.TIF

Family Events

WEDBELLS.TIF

ANNIVSRY.TIF

BALLNS.TIF

BDAYCAKE.TIF

GRAD1.TIF

BABYBOY.TIF

NEWBABY.TIF

WEDCAKE.TIF

BABYGIRL.TIF

GRADUATN.TIF

Religious Events

NATIVITY.TIF

BUNNY1.TIF

BUNNY2.TIF

EASTREGG.TIF

CROSS.TIF

CHANUKAH.TIF

PRIESTHD.TIF

HORN.TIF

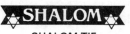

SHALOM.TIF

EASTRLLY.TIF

MINORAH.TIF

PROPHET.TIF

Borders and Mortises

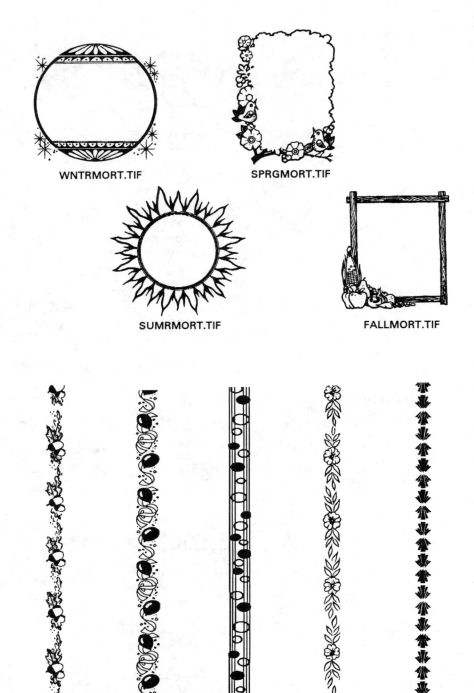

WNTRMORT.TIF

SPRGMORT.TIF

SUMRMORT.TIF

FALLMORT.TIF

ACORNBRD.TIF

BALLNBRD.TIF

CIRCLBRD.TIF

FLWRBRD1.TIF

RIBBNBRD.TIF

Education portfolio

School symbols

APPLE.TIF

GLOBE.TIF

LUNCHTRY.TIF

SUPPLIES.TIF

CLOCK.TIF

BIKE.TIF

PENCIL.TIF

PENCIL1.TIF

DONFRGET.TIF

School supplies

PAINT.TIF

MARK.TIF

SHARPENR.TIF

BOOKSTAC.TIF

STAPLER.TIF

TOOLS.TIF

CRAYONS.TIF

BINDERS.TIF

PUSHPINS.TIF

TAPE2.TIF

NTBKRULE.TIF

Students

READING.TIF

SCHOOL2.TIF

LUNCH1.TIF

3STUDENT.TIF

2STUDENT.TIF

GIRLBOY.TIF

CLASS2.TIF

CLASS1.TIF

School Personnel

BUSDRVR.TIF

TEACHER2.TIF

PRINCPAL.TIF

NURSE.TIF

JANITOR.TIF

POLICE.TIF

PATROL.TIF

TEACHER1.TIF

FIREMAN.TIF

School events

PROM1.TIF

PROM2.TIF

GRAD2.TIF

CARWASH.TIF

SCHLRING.TIF

GRAD3.TIF

HOTDOG.TIF

HMCOMING.TIF

Theater and music

JESTER.TIF

ACTOR.TIF

CLPBOARD.TIF

BANDPLYR.TIF

DIRECTOR.TIF

GRLPIANO.TIF

DRUMS.TIF

TRUMPET.TIF

MINIBAND.TIF

VIOLIN.TIF

CLEF.TIF

Clubs

ARTCLUB.TIF

DANCECLB.TIF

PHOTOCLB.TIF

SCOUTS3.TIF

SCOUTS4.TIF

4HCLUB.TIF

CHESSCLB.TIF

SCOUTS1.TIF

SCOUTS2.TIF

Cartoon Animals

BIRD.TIF

LION.TIF

NUT.TIF

RAIN.TIF

OWL.TIF

BEAVER.TIF

FISH.TIF

MOUSE.TIF

Female Athletes

CHEERLDR.TIF

SOCCER1.TIF

GRLBASKT.TIF

SKIING.TIF

GIRLGYM.TIF

RELAYRAC.TIF

GRLTENNS.TIF

DIVING.TIF

Male Athletes

HURDLER.TIF

TOUCHDWN.TIF

BOYSOCCR.TIF

BOYGYM.TIF

WRESTLNG.TIF

BOYSWIMG.TIF

BOYVLLEY.TIF

HOMERUN.TIF

BOYBSKT.TIF

Sports equipment

WHISTLE.TIF

SOCCER.TIF

FOOTBALL.TIF

BSKTBALL.TIF

BBALEQIP.TIF

TENNIS.TIF

GOLF.TIF

Borders and mortises

BINDER1.TIF

MEGPHONE.TIF

BLKBOARD.TIF

SCHHOUSE.TIF

BALLOON.TIF

PENNANT.TIF

ROSE.TIF

SUPPLYBD.TIF

Additional fonts

Adding fonts to your system dramatically increases your design options. Express Fonts™ font portfolios each contain two complete Express Publisher fonts. Like CG Times and CG Triumvirate, these fonts:

- are scalable from 6 to 144 points
- display clearly and accurately on the screen
- support bold, italic, bold italic underline, monospace, small cap, superscript, and subscript attributes
- can print on any supported printer.

Product	Item # 5.25" disk	Item # 3.5" disk	price
Express Fonts, Classic	2442B	2442A	$79.95
Includes CG Palacio™ and CG Triumvirate™ Condensed			
Express Fonts, Stylist	2444 B	2444A	$79.95
Inlcudes CG Century Schoolbook™ and CG Omega™			
Express Fonts, Flair	2454B	2454A	$79.95
Includes Park Avenue and Brush fonts			

You can find Express Fonts™ at your local software store, or you can order them directly from Power Up by sending a check or money order along with the item number of the portfolio you wish to the following address:

Power Up Software Corporation
PO Box 7600
San Mateo, CA 94403-7600

Add $4.95 for shipping and handling, CA, MA, NY, PA, and WA residents add the appropriate sales tax.

Express Fonts Classic

CG Palacio

CG Palacio is a classic serif typeface. Its formal elegance adds grace and prestige to important business documents.

CG Triumvirate Condensed

CG Triumvirate Condensed is a compact sans serif typeface that provides clarity and utility. It is perfect for assertive, credible headlines and section headings in minimal space.

Express Fonts Stylist

CG Century Schoolbook

CG Century Schoolbook is a distinctive serif typeface that was designed for readability. It is perfect for plain spoken headlines and friendly text.

CG Omega

CG Omega is a versatile face that bridges the gap between serif and sans serif design. Its elegant lines make it perfect for documents that require a touch of distinction.

Express Fonts Flair

Park Avenue

Park Avenue is a beautiful typeface with classic style and grace.

Brush

Brush combines the bold strength of a headline typeface with the fluidity of a script font. It attracts immediate attention.

Alternate characters

Express Publisher provides a standard set of keyboard characters as well as an extended, or alternate set. These alternate characters work for all Express Publisher Compugraphic fonts. The alternate characters for native printer fonts will not match the following list.

You cannot use the alternate character sets with TextEffects or in any dialog box.

To insert an alternate character, refer to the chart below and follow these steps:

1. Press SHIFT-F10.

2. Press the key corresponding to the alternate character you wish to insert.

SHIFT-F10 lets you insert one special character at a time. As soon as you have typed one character, your keyboard returns to normal and you can type the normal alphabetic characters.

Alternate characters

!	¶	3	‰	E	'	X	¿	j	œ
"	§	4	•	F	"	Y	Pt	k	Œ
#	†	5	●	G	¼	Z	ℓ	l	ø
$	‡	6	○	H	½	[	£	m	Ø
%	©	7	○	I	¾	\	¥	n	þ
&	®	8	■	J	¹	]	¤	o	Þ
'	™	9	■	K	²	^	ƒ	p	`
(	‰	:	□	L	³		ß	q	'
)	¢	;	□	M	/		a	r	^
*	–	<	'	P	‹	¯	a	s	¨
+	—	=	¬	Q	›	b	æ	t	~
,	…	>	|	R	«	c	Æ	u	'
-	fi	?	‗	S	»	d	ð	v	ˇ
.	fl	@	=	T	,	e	Đ	w	˘
0	"	A	±	U	„	f	ij	x	˙
1	"	B	×	V	°	g	IJ	y	˚
2	µ	C	÷	W	¡	h	ł	z	¯
		D	°			i	Ł		

PostScript alternate characters

The preceding characters are designed for use with our Com-pugraphic fonts only. These alternate characters generally will not map directly to the alternate characters supported by other fonts. The following chart identifies how our alternate characters will map to alphabetic PostScript fonts.

A	Ù	e	˒	9	Ï
B	Š	g	˝	0	Á
C	Ÿ	h	˓	-	ı
D	—	i	ˇ	=	Ò
E	Ž	j	—	]	´
G	õ	k	Ł	\	`
H	š	l	Ø	;	Ó
I	ž	m	ı	'	º
J	/	n	ł	.	«
K	§	o	ø	!	í
L	¤	u	ã	@	Û
M	'	x	°	#	ú
P	›	y	•	$	ñ
S	–	z	·	%	Ñ
T	†	`	–	^	^
U	‡	1	Â	&	ª
X	„	2	À	(	¿
Y	″	3	Ã	:	~
Z	…	4	Ê	"	ì
a	ß	5	Ë	<	Ô
b	˘	6	È	>	Õ
c	˙	7	Í	?	Ú
d	¨	8	Î		

Utilities

Softfont utility

The Softfont utility modifies Express Publisher's HP Laser printer drivers and adds Bitstream, HP soft fonts, and MicroLogic's More Fonts to these drivers. It adds your existing HP Laser fonts to Express Publisher printer drivers so that you can use these fonts from within Express Publisher. The Softfont utility also builds a batch file that downloads the fonts to your printer. You will run this batch file before printing your document.

Installing soft fonts

You must run the Softfont utility from the same directory as the printer driver you are modifying. This is C:\EXPRESS, unless you changed the default directory to something else.

1. To run the Softfont utility, type Softfont and press ENTER. (Unless stated otherwise on the screen, you can press ESC at any time during the installation to exit the utility.)

2. If you have an HP Laserjet printer driver in the directory, you will see a list of printer drivers to modify. Select the printer driver you want to modify and press ENTER. You will see the fonts that are currently installed for that print driver. Press ENTER to go on to the next screen, ESC to go back to the previous screen.

3. When you press ENTER, you will be prompted for the pathname to your soft fonts. Type in the pathname to where the fonts are located and press ENTER. The Softfont utility looks through that directory for HP soft fonts. It detects any Bitstream-compatible HP soft font files ready for downloading to a compatible HP laser printer.

4. A list of the soft font files appears in the designated directory. Each file will contain one font (a typeface is a family of fonts: Times 14 point Italic is a font, Times is the typeface.). Highlight a desired font and press ENTER. Softfont will prompt you

to accept the given font name or enter a new one. This will be the name that will appear in the Choose Font dialog box in Express Publisher. Some fonts have incomplete or missing names; make sure to give the font a name that you understand. After entering the name, press ENTER and the selected HP printer driver will be updated with the new font.

5. A message tells you the program has inserted the font into the PRD file and to press any key to add more fonts or ESC to exit. Press ESC only if you are done adding fonts. You can add more fonts from the same directory to the printer driver at this time by pressing any key and selecting additional fonts from the current directory. Each font will be marked with a check mark once it has been inserted into the printer driver. You can add as many fonts as you like to a selected printer driver, but keep in mind that each font downloaded into your printer takes up memory in your printer's RAM. That leaves less memory for printing your document.

6. When you are finished adding the fonts from the current directory, press ESC. At this time you may enter another directory where soft font files are located and add them to the printer driver. When you are finished adding soft fonts, you will be prompted to name the printer driver. You can give the new driver any legal DOS name. For example, if you modify the driver HPIII.PRD, you might call the new driver HPIIISFT.PRD so that you can easily identify it.

When you exit the Softfont utility, a batch file is generated that will download a copy of the soft fonts to the printer. The batch file will have the same name as the printer driver file. For example, if you create a new printer driver called HPLETTER.PRD, a batch file will be created called HPLETTER.BAT. This batch file contains the location of the soft fonts that you have selected to add to your printer driver. Remember, you must run this batch file before printing a document that uses soft fonts so that the fonts are downloaded to the printer.

Note   Do not duplicate the names of the original Express Publisher printer drivers because you will overwrite those files. If you do so, you will have to run SETUPEP to recopy the file.

Tips on using soft fonts

When you print a document that includes soft fonts, you must use the same printer driver that you selected when you created the document. Ideally, you should create a printer driver for every combination of soft fonts desired. If you use a printer driver to create a document and then use a different printer driver to print it, your document will probably not print correctly, even if both printer drivers contain the fonts that you used.

When soft fonts are downloaded, the printer labels them as S01, S02, S03, and so on. When you send the document to the printer, it searches for these labels. The fonts are labeled in the order that they were downloaded, which is the order in which they modified the printer driver. If the fonts do not have the same labels as when the document was created, they will not print correctly. Express Publisher will change the fonts to either a CG font or to another soft font.

The Softfont utility creates printer fonts, not screen fonts. When you change a block of text in Express Publisher to an installed soft font, it will appear on screen as either CG Times or CG Triumvirate, depending on whether it is a serif or sans serif font. The spacing of the characters may appear strange on the screen, because the spacing rules (width tables) for the soft font are different than those for the displayed CG font. The spacing in the printed document will be correct.

You may want to keep a library of the soft fonts that you use frequently. After you run the batch file that downloads the soft fonts, do a font print out by taking the printer off-line and pressing the PRINT FONTS button on the front panel of the printer. Write the name of the printer driver/batch file on the print out so you know which fonts have been downloaded (you won't see them on screen).

When you add soft fonts to a printer driver, you are adding specific point sizes and attributes as well. These fonts are not scalable: You can't add attributes, such as bold and underline, that you can add to the CG fonts.

The batch file that is created does not contain the soft font files themselves; it merely copies the appropriate files to the printer. If, after creating a soft font batch file, you move the soft font files to a different directory or remove them altogether, the batch file won't be able to find them or download them to the printer. A "file not found" message appears when you run the batch file, and the fonts will not be downloaded.

The only way to install soft fonts into the Express Publisher printer drivers is with SOFTFONT.EXE. Soft fonts installed or downloaded with anything other than the Softfont utility will probably not work with Express Publisher.

Remember that Express Publisher will only recognize up to 20 printer drivers in your EXPRESS directory at any time. If you are working with many different printer drivers, you may have to copy some to a different subdirectory while you are not using them so that you do not go over the limit.

Error Conditions   The Softfont utility does not detect when your hard disk is full. When the disk-full condition is reached, a blank screen appears, with a blinking cursor in the middle. Restart your system and make more space on your hard disk if this happens. Express Publisher requires 135K of free space, so running out of space is unlikely.

If you choose a soft font from within Express Publisher that has not been downloaded to the printer or has been downloaded in a different order, the font will be changed on your output to either a CG font or a soft font that has been downloaded. If you create a document with soft fonts, and then choose an unmodified printer driver, the sections of the document that contain soft fonts will be changed to whichever font is used for the screen display.

Laserjet Series II note: After downloading a soft font, a residual form feed is left on the printer (the form feed light is on). Take the printer off line and press the form feed button. Or wait for your next document to print; it will be preceded by a blank page.

If you have a soft font that has a background around the characters (which has the effect of the letters being tiles), the line spacing may be such that the tiles will overlap. To correct this, you can change the line spacing or add blank lines.

CGM2TIF utility

The CGM2TIF utility allows you to convert charts and images created with programs such as Harvard Graphics, Applause II, Freelance Plus, and Corel Draw to TIFF files, so they can be used with Express Publisher. Once you have created your chart or illustration in one of the supported programs, export it as a file in the CGM format. Refer to your graphics program user manual for information on exporting files in the CGM format.

When you create the chart, use only black and white colors for the best results. The CGM2TIF utility converts colors other than black or white to a shade of gray.

You'll find the CGM2TIF utility in your \EXPRESS directory, unless you changed the default directory during setup.

1. Type CGM2TIF to open the CGM2TIF utility. To move through the program from screen to screen, press ENTER. Press ESC at any time to exit the program.

2. Select Create TIF File.

3. Type the drive or directory name where the CGM file you want to convert is located and press ENTER.

4. Select the desired CGM file from the list that appears and press ENTER.

5. Choose the name of the application that you used to create and export the CGM image and press enter. If the name of the application is not listed, choose Others.

6. The first time you convert a CGM file you need to change the conversion options, so select the option to edit the conversion file and press ENTER.

   If you convert a file without making the changes, your file will be converted to a TIFF file 3.5" by 3.5". This means when you import the file into Express Publisher, it probably won't be able to show it on the screen, except as a gray box. So you should determine the size you want the chart to be in your document, then change the width and height conversion options.

   The default background color option is white; the foreground is black. If you want different colors enter 0 for black and 64 for white, 1 thru 63 are varying shades of gray. If you are using shades of gray, you may have to convert the file more than once with different gray values to arrive at the correct shading.

7. Once you have your conversion options set, press F10.

8. Select Transparency if you want the background of your chart to be transparent. If you choose Landscape orientation, Express Publisher converts your chart with its horizontal and vertical axes inverted, creating a Landscape orientation. Press F10 to continue.

9. If you plan to convert other charts created with the same application and want to use the same conversion options,

choose Save Config File and press ENTER. After you have saved the conversion options, select Continue and press ENTER. Once you save the conversion options for any of the listed applications, you can skip steps 5 through 8 and continue with step 9.

If you do not want to save the conversion options, choose Continue and press ENTER.

10. Type the drive or directory to which you want the CGM-converted TIFF file saved and press ENTER.

11. Choose Exit Conversion program or press ESC to exit the CGM2TIF utility and return to DOS.

Note When you import an image that was converted with CGM2TIF, it comes in as a transparent object. You can choose Filled in the Object Specs menu to change its setting. However, you can't go back and make the filled object transparent again.

Some programs create documents that default to white text on a black background. With these documents, import the converted file, then choose Reverse Colors from the Objects menu.

Glossary

..	The symbol in the directory structure that indicates the parent directory, which is one level above the current directory. For example, in the directory structure C:\Express\Art, Express is the parent directory of Art, and C:\ (the root directory) is the parent directory of Express.
$$$ file	A file with an extension of $$$ is a temporary file that was written to your hard disk. When using Express Publisher you can erase these files.
alternate characters	The set of characters not found on standard keyboards that can be accessed by pressing special key combinations. In Express Publisher, press SHIFT-F10.
anchor point	The beginning point when using the drawing tool to draw an object.
Arrow pointer	The mouse pointer used in Express Publisher to select objects.
art	*See* graphics file format.
ASCII	A standard code for representing characters as binary numbers. An ASCII text file is a basic text file that can be read by virtually any software application.
attribute (font)	An enhancement such as bold or italic added to a particular font (a typeface in one size) that changes how it looks.
AUTOEXEC.BAT	A batch file that a DOS computer runs automatically upon start-up. This file can be used to instruct DOS to handle some basic functions such as setting paths, and displaying the prompt, date, and time.
bit map	A computer image that consists of dots that are on (black) or off (white). These dots are stored together to form a picture.
buffers	*See* CONFIG.SYS.
CGA	*See* graphics display adapter.
character spacing	The number of blank points between individual letters, puncuation marks, numbers, and symbols. *See also* kerning.

click	To position the pointer on something, then press and quickly release the mouse button.
clip art	Graphic images that are stored in a file format that a computer can read.
clipboard	A temporary storage place for text or graphics. Access the clipboard through the Cut, Copy, and Paste commands.
COM1, COM2, etc.	Serial port(s) on a computer. A serial device, such as a modem or a serial printer, connects to your computer through a serial port.
CONFIG.SYS	A system configuration file that tells DOS how your computer system is set up. There are special commands you can use in these batch files, including these two commands: **Buffers=20** Sets the maximum number of buffers in your system. Disk buffers reduce the number of times your system must read and write to the disk, which improves performance. **Files=20** Sets the maximum number of files a program can open and use at one time. The default is usually 8.
crop	To cut out and retain part of an image while discarding the rest of it.
crop marks	Printed marks on the outside edges of a document indicating where paper should be cut to attain the desired page size.
cropping pointer	The pointer that indicates the program is ready to crop an image. *See* crop.
cursor	The symbol indicating the insertion point for text. In Express Publisher, this is also called the I-beam pointer.
Cut command	To remove a selected object or body of highlighted text from your document. The deleted item is moved to the clipboard.
DCX file	A graphics file type that is like a series of PCX files appended together. You can send an Express Publisher document saved as a DCX file to another Express Publisher user with an Intel Connection Co-processor.
default	An assumption that is made unless specific instructions to the contrary are given. For example, if you start Express Publisher without specifying a file to work with, it defaults to a new one page, one column, blank document.
dialog box	A pop-up window that requests information, contains user-adjustable settings, alerts you to problems, or presents options. Normally you must respond to the dialog box by accepting the options or cancelling the action.
directory	A location on disk where any number of files are grouped together.

disk printer file A file that has intercepted all of the information normally sent to a printer when printing a document. This enables you to actually print your document at a different time without running Express Publisher, by sending the disk printer file to a printer with the DOS Print command.

DOS (Disk Operating System) The software that handles all communication between your computer hardware and your application software.

dot-matrix printer A printer that forms letters and graphic images by printing patterns of tiny dots.

double click To click the mouse quickly, twice in succession. This is one way to select a file to be opened.

DPI dots per inch. *See also* resolution.

dragging The act of holding down the mouse button while moving the mouse. *Drag* the mouse over a body of text to select it.

drawing pointer A mouse pointer that looks like a pencil; it indicates that the drawing functions are enabled.

EGA *See* graphics display adapter.

EPS *See* graphics file format.

Escape key The key that can sometimes be used to cancel a command. For example, when printing, press ESCAPE to cancel the print job.

expanded memory (LIM EMS) Extra memory (RAM) above the standard 640K that adheres to the Lotus-Intel-Microsoft Expanded Memory Specification. You can add expanded memory to a 286-class or greater machine by adding an expanded memory board or by converting extended memory to EMS.

export To transfer data with certain characteristics intact from one program so that it can be used in a different program.

extended memory Extra memory (RAM) above the standard DOS limitation of 640K.

extension Optional characters (up to three) after the period in a DOS filename. The extension often indicates the file type.

font A complete set of characters in one size, face and style. 12 point CG Times italic is a font; CG Times is a typeface. *See also* typestyle, typeface. Fonts (or typefaces) are either *serif* or *sans serif*.
serif A fine line finishing off the main strokes of a letter. This letter A has serifs at the bottom; this letter A does not.
sans serif A typeface without serifs.

four-headed arrow pointer	The cursor that indicates that the selected object will move when the mouse is moved.
function keys	Keys along the top or left-hand side of a keyboard that begin with F, such as F1. These keys have particular tasks assigned to them within a software application.
GIF	*See* graphics file format.
graphics display adapter	A board that makes your computer capable of displaying graphics on your graphics monitor. Express Publisher supports Hercules (HGC), CGA, EGA, MCGA, and VGA.
graphics file format	The arrangement or layout of graphics data on disk. Software applications that produce pictures usually create data using one or more of these common formats. Express Publisher supports the following graphics file formats: ART, GIF, IMG (Gem), EPS, MAC, NAM, TIFF, and PCX.
grid	A set of vertical and horizontal points on screen that help you align objects. When Snap To Grid is on, Express Publisher aligns any object that is drawn or moved to the closest grid marker.
gutter width	The space between two columns of text.
Hercules	*See* graphics display adapter.
hot key	The key, corresponding to the underlined letter on Express Publisher menus, that you can press as a shortcut. For example, to pull down the File menu in Express Publisher, press ALT-F. Then, to Open a file, press O. (The underlined letter is the hot key.)
I-beam pointer	The cursor that indicates that Express Publisher is in text mode.
icon	A graphic representation of an object or a concept.
Illegal filename characters	Characters that DOS has reserved for its own use and that can't be used in filenames: *?/.,;[]+=\:<>
image orientation	The way data is printed on the page. Landscape is the orientation of a page so that the horizontal dimension is greater than the vertical one. For example, if a letter-sized sheet has Landscape orientation, the printer prints across the 11 inch width. (sideways printing). Portrait is the orientation of a page so that the vertical dimension is greater than the horizontal. Portrait is the normal orientation of letter-sized paper.
IMG (GEM)	*See* graphics file format.
Import	To bring data, with certain characteristics intact, from one program into the application you are currently using.

K	An abbreviation for kilobyte, as in 135K.
kerning	Making certain pairs of letters sit closer to each other on a line. For example, due to their shapes, the letters WA appear have more space between them than the letters IO. Kerning corrects this by placing W and A closer to each other.
landscape	*See* image orientation
laser printer	A printer that uses a laser beam to generate an image, then transfers it to paper electrostatically.
leading	The number of points between lines (line spacing).
list box	A type of dialog box that presents choices in a list format. You use the scroll bar to view the list of choices, select the item(s) you want with the mouse, and click OK.
LPT1, LPT2 etc.	Parallel ports found in the back of your computer that transfer data in 8- and 16-bit groups. Parallel printers connect to your computer through a parallel port.
MAC	*See* graphics file format.
MCGA	*See* graphics display adapter.
megabyte (MB)	One thousand kilobytes (1000K).
memory resident	A type of software program that is sitting in memory but inactive until you choose to activate it. You can usually use it on top of other underlying programs.
Menu bar	The horizontal strip at the top of the screen that contains the menu options.
Message line	The horizontal strip at the bottom of the screen that contains pertinent information on the current action.
monospace	A font attribute that makes the spaces between letters as large as the letters themselves.
more text marker	An arrow at the bottom of a text frame indicating there is more text in the story than will fit in the frame.
mouse	A special input device connected to the computer that rolls along the desktop and controls cursor movement.
mouse driver	The software that allows your mouse to communicate with your computer.
MOUSE.COM	A file that is often used as a mouse driver. You can place it in your AUTOEXEC.BAT file to insure that it is run automatically when the computer starts up.

MOUSE.SYS	A file that is often used as a mouse driver. It can be placed in your CONFIG.SYS to insure that it is run automatically when the computer starts up.
NAM graphics	*See* graphics file format.
outdent	(Also *hanging indent*) An indent that hangs out to the left of the margin.
paragraph spacing	The line spacing between paragraphs. When you set paragraph spacing for text, you are setting the amount of extra space that will be inserted after the carriage return.
Paste	To place something from the clipboard into your document.
pathname	The route that shows the way from the disk's root directory to some other location (subdirectory) on the disk. For example, if EXPRESS is a subdirectory off of the root of drive C, the pathname is C:\EXPRESS.
PCX	*See* graphics file format.
pica	A unit of measure. One pica is equal to twelve points. *See* point.
point	The printer's basic unit of type measurement, approximately 1/72 of an inch.
portrait	*See* image orientation.
PostScript printer	A printer that uses the PostScript language to produce text and graphics.
printer driver	The file that controls how the printer will interpret the printing commands from the software.
printer emulation	A printer driver that correctly interprets the commands designed for a different printer. This enables a printer to produce output just like the printer it is imitating.
printer fonts (native)	Fonts that are built in to the printer. No software is needed to tell the printer how these characters should look because the printer already has these fonts.
printer margins	The area on the outer edge of the page where the printer will not print.
printer port	The plug in the back of the computer where you connect the printer to the computer.
print spooler	A temporary storage place for information being sent to the printer. The print spooler holds information while the printer is busy processing something else.
prompt	A symbol that signals to the user that the computer is ready to receive input.

RAM	The computer's temporary memory, it functions only when the computer is on (as opposed to hard disk memory). A software application is loaded into RAM upon start-up. Any changes you make to a document are stored only in RAM until you save the document on disk.
reboot	To restart a computer. To reboot, simultaneously press CTRL-ALT-DELETE.
resolution	The number of dots per inch (dpi) used to represent graphics or text.
sans serif	*See* font.
scroll bar	The shaded rectangle on the right side and bottom of the Express Publisher screen. Click the scroll bar to move to the corresponding part of the page. Or drag the thumb (the white box) to scroll to a different section of the page. You can also click the arrows at either end of the scroll bar to move in that direction.
serif	*See* font.
shift-click	To hold down the SHIFT key while clicking the mouse.
small caps	A font attribute where all the letters are capitalized, but at the height of that font's lowercase letters (smaller than the regular capital letters of that font). THIS SENTENCE IS IN SMALL CAPS.
Style	A group of formatting commands saved under one name, which can then be applied to multiple paragraphs.
subscript	Letters that print below the baseline (where the other letters sit). This is normal, and this is subscript.
superscript	Letters that print above the baseline (where the other letters sit). This is normal, and this is superscript.
template	A file that contains the basic page elements of a document that you produce regularly, like a newsletter. The template is your starting point, but you use Save As to save it as a regular document and produce the newsletter.
text cursor	*See* I-beam cursor.
thumb	The white box on the scroll bar that you can drag to quickly move to a different part of the page.
TIFF	*See* graphics file format.
typeface	A named type design, such as CG Times.
type size	The size of type in points (10 point).
typestyle	The font attribute applied to a particular typeface, such as bold or italic. *See also* font.

VGA	*See* graphics display adapter.
watch pointer	Indicates that Express Publisher is processing information. When the pointer turns into the Watch pointer, Express Publisher will not recognize any commands from the keyboard or the mouse.
wild card characters	Also known as global filename characters, wild card characters such as * and ? give you a method of specifying part of a filename so that several files may match the specification. See your DOS manual for more information on wildcard characters.

Index

exiting 50
fill patterns 172
font size 162
formatting 49–50
headlines 160
Help system 161
importing 183
justification 169
kerning 170
line types 50, 173
lines and 166
margins 169
maximum characters 184
menus 159
moving headlines 174
non-printing lines 173
opening 161
opening saved headlines 181
pasting 178
placing headlines 161
principles of 184
print resolution 179
quitting 182
rotating text 174
saving 48–49, 179
scaling text vs. objects 175
shearing 168

stacking order 178
tools 162
transparent objects 173
undoing 179
Thumb 4, 5
TIF and TextEffects 183
TIFF picture 104–105
titles, on galleys 57
Toolbox 3, 12–13
    putting away 71
tools 12
transparent 173
triangles. *See*
    polygons; TextEffects
troubleshooting 221–236
TSRs 212

U

Undo Move command 70, 179
units of measure 71–72
Unlink tool 125
upgrading xv
utilities
    CGM2TIF 284
    Softfont 281

V

viewing document 66–68

W

white space 195
width of column 57
wild card characters 11–12, 63
Windows, using with xvii
word processing programs 126
WordPerfect 126, 127
WordStar 126, 127
wrapping text around
    pictures 50–52, 155–156

X

X Offset (and shadows) 167

Y

Y Offset (and shadows) 167

Z

Zoom In command 66
Zoom Out command 66